Learn to Code
HTML & CSS

Develop & Style Websites

Shay Howe

New Riders
VOICES THAT MATTER™

LEARN TO CODE HTML & CSS: DEVELOP & STYLE WEBSITES
Shay Howe

NEW RIDERS
www.newriders.com

To report errors, please send a note to errata@peachpit.com
New Riders is an imprint of Peachpit, a division of Pearson Education.
Copyright © 2014 by W. Shay Howe

Project Editors: Michael J. Nolan and Nancy Peterson
Development Editor: Jennifer Lynn
Production Editor: David Van Ness
Copyeditor: Jennifer Needham
Technical Editor: Chris Mills
Indexer: Karin Arrigoni
Proofreader: Darren Meiss
Cover Designer: Shay Howe
Interior Designer: Mimi Heft
Compositor: WolfsonDesign

ISBN 13: 978-0-321-94052-0
ISBN 10:   0-321-94052-0

9 8 7 6 5 4 3 2 1

Printed and bound in the United States of America

For you.

One way or another this book ended up in your hands. I'm excited to see what you do with it, and I hope the knowledge within this book makes as large an impact on your life as it has on my own.

About the Author

 Born and raised in the small town of Lima, Ohio, Shay Howe grew up disassembling remote controls and other electronics in hopes of learning how they worked. When the Internet was introduced, he was fascinated and immediately began learning all he could about it. Upon graduating from high school, he moved to Tempe, Arizona, where he attended the University of Advancing Technology and received a Bachelor of Arts degree in digital multimedia with a focus in web design.

Currently living in Chicago, Illinois, Shay is a designer and front-end developer with a passion for solving problems while building creative and intuitive websites. He specializes in web and product design and front-end development, specialties that he regularly writes and speaks about.

Shay is co-founder of Chicago Camps, which hosts low-cost, high-value technology events in the Chicago area. He is also co-organizer of Refresh Chicago and UX Happy Hour, which help to refresh the creative, technical, and professional culture of New Media endeavors.

Perhaps most importantly, though, Shay is the undisputed office table tennis champion.

Acknowledgments

To everyone who helped make this book a reality, from the bottom of my heart, I cannot thank you enough!

There are so many people who have helped me in my career and with this book that it's going to be impossible to thank them all. I will undoubtedly forget someone important, and I apologize to whoever that may be. That said, I have to begin by thanking my family and friends. There's no way this book would ever exist without their help and support.

My wife, Becky, was encouraging from day one and has always been supportive of my endeavors, no matter if they seemed like good ideas or not. Our pup, Gatsby, who makes me smile every day, kept my feet warm all winter while I was writing, using them as his bed under my desk. All of the thanks in the world would not be enough for my parents, Wes and Deb, who have provided me with more support and guidance than I could have ever dreamed. I love them all.

Before this was a book it was a website, and that website received feedback from some of the best in the business. I'm incredibly thankful to Jeff Cohen, Mike Gibson, Scott Robbin, Christopher Webb, Russell Schoenbeck, Dan Kim, Chris Mills, Bruce Lawson, Christian Heilmann, and many others for their initial feedback on these lessons. Of course the website itself wouldn't have existed without the help of Darby Frey, who has had my back for years and is easily one of the best guys I know.

I tapped on quite a few friends for content for this book, and I was overwhelmed by all of their contributions. I owe two-handed high fives to Aaron Irizarry, Adam Connor, AJ Self, Arman Ghosh, Bermon Painter, Brad Smith, Candi Lemoine, Carolyn Chandler, Chris Mills, Dan Denney, Darby Frey, Erica Decker, Estelle Weyl, Jen Myers, Jenn Downs, Jennifer Jones, Leslie Jensen-Inman, Maya Bruck, Russ Unger, Tessa Harmon, Victoria Pater, Vitaly Friedman, and Zoe Mickley Gillenwater. Next time I see each of them the high fives are payable in full, and dinner is on me.

I owe a ton of thanks to the New Riders family who helped bring this all together. Michael Nolan eased my fear of writing a book and gave me a gracious introduction to New Riders. Jennifer Lynn deserves an award for keeping this book on track and helping make sense of the content within it. Chris Mills did a fantastic job of making sure all of the right topics were covered in an understandable manner. Jennifer Needham put my words to work, making me sound better than I ever imagined. Mimi Heft always went the extra mile and was incredibly patient with me. Nancy Peterson handled every request I threw at her with ease and kept the entire team on the same page. They're all superheroes in my eyes, and they made writing this book an amazing experience.

Much of the content within this book has been heavily influenced by those who have written books and publications before me, and who continue to be thought leaders within the industry. Without the contributions of Jeffrey Zeldman, Eric Meyer, Dan Cederholm, Dave Shea, Andy Budd, Jeremy Keith, Cameron Moll, Ethan Marcotte, Chris Coyier, and others, it's hard to say what I'd know.

Today the Mozilla Developer Network and Dev.Opera communities are publishing some of best content on HTML and CSS; they have become staples within a long list of great resources. They must be thanked, too, for their amazing contributions.

When not in the office I do my best to stay involved in the community, and to that end I help organize a handful of different events in the Chicago area. While writing this book I fell behind on my duties, and I must thank Russ Unger and Brad Simpson from Chicago Camps and Jon Buda and Anthony Zinni from Refresh Chicago for picking up my slack. They all helped to carry my portion of the work without hesitation, and I'm thankful and honored to have them as partners in crime.

Many people have generously offered words of wisdom and lent an ear from time to time. For that, I must thank Bill DeRouchey, Bill Scott, Brad Wilkening, Braden Kowitz, Brandon Satrom, Carl Smith, Chris Courtney, Chris Eppstein, Crystal Shuller, Dale Sande, Dave Giunta, Dave Hoover, Debra Levin Gelman, Derek Featherstone, Dustin Anderson, Fabian Alcantara, Greg Baugues, Hampton Catlin, Jack Toomey, Jason Kunesh, Jason Ulaszek, JC Grubbs, Jim and Jen Remsik, Jonathan Snook, Keith Norman, Luis D. Rodriguez, Michael Boeke, Michael "Doc" Norton, Michael Parenteau, Milton Jackson, Nishant Kothary, Peter Merholz, Sam Rosen, Samantha Soma, Tim Frick, Todd Larsen, and Todd Zaki Warfel.

Last, but certainly not least, I must thank the late Matt Puchlerz. He taught me more than he'll ever know, and I wouldn't be where I am today without him. I am forever grateful for Matt's friendship, and I miss him dearly.

Contents

Introduction

I come from a family of educators. My parents are both teachers, as is my brother. I was the only one in my family not to become a teacher. That said, I love helping others, spreading the knowledge I have about web design, and teaching when possible. To that end, I often speak at different conferences and schools, as well as host the occasional workshop. When doing so, I continually receive questions about HTML and CSS. So, I wrote this book to be that ideal, all-encompassing resource for learning HTML and CSS.

Traditionally, you'll see books that teach HTML first and then CSS, keeping the two languages completely separate. But when they're taught independently, things don't really come together until the very end, which is frustrating for someone new to HTML and CSS. I wanted to take a different approach, teaching both languages at the same time so that you can see the fruits of your labor sooner rather than later. This book aims to bring instant gratification to the web design process.

It was also important to me that the book be project based, providing a completed website for readers who work through the book from start to finish. Not everyone learns by reading alone, so I wanted to provide a tangible website to allow people to learn experientially.

And let's face it, HTML and CSS can be a little daunting at first. After all, the languages are ever changing, and the evolution requires a steady stream of up-to-date material. This book is written in a workshop-style format, with 12 easy-to-digest lessons. Starting with the basics, each lesson builds upon the previous one and breaks down the barriers to entry, showing you how you can start writing HTML and CSS today in practical examples. In fact, you build a simple web page in the first lesson. Then, in subsequent lessons, you learn not only how to make this web page more robust, but also how to create additional design-savvy and interactive web pages that, when combined, form an entire functional website.

Learn to Code HTML & CSS covers the latest technologies as well as the foundations of HTML and CSS that were set years ago. It also covers a range of topics and skills, from beginning to advanced. So if you're looking to become a web designer or developer and you want to learn HTML and CSS, then this book is for you.

Lesson 1

Building Your First Web Page

If you can, imagine a time before the invention of the Internet. Websites didn't exist, and books, printed on paper and tightly bound, were your primary source of information. It took a considerable amount of effort—and reading—to track down the exact piece of information you were after.

Today you can open a web browser, jump over to your search engine of choice, and search away. Any bit of imaginable information rests at your fingertips. And chances are someone somewhere has built a website with your exact search in mind.

Within this book I'm going to show you how to build your own websites using the two most dominant computer languages— HTML and CSS.

Before we begin our journey to learn how to build websites with HTML and CSS, it is important to understand the differences between the two languages, the syntax of each language, and some common terminology.

What Are HTML & CSS?

HTML, HyperText Markup Language, gives content structure and meaning by defining that content as, for example, headings, paragraphs, or images. *CSS*, or Cascading Style Sheets, is a presentation language created to style the appearance of content—using, for example, fonts or colors.

The two languages—HTML and CSS—are independent of one another and should remain that way. CSS should not be written inside of an HTML document and vice versa. As a rule, HTML will always represent content, and CSS will always represent the appearance of that content.

With this understanding of the difference between HTML and CSS, let's dive into HTML in more detail.

Understanding Common HTML Terms

While getting started with HTML, you will likely encounter new—and often strange— terms. Over time you will become more and more familiar with all of them, but the three common HTML terms you should begin with are *elements*, *tags*, and *attributes*.

Elements

Elements are designators that define the structure and content of objects within a page. Some of the more frequently used elements include multiple levels of headings (identified as `<h1>` through `<h6>` elements) and paragraphs (identified as the `<p>` element); the list goes on to include the `<a>`, `<div>`, `<span>`, `<strong>`, and `<em>` elements, and many more.

Elements are identified by the use of less-than and greater-than angle brackets, `< >`, surrounding the element name. Thus, an element will look like the following:

```
1.    <a>
```

Tags

The use of less-than and greater-than angle brackets surrounding an element creates what is known as a *tag*. Tags most commonly occur in pairs of opening and closing tags.

An *opening tag* marks the beginning of an element. It consists of a less-than sign followed by an element's name, and then ends with a greater-than sign; for example, `<div>`.

A *closing tag* marks the end of an element. It consists of a less-than sign followed by a forward slash and the element's name, and then ends with a greater-than sign; for example, `</div>`.

The content that falls between the opening and closing tags is the content of that element. An anchor link, for example, will have an opening tag of `<a>` and a closing tag of `</a>`. What falls between these two tags will be the content of the anchor link.

So, anchor tags will look a bit like this:

```
1.  <a>...</a>
```

Attributes

Attributes are properties used to provide additional information about an element. The most common attributes include the `id` attribute, which identifies an element; the `class` attribute, which classifies an element; the `src` attribute, which specifies a source for embeddable content; and the `href` attribute, which provides a hyperlink reference to a linked resource.

Attributes are defined within the opening tag, after an element's name. Generally attributes include a name and a value. The format for these attributes consists of the attribute name followed by an equals sign and then a quoted attribute value. For example, an `<a>` element including an `href` attribute would look like the following:

```
1.  <a href="http://shayhowe.com/">Shay Howe</a>
```

The preceding code will display the text "Shay Howe" on the web page (see **Figure 1.1**) and will take users to http://shayhowe.com/ upon clicking the "Shay Howe" text. The anchor element is declared with the opening `<a>` and closing `</a>` tags encompassing the text, and the hyperlink reference attribute and value are declared with `href="http://shayhowe.com"` in the opening tag (see **Figure 1.2**).

Shay Howe

Figure 1.1 An anchor element creating a "Shay Howe" hyperlink

Figure 1.2 HTML syntax outline including an element, attribute, and tag

Now that you know what HTML elements, tags, and attributes are, let's take a look at putting together our first web page. If anything looks new here, no worries—we'll decipher it as we go.

Setting Up the HTML Document Structure

HTML documents are plain text documents saved with an .html file extension rather than a .txt file extension. To begin writing HTML, you first need a plain text editor that you are comfortable using. Sadly this does not include Microsoft Word or Pages, as those are rich text editors. Two of the more popular plain text editors for writing HTML and CSS are Dreamweaver and Sublime Text. Free alternatives also include Notepad++ for Windows and TextWrangler for Mac.

All HTML documents have a required structure that includes the following declaration and elements: <!DOCTYPE html>, <html>, <head>, and <body>.

The document type declaration, or <!DOCTYPE html>, informs web browsers which version of HTML is being used and is placed at the very beginning of the HTML document. Because we'll be using the latest version of HTML, our document type declaration is simply <!DOCTYPE html>. Following the document type declaration, the <html> element signifies the beginning of the document.

Inside the <html> element, the <head> element identifies the top of the document, including any metadata (accompanying information about the page). The content inside the <head> element is not displayed on the web page itself. Instead, it may include the document title (which is displayed on the title bar in the browser window), links to any external files, or any other beneficial metadata.

All of the visible content within the web page will fall within the <body> element. A breakdown of a typical HTML document structure looks like this:

```
1.   <!DOCTYPE html>
2.   <html lang="en">
3.     <head>
4.       <meta charset="utf-8">
```

```
5.      <title>Hello World</title>
6.      </head>
7.      <body>
8.        <h1>Hello World</h1>
9.        <p>This is a web page.</p>
10.     </body>
11.   </html>
```

The preceding code shows the document beginning with the document type declaration, `<!DOCTYPE html>`, followed directly by the `<html>` element. Inside the `<html>` element come the `<head>` and `<body>` elements. The `<head>` element includes the character encoding of the page via the `<meta charset="utf-8">` tag and the title of the document via the `<title>` element. The `<body>` element includes a heading via the `<h1>` element and a paragraph via the `<p>` element. Because both the heading and paragraph are nested within the `<body>` element, they are visible on the web page (see **Figure 1.3**).

Hello World

This is a web page.

Figure 1.3 A simple web page

When an element is placed inside of another element, also known as *nested*, it is a good idea to indent that element to keep the document structure well organized and legible. In the previous code, both the `<head>` and `<body>` elements were nested—and indented—inside the `<html>` element. The pattern of indenting for elements continues as new elements are added inside the `<head>` and `<body>` elements.

Self-Closing Elements

In the previous example, the `<meta>` element had only one tag and didn't include a closing tag. Fear not, this was intentional. Not all elements consist of opening and closing tags. Some elements simply receive their content or behavior from attributes within a single tag. The `<meta>` element is one of these elements. The content of the previous `<meta>` element is assigned with the use of the `charset` attribute and value. Other common self-closing elements include

- `<br>`
- `<embed>`
- `<hr>`
- `<img>`
- `<input>`
- `<link>`
- `<meta>`
- `<param>`
- `<source>`
- `<wbr>`

The structure outlined here, making use of the <!DOCTYPE html> document type and <html>, <head>, and <body> elements, is quite common. We'll want to keep this document structure handy, as we'll be using it often as we create new HTML documents.

Code Validation

No matter how careful we are when writing our code, we will inevitably make mistakes. Thankfully, when writing HTML and CSS we have validators to check our work. The W3C has built both HTML (http://validator.w3.org/) and CSS validators (http://jigsaw.w3.org/css-validator/) that will scan code for mistakes. Validating our code not only helps it render properly across all browsers, but also helps teach us the best practices for writing code.

In Practice

As web designers and front-end developers, we have the luxury of attending a number of great conferences dedicated to our craft. We're going to make up our own conference, Styles Conference, and build a website for it throughout the following lessons. Here we go!

1. Let's open our text editor, create a new file named index.html, and save it to a location we won't forget. I'm going to create a folder on my Desktop named "styles-conference" and save this file there; feel free to do the same.

2. Within the index.html file, let's add the document structure, including the <!DOCTYPE html> document type and the <html>, <head>, and <body> elements.

```
1.   <!DOCTYPE html>
2.   <html lang="en">
3.     <head>
4.     </head>
5.     <body>
6.     </body>
7.   </html>
```

3. Inside the <head> element, let's add <meta> and <title> elements. The <meta> element should include the proper charset attribute and value, while the <title> element should contain the title of the page—let's say "Styles Conference."

```
1.  <head>
2.    <meta charset="utf-8">
3.    <title>Styles Conference</title>
4.  </head>
```

4. Inside the <body> element, let's add <h1> and <p> elements. The <h1> element should include the heading we wish to include—let's use "Styles Conference" again—and the <p> element should include a simple paragraph to introduce our conference.

```
1.  <body>
2.    <h1>Styles Conference</h1>
3.    <p>Every year the brightest web designers and front-end
       developers descend on Chicago to discuss the latest
       technologies. Join us this August!</p>
4.  </body>
```

5. Now it's time to see how we've done! Let's go find our index.html file (mine is within the "styles-conference" folder on my Desktop). Double-clicking this file or dragging it into a web browser will open it for us to review. It should look like **Figure 1.4**.

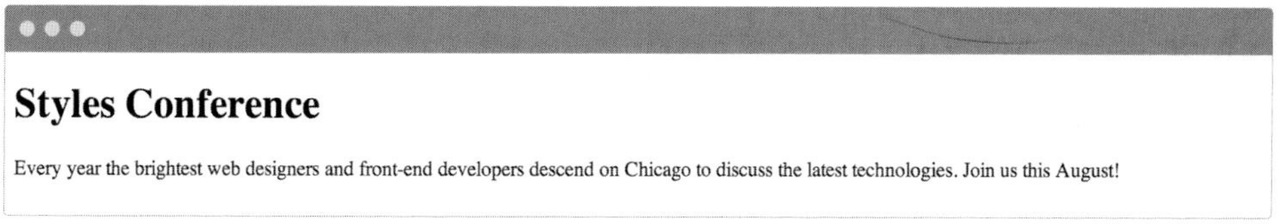

Styles Conference

Every year the brightest web designers and front-end developers descend on Chicago to discuss the latest technologies. Join us this August!

Figure 1.4 Our first steps into building our Styles Conference website

Let's switch gears a bit, moving away from HTML, and take a look at CSS. Remember, HTML will define the content and structure of our web pages, while CSS will define the visual style and appearance of our web pages.

Understanding Common CSS Terms

In addition to HTML terms, there are a few common CSS terms you will want to familiarize yourself with. These terms include *selectors*, *properties*, and *values*. As with the HTML terminology, the more you work with CSS, the more these terms will become second nature.

Selectors

As elements are added to a web page, they may be styled using CSS. A *selector* desig-
nates exactly which element or elements within our HTML to target and apply styles
(such as color, size, and position) to. Selectors may include a combination of different
qualifiers to select unique elements, all depending on how specific we wish to be. For
example, we may want to select every paragraph on a page, or we may want to select
only one specific paragraph on a page.

Selectors generally target an attribute value, such as an id or class value, or target the
type of element, such as <h1> or <p>.

Within CSS, selectors are followed with curly brackets, {}, which encompass the styles to
be applied to the selected element. The selector here is targeting all <p> elements.

```
1.   p { ... }
```

Properties

Once an element is selected, a *property* determines the styles that will be applied to that
element. Property names fall after a selector, within the curly brackets, {}, and immediately
preceding a colon, :. There are numerous properties we can use, such as background,
color, font-size, height, and width, and new properties are often added. In the following code, we are defining the color and font-size properties to be applied to all
<p> elements.

```
1.   p {
2.     color: ...;
3.     font-size: ...;
4.   }
```

Values

So far we've selected an element with a selector and determined what style we'd like to
apply with a property. Now we can determine the behavior of that property with a *value*.
Values can be identified as the text between the colon, :, and semicolon, ;. Here we are
selecting all <p> elements and setting the value of the color property to be orange and
the value of the font-size property to be 16 pixels.

```
1.  p {
2.    color: orange;
3.    font-size: 16px;
4.  }
```

To review, in CSS our rule set begins with the selector, which is immediately followed by curly brackets. Within these curly brackets are declarations consisting of property and value pairs. Each declaration begins with a property, which is followed by a colon, the property value, and finally a semicolon.

It is a common practice to indent property and value pairs within the curly brackets. As with HTML, these indentations help keep our code organized and legible.

All of these common CSS terms combine in this manner (see **Figure 1.5**).

Knowing a few common terms and the general syntax of CSS is a great start, but we have a few more items to learn before jumping in too deep. Specifically, we need to take a closer look at how selectors work within CSS.

```
Selector
   ┴                    Value
   p {
       color: orange;
       font-size: 16px;
   }
          Property
```

Figure 1.5 CSS syntax outline including a selector, properties, and values

Working with Selectors

Selectors, as previously mentioned, indicate which HTML elements are being styled. It is important to fully understand how to use selectors and how they can be leveraged. The first step is to become familiar with the different types of selectors. We'll start with the most common selectors: *type*, *class*, and *ID* selectors.

Type Selectors

Type selectors target elements by their element type. For example, should we wish to target all division elements, <div>, we would use a type selector of div. The following code shows a type selector for division elements as well as the corresponding HTML it selects.

CSS

```
1.  div { ... }
```

HTML

```
1.  <div>...</div>
2.  <div>...</div>
```

Class Selectors

Class selectors allow us to select an element based on the element's `class` attribute value. Class selectors are a little more specific than type selectors, as they select a particular group of elements rather than all elements of one type.

Class selectors allow us to apply the same styles to different elements at once by using the same `class` attribute value across multiple elements.

Within CSS, classes are denoted by a leading period, `.`, followed by the `class` attribute value. Here the class selector will select any element containing the `class` attribute value of `awesome`, including both division and paragraph elements.

CSS

```
1.  .awesome { ... }
```

HTML

```
1.  <div class="awesome">...</div>
2.  <p class="awesome">...</p>
```

ID Selectors

ID selectors are even more precise than class selectors, as they target only one unique element at a time. Just as class selectors use an element's `class` attribute value as the selector, ID selectors use an element's `id` attribute value as a selector.

Regardless of which type of element they appear on, `id` attribute values can only be used once per page. If used they should be reserved for significant elements.

Within CSS, ID selectors are denoted by a leading hash sign, #, followed by the `id` attribute value. Here the ID selector will only select the element containing the `id` attribute value of `shayhowe`.

CSS

```
1.  #shayhowe { ... }
```

HTML

```
1.  <div id="shayhowe">...</div>
```

Additional Selectors

Selectors are extremely powerful, and the selectors outlined here are the most common selectors we'll come across. These selectors are also only the beginning. Many more advanced selectors exist and are readily available. When you feel comfortable with these selectors, don't be afraid to look into some of the more advanced selectors.

All right, everything is starting to come together. We add elements to a page inside our HTML, and we can then select those elements and apply styles to them using CSS. Now let's connect the dots between our HTML and CSS, and get these two languages working together.

Referencing CSS

In order to get our CSS talking to our HTML, we need to reference our CSS file within our HTML. The best practice for referencing our CSS is to include all of our styles in a single external style sheet, which is referenced from within the <head> element of our HTML document. Using a single external style sheet allows us to use the same styles across an entire website and quickly make changes sitewide.

Other Options for Adding CSS

Other options for referencing CSS include using internal and inline styles. You may come across these options in the wild, but they are generally frowned upon, as they make updating websites cumbersome and unwieldy.

To create our external CSS style sheet, we'll want to use our text editor of choice again to create a new plain text file with a .css file extension. Our CSS file should be saved within the same folder, or a subfolder, where our HTML file is located.

Within the <head> element of the HTML document, the <link> element is used to define the relationship between the HTML file and the CSS file. Because we are linking to CSS, we use the rel attribute with a value of stylesheet to specify their relationship. Furthermore, the href (or hyperlink reference) attribute is used to identify the location, or path, of the CSS file.

Consider the following example of an HTML document `<head>` element that references a single external style sheet.

```
1.   <head>
2.     <link rel="stylesheet" href="main.css">
3.   </head>
```

In order for the CSS to render correctly, the path of the `href` attribute value must directly correlate to where our CSS file is saved. In the preceding example, the `main.css` file is stored within the same location as the HTML file, also known as the root directory.

If our CSS file is within a subdirectory or subfolder, the `href` attribute value needs to correlate to this path accordingly. For example, if our `main.css` file were stored within a subdirectory named `stylesheets`, the `href` attribute value would be `stylesheets/main.css`, using a forward slash to indicate moving into a subdirectory.

At this point our pages are starting to come to life, slowly but surely. We haven't delved into CSS too much, but you may have noticed that some elements have default styles we haven't declared within our CSS. That is the browser imposing its own preferred CSS styles for those elements. Fortunately we can overwrite these styles fairly easily, which is what we'll do next using CSS resets.

Using CSS Resets

Every web browser has its own default styles for different elements. How Google Chrome renders headings, paragraphs, lists, and so forth may be different from how Internet Explorer does. To ensure cross-browser compatibility, CSS resets have become widely used.

CSS resets take every common HTML element with a predefined style and provide one unified style for all browsers. These resets generally involve removing any sizing, margins, paddings, or additional styles and toning these values down. Because CSS cascades from top to bottom—more on that soon—our reset needs to be at the very top of our style sheet. Doing so ensures that those styles are read first and that all of the different web browsers are working from a common baseline.

There are a bunch of different resets available to use, all of which have their own fortes. One of the most popular resets is Eric Meyer's reset (http://meyerweb.com/eric/tools/css/reset/), which has been adapted to include styles for the new HTML5 elements.

If you are feeling a bit more adventurous, there is also Normalize.css (http://necolas.github.io/normalize.css/), created by Nicolas Gallagher. Normalize.css focuses not on using a hard reset for all common elements, but instead on setting common styles for these elements. It requires a stronger understanding of CSS, as well as awareness of what you'd like your styles to be.

Cross-Browser Compatibility & Testing

As previously mentioned, different browsers render elements in different ways. It's important to recognize the value in cross-browser compatibility and testing. Websites don't need to look exactly the same in every browser, but they should be close. Which browsers you wish to support, and to what degree, is a decision you will need to make based on what is best for your website.

In all there are a handful of things to be on the lookout for when writing CSS. The good news is that anything is possible, and with a little patience we'll figure it all out.

In Practice

Picking back up where we last left off on our conference website, let's see if we can add in a bit of CSS.

1. Inside of our "styles-conference" folder, let's create a new folder named "assets." We'll store all of the assets for our website, such as our style sheets, images, videos, and so forth, in this folder. For our style sheets, let's go ahead and add another folder named "stylesheets" inside the "assets" folder.

2. Using our text editor, let's create a new file named `main.css` and save it within the "stylesheets" folder we just created.

3. Looking at our `index.html` file in a web browser, we can see that the <h1> and <p> elements each have default CSS styles. Specifically, they each have a unique font size and spacing around them. Using Eric Meyer's reset, we can tone down these styles, allowing each of them to be styled from the same base. To do this let's head over to Eric's website (http://meyerweb.com/eric/tools/css/reset/), copy his reset, and paste it at the top of our `main.css` file.

```
1.   /* http://meyerweb.com/eric/tools/css/reset/
2.      v2.0 | 20110126
```

continues

```
3.    License: none (public domain)
4.  */
5.
6.  html, body, div, span, applet, object, iframe,
7.  h1, h2, h3, h4, h5, h6, p, blockquote, pre,
8.  a, abbr, acronym, address, big, cite, code,
9.  del, dfn, em, img, ins, kbd, q, s, samp,
10. small, strike, strong, sub, sup, tt, var,
11. b, u, i, center,
12. dl, dt, dd, ol, ul, li,
13. fieldset, form, label, legend,
14. table, caption, tbody, tfoot, thead, tr, th, td,
15. article, aside, canvas, details, embed,
16. figure, figcaption, footer, header, hgroup,
17. menu, nav, output, ruby, section, summary,
18. time, mark, audio, video {
19.   margin: 0;
20.   padding: 0;
21.   border: 0;
22.   font-size: 100%;
23.   font: inherit;
24.   vertical-align: baseline;
25. }
26. /* HTML5 display-role reset for older browsers */
27. article, aside, details, figcaption, figure,
28. footer, header, hgroup, menu, nav, section {
29.   display: block;
30. }
31. body {
32.   line-height: 1;
33. }
34. ol, ul {
35.   list-style: none;
36. }
37. blockquote, q {
38.   quotes: none;
39. }
40. blockquote:before, blockquote:after,
41. q:before, q:after {
```

```
42.     content: '';
43.     content: none;
44.   }
45.   table {
46.     border-collapse: collapse;
47.     border-spacing: 0;
48.   }
```

4. With our `main.css` file starting to take shape, let's connect it to our `index.html` file. Opening the `index.html` file in our text editor, let's add the `<link>` element within our `<head>` element, just after the `<title>` element.

5. Because we'll be referencing a style sheet within the `<link>` element, let's add the relation attribute, `rel`, with a value of `stylesheet`.

6. We also want to include a hyperlink reference, using the `href` attribute, to our `main.css` file. Remember, our `main.css` file is saved within the "stylesheets" folder, which is inside the "assets" folder. Therefore, the `href` attribute value, which is the path to our `main.css` file, needs to be `assets/stylesheets/main.css`.

```
1.   <head>
2.     <meta charset="utf-8">
3.     <title>Styles Conference</title>
4.     <link rel="stylesheet" href="assets/stylesheets/main.css">
5.   </head>
```

Time to check out our work and see if our HTML and CSS are getting along. Now opening our index.html file (or refreshing the page if it's already opened) within a web browser should show slightly different results than before. Currently our website should look like **Figure 1.6**.

Styles Conference
Every year the brightest web designers and front-end developers descend on Chicago to discuss the latest technologies. Join us this August!

Figure 1.6 Our Styles Conference website with a CSS reset

The source code for the exercises within this lesson can be found at http://learn.shayhowe.com/html-css/building-your-first-web-page.

Summary

So far, so good! We've taken a few big steps in this lesson.

Just think, you now know the basics of HTML and CSS. As we continue and you spend more time writing HTML and CSS, you'll become much more comfortable with the two languages.

To recap, so far we've covered the following:

- The difference between HTML and CSS
- Getting acquainted with HTML elements, tags, and attributes
- Setting up the structure of your first web page
- Getting acquainted with CSS selectors, properties, and values
- Working with CSS selectors
- Referencing CSS in your HTML
- The value of CSS resets

Now let's take a closer look at HTML and learn a little about semantics.

Lesson 2

Getting to Know HTML

With our introduction to HTML and CSS complete, it's time to dig a little deeper into HTML and examine the different components that make up this language.

In order to start building websites, we need to learn a little about which HTML elements are best used to display different types of content. It's also important to understand how elements are visually displayed on a web page, as well as what different elements mean semantically.

Using the proper element for the job goes a long way, and we'll want to make well-informed decisions in the process.

Semantics Overview

So what exactly are semantics? Semantics within HTML is the practice of giving content on the page meaning and structure by using the proper element. Semantic code describes the value of content on a page, regardless of the style or appearance of that content. There are several benefits to using semantic elements, including enabling computers, screen readers, search engines, and other devices to adequately read and understand the content on a web page. Additionally, semantic HTML is easier to manage and work with, as it shows clearly what each piece of content is about.

Moving forward, as new elements are introduced, we'll talk about what those elements actually mean and the type of content they best represent. Before we do that, though, let's look at two elements—<div>s and <span>s—that actually don't hold any semantic value. They exist for styling purposes only.

Identifying Divisions & Spans

Divisions, or <div>s, and <span>s are HTML elements that act as containers solely for styling purposes. As generic containers, they do not come with any overarching meaning or semantic value. Paragraphs are semantic in that content wrapped within a <p> element is known and understood as a paragraph. <div>s and <span>s do not hold any such meaning and are simply containers.

Block vs. Inline Elements

Most elements are either block- or inline-level elements. What's the difference?

Block-level elements begin on a new line, stacking one on top of the other, and occupy any available width. Block-level elements may be nested inside one another and may wrap inline-level elements. We'll most commonly see block-level elements used for larger pieces of content, such as paragraphs.

Inline-level elements do not begin on a new line. They fall into the normal flow of a document, lining up one after the other, and only maintain the width of their content. Inline-level elements may be nested inside one another; however, they cannot wrap block-level elements. We'll usually see inline-level elements with smaller pieces of content, such as a few words.

Both <div>s and <span>s, however, are extremely valuable when building a website in that they give us the ability to apply targeted styles to a contained set of content.

A <div> is a block-level element that is commonly used to identify large groupings of content, and which helps to build a web page's layout and design. A <span>, on the other hand, is an inline-level element commonly used to identify smaller groupings of text within a block-level element.

We'll commonly see <div>s and <span>s with class or id attributes for styling purposes. Choosing a class or id attribute value, or name, requires a bit of care. We want to choose a value that refers to the content of an element, not necessarily the appearance of an element.

For example, if we have a <div> with an orange background that contains social media links, our first thought might be to give the <div> a class value of orange. What happens if that orange background is later changed to blue? Having a class value of orange no longer makes sense. A more sensible choice for a class value would be social, as it pertains to the contents of the <div>, not the style.

```
1.  <!-- Division -->
2.  <div class="social">
3.    <p>I may be found on...</p>
4.    <p>Additionally, I have a profile on...</p>
5.  </div>
6.
7.  <!-- Span -->
8.  <p>Soon we'll be <span class="tooltip">writing HTML</span> with
    the best of them.</p>
```

Comments within HTML & CSS

The previous code includes exclamation points within the HTML, and that's all right. Those are not elements, those are comments.

HTML and CSS give us the ability to leave comments within our code, and any content wrapped within a comment will not be displayed on the web page. Comments help keep our files organized, allow us to set reminders, and provide a way for us to more effectively manage our code. Comments become especially useful when there are multiple people working on the same files.

HTML comments start with <!-- and end with -->. CSS comments start with /* and end with */.

Using Text-Based Elements

Many different forms of media and content exist online; however, text is predominant. Accordingly, there are a number of different elements for displaying text on a web page. For now we'll focus on the more popular elements, including headings, paragraphs, bold text to show importance, and italics for emphasis. Later, within Lesson 6, "Working with Typography," we'll take a closer look at how to style text.

Headings

Headings are block-level elements, and they come in six different rankings, `<h1>` through `<h6>`. Headings help to quickly break up content and establish hierarchy, and they are key identifiers for users reading a page. They also help search engines to index and determine the content on a page.

Headings should be used in an order that is relevant to the content of a page. The primary heading of a page or section should be marked up with an `<h1>` element, and subsequent headings should use `<h2>`, `<h3>`, `<h4>`, `<h5>`, and `<h6>` elements as necessary.

Each heading level should be used where it is semantically valued, and should not be used to make text bold or big—there are other, better ways to do that.

Here is an example of HTML for all the different heading levels and the resulting display on a web page (see **Figure 2.1**).

```
1.  <h1>Heading Level 1</h1>
2.  <h2>Heading Level 2</h2>
3.  <h3>Heading Level 3</h3>
4.  <h4>Heading Level 4</h4>
5.  <h5>Heading Level 5</h5>
6.  <h6>Heading Level 6</h6>
```

Heading Level 1

Heading Level 2

Heading Level 3

Heading Level 4

Heading Level 5

Heading Level 6

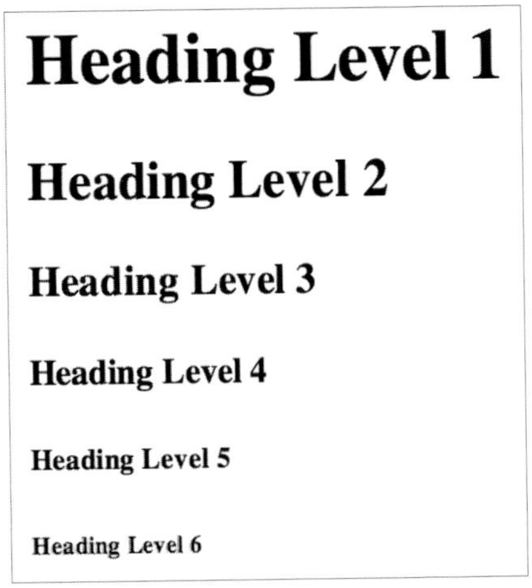

Figure 2.1 Various heading levels as displayed on a web page

Paragraphs

Headings are often followed by supporting paragraphs. Paragraphs are defined using the `<p>` block-level element. Paragraphs can appear one after the other, adding information to a page as desired. Here is example of how to set up paragraphs (see **Figure 2.2**).

```
1.   <p>Steve Jobs was a co-founder and longtime chief executive
     officer at Apple. On June 12, 2005, Steve gave the commencement
     address at Stanford University.</p>
2.
3.   <p>In his address Steve urged graduates to follow their dreams and,
     despite any setbacks, to never give up&ndash;advice which he
     sincerely took to heart.</p>
```

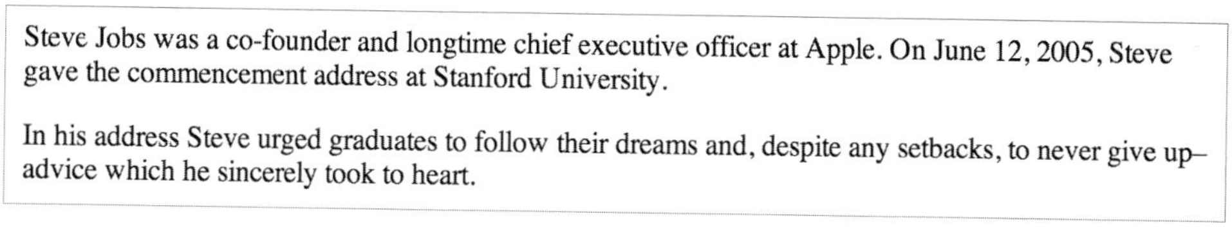

> Steve Jobs was a co-founder and longtime chief executive officer at Apple. On June 12, 2005, Steve gave the commencement address at Stanford University.
>
> In his address Steve urged graduates to follow their dreams and, despite any setbacks, to never give up–advice which he sincerely took to heart.

Figure 2.2 Two paragraphs as displayed on a web page

Bold Text with Strong

To make text bold and place a strong importance on it, we'll use the `<strong>` inline-level element. There are two elements that will bold text for us: the `<strong>` and `<b>` elements. It is important to understand the semantic difference between the two.

The `<strong>` element is semantically used to give *strong importance* to text, and is thus the most popular option for bolding text. The `<b>` element, on the other hand, semantically means to *stylistically offset* text, which isn't always the best choice for text deserving prominent attention. We have to gauge the significance of the text we wish to set as bold and to choose an element accordingly.

Here are the two HTML options for creating bold text in action (see **Figure 2.3**):

```
1.  <!-- Strong importance -->
2.  <p><strong>Caution:</strong> Falling rocks.</p>
3.
4.  <!-- Stylistically offset -->
5.  <p>This recipe calls for <b>bacon</b> and <b>baconnaise</b>.</p>
```

> **Caution:** Falling rocks.
>
> This recipe calls for **bacon** and **baconnaise**.

Figure 2.3 Using the <strong> and <b> elements to bold text properly, the word "Caution:" is semantically interpreted as having *strong importance*, and the words "bacon" and "baconnaise" are semantically interpreted as being *stylistically offset*

Italicize Text with Emphasis

To italicize text, thereby placing emphasis on it, we'll use the <em> inline-level element. As with the elements for bold text, there are two different elements that will italicize text, each with a slightly different semantic meaning.

The <em> element is used semantically to place a *stressed emphasis* on text; it is thus the most popular option for italicizing text. The other option, the <i> element, is used semantically to convey text in an *alternative voice or tone*, almost as if it were placed in quotation marks. Again, we will need to gauge the significance of the text we want to italicize and choose an element accordingly.

Here's the HTML code for italicizing text (see Figure 2.4):

```
1.  <!-- Stressed emphasis -->
2.  <p>I <em>love</em> Chicago!</p>
3.
4.  <!-- Alternative voice or tone -->
5.  <p>The name <i>Shay</i> means a gift.</p>
```

> I *love* Chicago!
>
> The name *Shay* means a gift.

Figure 2.4 Using the <em> and <i> elements to italicize text properly, the word "love" is semantically interpreted as having *stressed emphasis*, and the word "Shay" is semantically interpreted as having an *alternative voice or tone*

These text-level elements are quite handy for bringing our content to life. In addition to these, there are structurally based elements. Whereas text-based elements identify headings and paragraphs, structural elements identify groupings of content such as headers, articles, footers, and so forth. Let's take a look.

Building Structure

For the longest time the structure of a web page was built using divisions. The problem was that divisions provide no semantic value, and it was fairly difficult to determine the intention of these divisions. Fortunately HTML5 introduced new structurally based elements, including the <header>, <nav>, <article>, <section>, <aside>, and <footer> elements.

All of these new elements are intended to give meaning to the organization of our pages and improve our structural semantics. They are all block-level elements and do not have any implied position or style. Additionally, all of these elements may be used multiple times per page, so long as each use reflects the proper semantic meaning.

Let's roll up our sleeves and take a closer look.

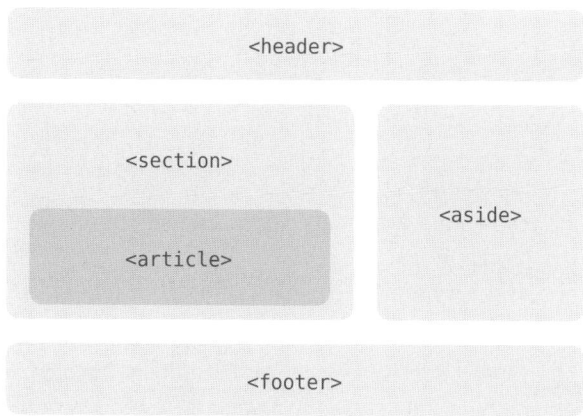

Figure 2.5 One possible example of HTML5 structural elements giving meaning to the organization of our pages

Header

The `<header>` element, like it sounds, is used to identify the top of a page, article, section, or other segment of a page. In general, the `<header>` element may include a heading, introductory text, and even navigation.

```
1.    <header>...</header>
```

`<header>` vs. `<head>` vs. `<h1>` through `<h6>` Elements

It is easy to confuse the `<header>` element with the `<head>` element or the heading elements, `<h1>` through `<h6>`. They all have different semantic meanings and should be used according to their meanings. For reference...

The `<header>` element is a structural element that outlines the heading of a segment of a page. It falls within the `<body>` element.

The `<head>` element is not displayed on a page and is used to outline metadata, including the document title, and links to external files. It falls directly within the `<html>` element.

Heading elements, `<h1>` through `<h6>`, are used to designate multiple levels of text headings throughout a page.

Navigation

The `<nav>` element identifies a section of major navigational links on a page. The `<nav>` element should be reserved for primary navigation sections only, such as global navigation, a table of contents, previous/next links, or other noteworthy groups of navigational links.

Most commonly, links included within the `<nav>` element will link to other pages within the same website or to parts of the same web page. Miscellaneous one-off links should not be wrapped within the `<nav>` element; they should use the anchor element, `<a>`, and the anchor element alone.

```
1.    <nav>...</nav>
```

Article

The `<article>` element is used to identify a section of independent, self-contained content that may be independently distributed or reused. We'll often use the `<article>` element to mark up blog posts, newspaper articles, user-submitted content, and the like.

When deciding whether to use the `<article>` element, we must determine if the content within the element could be replicated elsewhere without any confusion. If the content within the `<article>` element were removed from the context of the page and placed, for example, within an email or printed work, that content should still make sense.

```
1.  <article>...</article>
```

Section

The `<section>` element is used to identify a thematic grouping of content, which generally, but not always, includes a heading. The grouping of content within the `<section>` element may be generic in nature, but it's useful to identify all of the content as related.

The `<section>` element is commonly used to break up and provide hierarchy to a page.

```
1.  <section>...</section>
```

Deciding Between `<article>`, `<section>`, or `<div>` Elements

At times it becomes fairly difficult to decide which element—`<article>`, `<section>`, or `<div>`—is the best element for the job based on its semantic meaning. The trick here, as with every semantic decision, is to look at the content.

Both the `<article>` and `<section>` elements contribute to a document's structure and help to outline a document. If the content is being grouped solely for styling purposes and doesn't provide value to the outline of a document, use the `<div>` element.

If the content adds to the document outline and it can be independently redistributed or syndicated, use the `<article>` element.

If the content adds to the document outline and represents a thematic group of content, use the `<section>` element.

Aside

The `<aside>` element holds content, such as sidebars, inserts, or brief explanations, that is tangentially related to the content surrounding it. When used within an `<article>` element, for example, the `<aside>` element may identify content related to the author of the article.

We may instinctively think of an `<aside>` element as an element that appears off to the left or right side of a page. We have to remember, though, that all of the structural elements, including the `<aside>` element, are block-level elements and as such will appear on a new line, occupying the full available width of the page or of the element they are nested within, also known as their parent element.

1. `<aside>...</aside>`

We'll discuss how to change the position of an element, perhaps placing it to the right or left of a group of content, in Lesson 5, "Positioning Content."

Footer

The `<footer>` element identifies the closing or end of a page, article, section, or other segment of a page. Generally the `<footer>` element is found at the bottom of its parent. Content within the `<footer>` element should be relative information and should not diverge from the document or section it is included within.

1. `<footer>...</footer>`

With structural elements and text-based elements under our belts, our HTML knowledge is really starting to come together. Now is a good time to revisit our Styles Conference website and see if we can provide it with a little better structure.

In Practice

Currently, our Styles Conference website lacks real structure—and content for that matter. Let's take some time to flesh out our home page a bit.

1. Using our existing `index.html` file, let's add in a `<header>` element. Our `<header>` element should include our existing `<h1>` element; let's also add an `<h3>` element as a tagline to support our `<h1>` element.

```
1.   <header>
2.     <h1>Styles Conference</h1>
3.     <h3>August 24&ndash;26th &mdash; Chicago, IL</h3>
4.   </header>
```

2. After our `<header>` element, let's add a new group of content, using the `<section>` element, that introduces our conference. We'll begin this section with a new `<h2>` element and end it with our existing paragraph.

```
1.   <section>
2.     <h2>Dedicated to the Craft of Building Websites</h2>
3.     <p>Every year the brightest web designers and front-end
         developers descend on Chicago to discuss the latest technologies.
         Join us this August!</p>
4.   </section>
```

3. Following the introduction to our conference, let's add another group of content that teases a few of the pages we'll be adding, specifically the Speakers, Schedule, and Venue pages. Each of the pages we're teasing should also reside within its own section and include supporting text.

   We'll group all of the teasers inside a `<section>` element, and each individual teaser will be wrapped within a `<section>` element as well. In all, we'll have three `<section>` elements inside another `<section>` element, which is all right.

```
1.   <section>
2.
3.     <section>
4.       <h5>Speakers</h5>
5.       <h3>World-Class Speakers</h3>
6.       <p>Joining us from all around the world are over twenty
           fantastic speakers, here to share their stories.</p>
7.     </section>
8.
9.     ...
10.
11. </section>
```

4. Lastly, let's add our copyright within the `<footer>` element at the end of our page. To do so let's use the `<small>` element, which semantically represents side comments and small print—perfect for our copyright.

   Generally, content within the `<small>` element will be rendered as, well, small, but our CSS reset will prevent that from happening.

```
1. <footer>
2.   <small>&copy; Styles Conference</small>
3. </footer>
```

Now we can see our home page beginning to come to life, as in **Figure 2.6**.

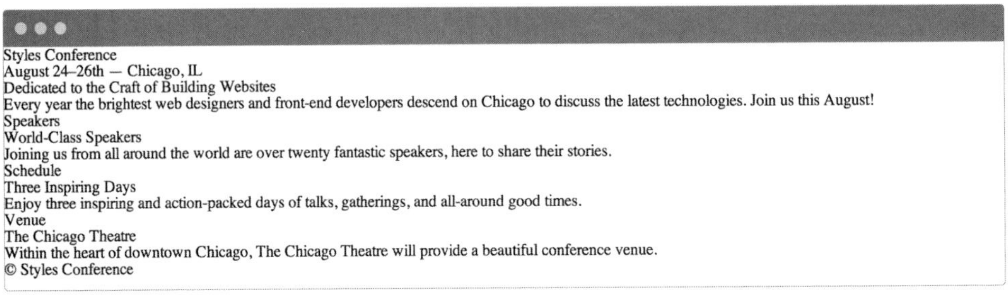

Styles Conference
August 24–26th — Chicago, IL
Dedicated to the Craft of Building Websites
Every year the brightest web designers and front-end developers descend on Chicago to discuss the latest technologies. Join us this August!
Speakers
World-Class Speakers
Joining us from all around the world are over twenty fantastic speakers, here to share their stories.
Schedule
Three Inspiring Days
Enjoy three inspiring and action-packed days of talks, gatherings, and all-around good times.
Venue
The Chicago Theatre
Within the heart of downtown Chicago, The Chicago Theatre will provide a beautiful conference venue.
© Styles Conference

Figure 2.6 Our home page after adding more content and structure

Encoding Special Characters

The `<h3>` element within our `<header>` element, as well as the `<small>` element within our `<footer>` element, has some interesting things going on. Specifically, a few special characters within these elements are being encoded.

Special characters include various punctuation marks, accented letters, and symbols. When typed directly into HTML, they can be misunderstood or mistaken for the wrong character; thus they need to be encoded.

Each encoded character will begin with an ampersand, &, and end with a semicolon, ;. What falls between the ampersand and semicolon is a character's unique encoding, be it a name or numeric encoding.

For example, we would encode the word "resumé" as `resum&eacute;`. Within our header we have encoded both en and em dashes, and within our footer we have encoded the copyright symbol. For reference, a long list of character encodings may be found at http://copypastecharacter.com.

With our home page taking shape, let's take a look at creating hyperlinks so that we may add additional pages and build out the rest of our website.

Creating Hyperlinks

Along with text, one of the core components of the Internet is the hyperlink, which provides the ability to link from one web page or resource to another. Hyperlinks are established using the anchor, <a>, inline-level element. In order to create a link from one page (or resource) to another, the href attribute, known as a hyperlink reference, is required. The href attribute value identifies the destination of the link.

For example, clicking the text "Shay," which is wrapped inside the anchor element with the href attribute value of http://shayhowe.com, will take users to my website (see Figure 2.7).

```
1.   <a href="http://shayhowe.com">Shay</a>
```

Shay

Figure 2.7 "Shay" used as hyperlink text referencing http://shayhowe.com

Wrapping Block-Level Elements with Anchors

By nature the anchor element, <a>, is an inline element, and, according to web standards, inline-level elements may not wrap block-level elements. With the introduction of HTML5, however, anchor elements specifically have permission to wrap either block-, inline-, or any other level elements. This is a break from the standard convention, but it's permissible in order to enable entire blocks of content on a page to become links.

Relative & Absolute Paths

The two most common types of links are links to *other pages* of the same website and links to *other websites*. These links are identified by their `href` attribute values, also known as their paths.

Links pointing to other pages of the same website will have a *relative path*, which does not include the domain (.com, .org, .edu, etc.) in the `href` attribute value. Because the link is pointing to another page on the same website, the `href` attribute value needs to include only the filename of the page being linked to: `about.html`, for example.

Should the page being linked to reside within a different directory, or folder, the `href` attribute value needs to reflect this as well. Say the `about.html` page resides within the `pages` directory; the relative path would then be `pages/about.html`.

Linking to other websites outside of the current one requires an *absolute path*, where the `href` attribute value must include the full domain. A link to Google would need the `href` attribute value of `http://google.com`, starting with `http` and including the domain, `.com` in this case.

Here clicking on the text "About" will open the `about.html` page inside our browser. Clicking the text "Google," on the other hand, will open `http://www.google.com/` within our browser.

```
1.  <!-- Relative Path -->
2.  <a href="/about.html">About</a>
3.
4.  <!-- Absolute Path -->
5.  <a href="http://www.google.com/">Google</a>
```

Linking to an Email Address

Occasionally we may want to create a hyperlink to our email address—for example, hyperlink text that says "Email Me," which when clicked opens a user's default email client and pre-populates part of an email. At a minimum the email address to which the email is being sent is populated; other information such as a subject line and body text may also be included.

To create an email link, the `href` attribute value needs to start with `mailto:` followed by the email address to which the email should be sent. To create an email link to shay@ awesome.com, for example, the `href` attribute value would be `mailto:shay@awesome.com`.

Additionally, subject, body text, and other information for the email may be populated. To add a subject line, we'll include the `subject=` parameter after the email address. The first parameter following the email address must begin with a question mark, `?`, to bind it to the hyperlink path. Multiple words within a subject line require that spaces be encoded using `%20`.

Adding body text works in the same way as adding the subject, this time using the `body=` parameter in the `href` attribute value. Because we are binding one parameter to another we need to use the ampersand, `&`, to separate the two. As with the subject, spaces must be encoded using `%20`, and line breaks must be encoded using `%0A`.

Altogether, a link to shay@awesome.com with the subject of "Reaching Out" and body text of "How are you" would require an `href` attribute value of

```
mailto:shay@awesome.com?subject=Reaching20%Out&body=How%20are%20you
```

Here's the full breakdown:

```
1.   <a href="mailto:shay@awesome.com?subject=Reaching20%Out&body=
     How%20are%20you">Email Me</a>
```

Opening Links in a New Window

One feature available with hyperlinks is the ability to determine where a link opens when clicked. Typically, links open in the same window from which they are clicked; however, links may also be opened in new windows.

To trigger the action of opening a link in a new window, use the `target` attribute with a value of `_blank`. The `target` attribute determines exactly where the link will be displayed, and the `_blank` value specifies a new window.

To open `http://shayhowe.com/` in a new window, the code would look like this:

```
1.   <a href="http://shayhowe.com/" target="_blank">Shay Howe</a>
```

Linking to Parts of the Same Page

Periodically we'll see hyperlinks that link to part of the same page the link appears on. A common example of these same-page links are "Back to top" links that return a user to the top of a page.

We can create an on-page link by first setting an ID attribute on the element we wish to link to, then using the value of that ID attribute within an anchor element's `href` attribute.

Using the "Back to top" link as an example, we can place an ID attribute value of `top` on the `<body>` element. Now we can create an anchor element with an `href` attribute value of #top, pound sign and all, to link to the beginning of the `<body>` element.

Our code for this same-page link would look like the following:

```
1.  <body id="top">
2.    ...
3.    <a href="#top">Back to top</a>
4.    ...
5.  </body>
```

Hyperlinks are incredibly useful and have revolutionized how we use the Internet. So far we've covered how to link to other pages or websites, as well as how to create email links and links to parts of the same page. Before we go any further, let's create some links of our own.

In Practice

It's time to take Styles Conference from a single-page website to a full-blown website with multiple pages, all of which will be linked together using hyperlinks.

1. We'll begin by making our "Styles Conference" text inside the `<h1>` element within our `<header>` element link to the `index.html` page.

    Because we are already on the `index.html` page, this may seem a little odd—and rightfully so—but as the header is replicated on other pages, linking back to the home page will make sense.

    ```
    1.  <h1>
    2.    <a href="index.html">Styles Conference</a>
    3.  </h1>
    ```

2. In order to navigate across all of the different pages, we're going add in a navigation menu, using the <nav> element, within our <header> element. We'll be creating Speakers, Schedule, Venue, and Register pages to go with our home page, so we should create links for all of them.

```
1.   <header>
2.
3.   ...
4.
5.     <nav>
6.       <a href="index.html">Home</a>
7.       <a href="speakers.html">Speakers</a>
8.       <a href="schedule.html">Schedule</a>
9.       <a href="venue.html">Venue</a>
10.      <a href="register.html">Register</a>
11.    </nav>
12.
13.  </header>
```

3. Let's also add the same navigation menu from our <header> element to our <footer> element for convenience.

```
1.   <footer>
2.
3.   ...
4.
5.     <nav>
6.       <a href="index.html">Home</a>
7.       <a href="speakers.html">Speakers</a>
8.       <a href="schedule.html">Schedule</a>
9.       <a href="venue.html">Venue</a>
10.      <a href="register.html">Register</a>
11.    </nav>
12.
13.  </footer>
```

4. Within the `<section>` element that introduces our conference, just below our header, we should also include a link to register for the conference. Placing a link below the paragraph will work perfectly.

```
1.  <section>
2.
3.    ...
4.
5.    <a href="register.html">Register Now</a>
6.
7.  </section>
```

5. We can't forget to add links to all of the sections teasing our other pages. Inside each section, let's wrap both the `<h3>` and `<h5>` elements within an anchor element linking to the proper page.

   We'll want to make sure we do this for every section accordingly.

```
1.  <section>
2.
3.    <section>
4.      <a href="speakers.html">
5.        <h5>Speakers</h5>
6.        <h3>World-Class Speakers</h3>
7.      </a>
8.      <p>Joining us from all around the world are over twenty
           fantastic speakers, here to share their stories.</p>
9.    </section>
10.
11.   ...
12.
13. </section>
```

6. Now we need to create a handful of new pages. Let's create `speakers.html`, `schedule.html`, `venue.html`, and `register.html` files. These files should live within the same folder as the `index.html` file, and, because we're keeping them inside the same folder, all of our links should work as expected.

   To ensure that all of our pages look the same, let's make sure that all of these new files have the same document structure and `<header>` and `<footer>` elements as the `index.html` file.

It's official, we're no longer working with a single page but indeed a full website. Our home page should now look like **Figure** 2.8.

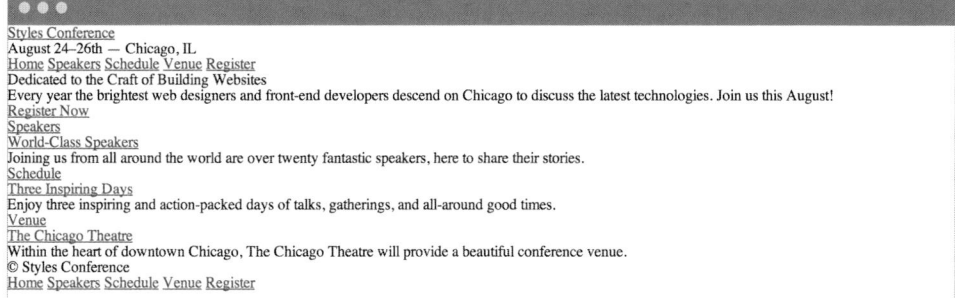

Figure 2.8 Our home page after all of the different links and navigation have been added

The source code for the exercises within this lesson can be found at http://learn.shayhowe.com/html-css/getting-to-know-html.

Summary

Semantics, as discussed within this lesson, are essential for providing our HTML with structure and meaning. Moving forward we'll periodically introduce new elements, all of which will come with their own semantic meaning. It is the meaning of all of these elements that will provide our content with the most value.

Once again, in this lesson we covered the following:

- What semantics are and why they are important
- `<div>`s and `<spans>`s, and the difference between block- and inline-level elements
- Which text-based elements best represent the content of a page
- The HTML5 structural elements and how to define the structure and organization of our content and page
- How to use hyperlinks to navigate between web pages or websites

Hopefully you're starting to feel pretty good about HTML. There is still quite a bit to learn, but the foundation is in place. Next up, we'll take a deeper look into CSS.

Lesson 3

Getting to Know CSS

CSS is a complex language that packs quite a bit of power. It allows us to add layout and design to our pages, and it allows us to share those styles from element to element and page to page. Before we can unlock all of its features, though, there are a few aspects of the language we must fully understand.

First, it's crucial to know exactly how styles are rendered. Specifically, we'll need to know how different types of selectors work and how the order of those selectors can affect how our styles are rendered. We'll also want to understand a few common property values that continually appear within CSS, particularly those that deal with color and length.

Let's look under the hood of CSS to see exactly what is going on.

The Cascade

We'll begin breaking down exactly how styles are rendered by looking at what is known as the *cascade* and studying a few examples of the cascade in action. Within CSS, all styles cascade from the top of a style sheet to the bottom, allowing different styles to be added or overwritten as the style sheet progresses.

For example, say we select all paragraph elements at the top of our style sheet and set their background color to orange and their font size to 24 pixels. Then towards the bottom of our style sheet, we select all paragraph elements again and set their background color to green, as seen here.

```
1.  p {
2.    background: orange;
3.    font-size: 24px;
4.  }
5.  p {
6.    background: green;
7.  }
```

Because the paragraph selector that sets the background color to green comes after the paragraph selector that sets the background color to orange, it will take precedence in the cascade. All of the paragraphs will appear with a green background. The font size will remain 24 pixels because the second paragraph selector didn't identify a new font size.

Cascading Properties

The cascade also works with properties inside individual selectors. Again, for example, say we select all the paragraph elements and set their background color to orange. Then directly below the orange background property and value declaration, we add another property and value declaration setting the background color to green, as seen here.

```
1.  p {
2.    background: orange;
3.    background: green;
4.  }
```

Because the green background color declaration comes after the orange background color declaration, it will overrule the orange background, and, as before, our paragraphs will appear with a green background.

All styles will cascade from the top of our style sheet to the bottom of our style sheet. There are, however, times where the cascade doesn't play so nicely. Those times occur when different types of selectors are used and the specificity of those selectors breaks the cascade. Let's take a look.

Calculating Specificity

Every selector in CSS has a specificity weight. A selector's specificity weight, along with its placement in the cascade, identifies how its styles will be rendered.

In Lesson 1, "Building Your First Web Page," we talked about three different types of selectors: the type, class, and ID selectors. Each of these selectors has a different specificity weight.

The type selector has the lowest specificity weight and holds a point value of 0-0-1. The class selector has a medium specificity weight and holds a point value of 0-1-0. Lastly, the ID selector has a high specificity weight and holds a point value of 1-0-0. As we can see, specificity points are calculated using three columns. The first column counts ID selectors, the second column counts class selectors, and the third column counts type selectors.

What's important to note here is that the ID selector has a higher specificity weight than the class selector, and the class selector has a higher specificity weight than the type selector.

Specificity Points

Specificity points are intentionally hyphenated, as their values are not computed from a base of 10. Class selectors do not hold a point value of 10, and ID selectors do not hold a point value of 100. Instead, these points should be read as 0-1-0 and 1-0-0 respectively. We'll take a closer look at why these point values are hyphenated shortly, when we combine selectors.

The higher the specificity weight of a selector, the more superiority the selector is given when a styling conflict occurs. For example, if a paragraph element is selected using a type selector in one place and an ID selector in another, the ID selector will take precedence over the type selector regardless of where the ID selector appears in the cascade.

HTML

```
1.  <p id="food">...</p>
```

CSS

```
1.  #food {
2.    background: green;
3.  }
4.  p {
5.    background: orange;
6.  }
```

Here we have a paragraph element with an ID attribute value of food. Within our CSS, that paragraph is being selected by two different kinds of selectors: one type selector and one ID selector. Although the type selector comes after the ID selector in the cascade, the ID selector takes precedence over the type selector because it has a higher specificity weight; consequently the paragraph will appear with a green background.

The specificity weights of different types of selectors are incredibly important to remember. At times styles may not appear on elements as intended, and chances are the specificity weights of our selectors are breaking the cascade, therefore our styles are not appearing properly.

Understanding how the cascade and specificity work is a huge hurdle, and we'll continue to cover this topic. For now, let's look at how to be a little more particular and intentional with our selectors by combining them. Keep in mind that as we combine selectors, we'll also be changing their specificity.

Combining Selectors

So far we've looked at how to use different types of selectors individually, but we also need to know how to use these selectors together. By combining selectors we can be more specific about which element or group of elements we'd like to select.

For example, say we want to select all paragraph elements that reside within an element with a class attribute value of hotdog and set their background color to brown. However, if one of those paragraphs happens to have the class attribute value of mustard, we want to set its background color to yellow. Our HTML and CSS may look like the following:

HTML

```
1.   <div class="hotdog">
2.     <p>...</p>
3.     <p>...</p>
4.     <p class="mustard">...</p>
5.   </div>
```

CSS

```
1.   .hotdog p {
2.     background: brown;
3.   }
4.   .hotdog p.mustard {
5.     background: yellow;
6.   }
```

When selectors are combined they should be read from right to left. The selector farthest to the right, directly before the opening curly bracket, is known as the *key selector*. The key selector identifies exactly which element the styles will be applied to. Any selector to the left of the key selector will serve as a prequalifier.

The first combined selector above, .hotdog p, includes two selectors: a class and a type selector. These two selectors are separated by a single space. The key selector is a type selector targeting paragraph elements. And because this type selector is prequalified with a class selector of hotdog, the full combined selector will only select paragraph elements that reside within an element with a class attribute value of hotdog.

The second selector above, `.hotdog p.mustard`, includes three selectors: two class selectors and one type selector. The only difference between the second selector and the first selector is the addition of the class selector of `mustard` to the end of the paragraph type selector. Because the new class selector, `mustard`, falls all the way to the right of the combined selector, it is the key selector, and all of the individual selectors coming before it are now prequalifiers.

Spaces Within Selectors

Within the previous combined selector, `.hotdog p.mustard`, there is a space between the `hotdog` class selector and the paragraph type selector but not between the paragraph type selector and the `mustard` class selector. The use, and omission, of spaces makes a large difference in selectors.

Since there isn't a space between the paragraph type selector and the `mustard` class selector that means the selector will only select paragraph elements with the class of `mustard`. If the paragraph type selector was removed, and the `mustard` class selector had spaces on both sides of it, it would select any element with the class of `mustard`, not just paragraphs.

The best practice is to not prefix a class selector with a type selector. Generally we want to select any element with a given class, not just one type of element. And following this best practice, our new combined selector would be better as `.hotdog .mustard`.

Reading the combined selector from right to left, it is targeting paragraphs with a class attribute value of `mustard` that reside within an element with the class attribute value of `hotdog`.

Different types of selectors can be combined to target any given element on a page. As we continue to write different combined selectors, we'll see their powers come to life. Before we do that, though, let's take a look at how combining selectors changes a selector's specificity weight.

Specificity Within Combined Selectors

When selectors are combined, so are the specificity weights of the individual selectors. These combined specificity weights can be calculated by counting each different type of selector within a combined selector.

Looking at our combined selectors from before, the first selector, `.hotdog p`, had both a class selector and a type selector. Knowing that the point value of a class selector is `0-1-0` and the point value of a type selector is `0-0-1`, the total combined point value would be `0-1-1`, found by adding up each kind of selector.

The second selector, `.hotdog p.mustard`, had two class selectors and one type selector. Combined, the selector has a specificity point value of `0-2-1`. The `0` in the first column is for zero ID selectors, the `2` in the second column is for two class selectors, and the `1` in the last column is for one type selector.

Comparing the two selectors, the second selector, with its two classes, has a noticeably higher specificity weight and point value. As such it will take precedence within the cascade. If we were to flip the order of these selectors within our style sheet, placing the higher-weighted selector above the lower-weighted selector as shown here, the appearance of their styles would not be affected due to each selector's specificity weight.

```
1.  .hotdog p.mustard {
2.    background: yellow;
3.  }
4.  .hotdog p {
5.    background: brown;
6.  }
```

In general we want to always keep an eye on the specificity weights of our selectors. The higher our specificity weights rise, the more likely our cascade is to break.

Layering Styles with Multiple Classes

One way to keep the specificity weights of our selectors low is to be as modular as possible, sharing similar styles from element to element. And one way to be as modular as possible is to layer on different styles by using multiple classes.

Elements within HTML can have more than one class attribute value so long as each value is space separated. With that, we can place certain styles on all elements of one sort while placing other styles only on specific elements of that sort.

We can tie styles we want to continually reuse to one class and layer on additional styles from another class.

Let's take a look at buttons, for example. Say we want all of our buttons to have a font size of 16 pixels, but we want the background color of our buttons to vary depending on where the buttons are used. We can create a few classes and layer them on an element as necessary to apply the desired styles.

HTML

```
1.  <a class="btn btn-danger">...</a>
2.
3.  <a class="btn btn-success">...</a>
```

CSS

```
1.  .btn {
2.    font-size: 16px;
3.  }
4.  .btn-danger {
5.    background: red;
6.  }
7.  .btn-success {
8.    background: green;
9.  }
```

Here you can see two anchor elements, both with multiple class attribute values. The first class, btn, is used to apply a font size of 16 pixels to each of the elements. Then, the first anchor element uses an additional class of btn-danger to apply a red background color while the second anchor element uses an additional class of btn-success to apply a green background color. Our styles here are clean and modular.

Using multiple classes, we can layer on as many styles as we wish, keeping our code lean and our specificity weights low. Much like understanding the cascade and calculating specificity, this is a practice that will take time to fully absorb, but we'll get better with each lesson.

Common CSS Property Values

We've used a handful of common CSS property values already, such as the keyword color values of red and green. You may not have thought too much about them; that's okay. We're going to take time now to go over some previously used property values as well as to explore some of the more common property values that we'll soon be using.

Specifically, we'll look at property values that relate to colors and length measurements.

Colors

All color values within CSS are defined on an sRGB (or standard red, green, and blue) color space. Colors within this space are formed by mixing red, green, and blue color channels together, mirroring the way that televisions and monitors generate all the different colors they display. By mixing different levels of red, green, and blue, we can create millions of colors—and find nearly any color we'd like.

Currently there are four primary ways to represent sRGB colors within CSS: keywords, hexadecimal notation, and RGB and HSL values.

Keyword Colors

Keyword color values are names (such as red, green, or blue) that map to a given color. These keyword names and their corresponding colors are determined by the CSS specification. Most common colors, along with a few oddities, have keyword names. A complete list of these keyword names can be found within the CSS specification (http://www.w3.org/TR/css3-color/), and a few of the more common keyword color values are listed in **Figure 3.1**.

Here we are applying a maroon background to any element with the task class attribute value and a yellow background to any element with the count class attribute value.

```
1.   .task {
2.     background: maroon;
3.   }
4.   .count {
5.     background: yellow;
6.   }
```

While keyword color values are simple in nature, they provide limited options and thus are not the most popular color value choice.

Figure 3.1 Some of the most common keyword color values, along with their hexadecimal, RGB, and HSL equivalents

	NAME	HEX VALUES	RGB VALUES	HSL VALUES
	black	#000000	rgb(0, 0, 0)	hsl(0, 0%, 0%)
	silver	#c0c0c0	rgb(192, 192, 192)	hsl(0, 0%, 75%)
	gray	#808080	rgb(128, 128, 128)	hsl(0, 0%, 50%)
	white	#ffffff	rgb(255, 255, 255)	hsl(0, 100%, 100%)
	maroon	#800000	rgb(128, 0, 0)	hsl(0, 100%, 25%)
	red	#ff0000	rgb(255, 0, 0)	hsl(0, 100%, 50%)
	purple	#800080	rgb(128, 0, 128)	hsl(300, 100%, 25%)
	fuschia	#ff00ff	rgb(255, 0, 255)	hsl(300, 100%, 50%)
	green	#008000	rgb(0, 128, 0)	hsl(120, 100%, 25%)
	olive	#00ff00	rgb(0, 255, 0)	hsl(120, 100%, 50%)
	lime	#808000	rgb(128, 128, 0)	hsl(60, 100%, 25%)
	yellow	#ffff00	rgb(255, 255, 0)	hsl(60, 100%, 50%)
	navy	#000080	rgb(0, 0, 128)	hsl(240, 100%, 25%)
	blue	#0000ff	rgb(0, 0, 255)	hsl(240, 100%, 50%)
	teal	#008080	rgb(0, 128, 128)	hsl(180, 100%, 25%)
	aqua	#00ffff	rgb(0, 255, 255)	hsl(180, 100%, 50%)

Hexadecimal Colors

Hexadecimal color values consist of a pound, or hash, #, followed by a three- or six-character figure. The figures use the numbers 0 through 9 and the letters a through f, upper or lower case. These values map to the red, green, and blue color channels.

In six-character notation, the first two characters represent the red channel, the third and fourth characters represent the green channel, and the last two characters represent the blue channel. In three-character notation, the first character represents the red channel, the second character represents the green channel, and the last character represents the blue channel.

If in six-character notation the first two characters are a matching pair, the third and fourth characters are a matching pair, and the last two characters are a matching pair, the six-character figure may be shortened to a three-character figure. To do this the repeated character from each pair should be used once. For example, a shade of orange represented by the hexadecimal color #ff6600 could also be written as #f60 (see **Figure 3.2**).

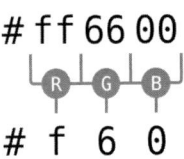

Figure 3.2 Six-character hexadecimal values may be written as three-character hexadecimal values when the red, green, and blue color channels each contain a repeating character

The character pairs are obtained by converting 0 through 255 into a base-16, or hexadecimal, format. The math is a little tricky—and worthy of its own book—but it helps to know that 0 equals black and F equals white.

The Millions of Hexadecimal Colors

There are millions of hexadecimal colors, over 16.7 million to be exact. Here's how…

There are 16 options for every character in a hexadecimal color, 0 through 9 and A through F. With the characters grouped in pairs, there are 256 color options per pair (16 multiplied by 16, or 16 squared).

And with three groups of 256 color options we have a total of over 16.7 million colors (256 multiplied by 256 multiplied by 256, or 256 cubed).

To create the same maroon and yellow background colors from before, we could replace the keyword color values with hexadecimal color values, as seen here.

```
1.   .task {
2.     background: #800;
3.   }
4.   .count {
5.     background: #ffff00;
6.   }
```

Hexadecimal color values have been around for a while, and they have become fairly popular because they offer a large number of color options. They are, however, a little difficult to work with, especially if you're not too familiar with them. Fortunately Adobe has created Adobe Kuler (https://kuler.adobe.com/), a free application that provides a color wheel to help us find any color we want and its corresponding hexadecimal value. Additionally, most image editing applications, such as Adobe Photoshop, provide the capability to locate hexadecimal color values (see **Figure 3.3**).

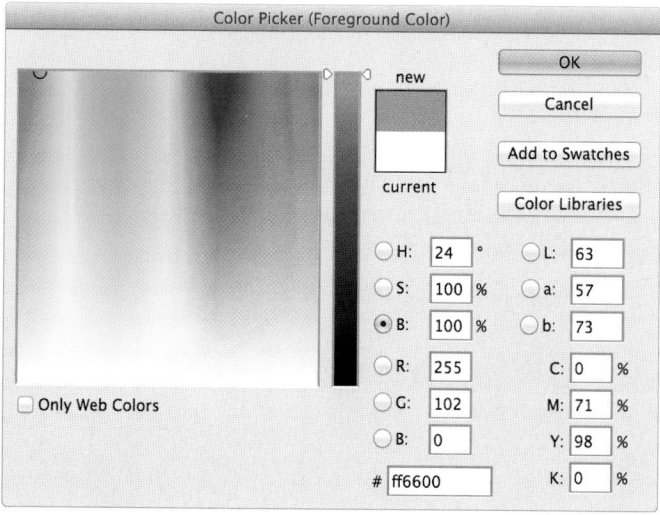

Figure 3.3 The color picker tool within Adobe Photoshop displays the hexadecimal, RGB, and HSL color values

RGB & RGBa Colors

RGB color values are stated using the `rgb()` function, which stands for red, green, and blue. The function accepts three comma-separated values, each of which is an integer from 0 to 255. A value of 0 would be pure black; a value of 255 would be pure white.

As we might expect, the first value within the `rgb()` function represents the red channel, the second value represents the green channel, and the third value represents the blue channel.

If we were to recreate the shade of orange from before as an RGB color value, it would be represented as `rgb(255, 102, 0)`.

Also, using the same maroon and yellow background colors from before, we could replace the keyword or hexadecimal color values with RGB color values.

```
1.   .task {
2.     background: rgb(128, 0, 0);
3.   }
4.   .count {
5.     background: rgb(255, 255, 0);
6.   }
```

RGB color values may also include an alpha, or transparency, channel by using the `rgba()` function. The `rgba()` function requires a fourth value, which must be a number between 0 and 1, including decimals. A value of 0 creates a fully transparent color, meaning it would be invisible, and a value of 1 creates a fully opaque color. Any decimal value in between 0 and 1 would create a semi-transparent color.

If we wanted our shade of orange to appear 50% opaque, we would use an RGBa color value of `rgba(255, 102, 0, .5)`.

We can also change the opacity of our `maroon` and `yellow` background colors. The following code sets the `maroon` background color to 25% opaque and leaves the `yellow` background color 100% opaque.

```
1.   .task {
2.     background: rgba(128, 0, 0, .25);
3.   }
4.   .count {
5.     background: rgba(255, 255, 0, 1);
6.   }
```

RGB color values are becoming more popular, especially due to the ability to create semi-transparent colors using RGBa.

HSL & HSLa Colors

HSL color values are stated using the `hsl()` function, which stands for hue, saturation, and lightness. Within the parentheses, the function accepts three comma-separated values, much like `rgb()`.

The first value, the hue, is a unitless number from 0 to 360. The numbers 0 through 360 represent the color wheel, and the value identifies the degree of a color on the color wheel.

The second and third values, the saturation and lightness, are percentage values from 0 to 100%. The saturation value identifies how saturated with color the hue is, with 0 being grayscale and 100% being fully saturated. The lightness identifies how dark or light the hue value is, with 0 being completely black and 100% being completely white.

Returning to our shade of orange, as an HSL color value it would be written as `hsl(24, 100%, 100%)`.

Our `maroon` and `yellow` background colors can also be stated as HSL color values, as shown here.

```
1.  .task {
2.    background: hsl(0, 100%, 50%);
3.  }
4.  .count {
5.    background: hsl(60, 100%, 100%);
6.  }
```

HSL color values, like RGBa, may also include an alpha, or transparency, channel with the use of the `hsla()` function. The behavior of the alpha channel is just like that of the `rgba()` function. A fourth value between 0 and 1, including decimals, must be added to the function to identify the degree of opacity.

Our shade of orange as an HSLa color set to 50% opaque would be represented as `hsl(24, 100%, 100%, .5)`.

The same 25% opaque `maroon` background color and 100% opaque `yellow` background color from before would look like the following as HSLa color values.

```
1.  .task {
2.    background: hsla(0, 100%, 50%, .25);
3.  }
4.  .count {
5.    background: hsla(60, 100%, 100%, 1);
6.  }
```

The HSL color value is the newest color value available within CSS. Due to its age and support within browsers, though, it isn't as widely used as the other values.

For the time being, hexadecimal color values remain the most popular as they are widely supported; though when an alpha channel for transparency is needed, RGBa color values are preferred. These preferences may change in the future, but for now we'll use hexadecimal and RGBa color values.

Lengths

Length values within CSS are similar to colors in that there are a handful of different types of values for length, all of which serve distinct purposes. Length values come in two different forms, absolute and relative, each of which uses different units of measurement.

We're going to stick to the more common—and more straightforward—values at the moment, as more complex values will provide much more power than we need for now.

Absolute Lengths

Absolute length values are the simplest length values, as they are fixed to a physical measurement, such as inches, centimeters, or millimeters. The most popular absolute unit of measurement is known as the pixel and is represented by the px unit notation.

Pixels

The pixel is equal to 1/96th of an inch; thus there are 96 pixels in an inch. The exact measurement of a pixel, however, may vary slightly between high-density and low-density viewing devices.

Pixels have been around for quite some time and are commonly used with a handful of different properties. The code here is using pixels to set the font size of all paragraphs to 14 pixels.

```
1.  p {
2.    font-size: 14px;
3.  }
```

With the changing landscape of viewing devices and their varying screen sizes, pixels have lost some of their popularity. As an absolute unit of measurement, they don't provide too much flexibility. Pixels are, however, trustworthy and great for getting started. We're going to lean on them quite a bit as we're learning the ropes of HTML and CSS.

Relative Lengths

In addition to absolute length values, there are also relative length values. Relative length values are a little more complicated, as they are not fixed units of measurement; they rely on the length of another measurement.

Percentages

Percentages, represented by the % unit notation, are one of the most popular relative values. Percentage lengths are defined in relation to the length of another object. For example, to set the width of an element to 50%, we have to know the width of its parent element, the element it is nested within, and then identify 50% of the parent element's width.

```
1.  .col {
2.    width: 50%;
3.  }
```

Here we've set the width of the element with the class attribute value of col to 50%. That 50% will be calculated relative to the width of the element's parent.

Percentages are extremely helpful for setting the height and width of elements and building out a web page's layout. We're going to rely on them often to help us out in these areas.

Em

The em unit is also a very popular relative value. The em unit is represented by the em unit notation, and its length is calculated based on an element's font size.

A single em unit is equivalent to an element's font size. So, for example, if an element has a font size of 14 pixels and a width set to 5em, the width would equal 70 pixels (14 pixels multiplied by 5).

```
1.  .banner {
2.    font-size: 14px;
3.    width: 5em;
4.  }
```

When a font size is not explicitly stated for an element, the em unit will be relative to the font size of the closest parent element with a stated font size.

The em unit is often used for styling text, including font sizes, as well as spacing around text, including margins and paddings. We'll explore text a bit more in Lesson 6, "Working with Typography."

There are a lot more absolute and relative units of measurement than those mentioned here. However, these three—pixels, percentages, and em units—are the most popular and the ones we're going to primarily use.

Summary

Sadly our Styles Conference website lay dormant this lesson. We focused on the foundations of CSS, covering exactly how it works and some common values we're sure to use.

To briefly recap, within this lesson we've discussed the following:

- How style sheets cascade from the top to the bottom of a file
- What specificity is and how we can calculate it
- How to combine selectors to target specific elements or groups of elements
- How to use multiple classes on a single element to layer on different styles for more modular code
- The different color values available to use within CSS, including keyword, hexadecimal, RGB, and HSL values
- The different length values available to use within CSS, including pixels, percentages, and em units

We still have a lot to cover, but the fundamentals are starting to fall into place. Within the next few lessons we'll continue to dive in to CSS, and our website will really begin to take shape.

Lesson 4

Opening the Box Model

We've familiarized ourselves with HTML and CSS; we know what they look like and how to accomplish some of the basics. Now we're going to go a bit deeper and look at exactly how elements are displayed on a page and how they are sized.

In the process we'll discuss what is known as the box model and how it works with HTML and CSS. We're also going to look at a few new CSS properties and use some of the length values we covered in Lesson 3. Let's begin.

How Are Elements Displayed?

Before jumping into the box model, it helps to understand how elements are displayed. In Lesson 2 we covered the difference between block-level and inline-level elements. To quickly recap, block-level elements occupy any available width, regardless of their content, and begin on a new line. Inline-level elements occupy only the width their content requires and line up on the same line, one after the other. Block-level elements are generally used for larger pieces of content, such as headings and structural elements. Inline-level elements are generally used for smaller pieces of content, such as a few words selected to be bold or italicized.

Display

Exactly how elements are displayed—as block-level elements, inline elements, or something else—is determined by the `display` property. Every element has a default display property value; however, as with all other property values, that value may be overwritten. There are quite a few values for the `display` property, but the most common are `block`, `inline`, `inline-block`, and `none`.

We can change an element's `display` property value by selecting that element within CSS and declaring a new `display` property value. A value of `block` will make that element a block-level element.

```
1.  p {
2.    display: block;
3.  }
```

A value of `inline` will make that element an inline-level element.

```
1.  p {
2.    display: inline;
3.  }
```

Things get interesting with the `inline-block` value. Using this value will allow an element to behave as a block-level element, accepting all box model properties (which we'll cover soon). However, the element will be displayed in line with other elements, and it will not begin on a new line by default.

```
1.  p {
2.    display: inline-block;
3.  }
```

Paragraph one. Paragraph two. Paragraph three.

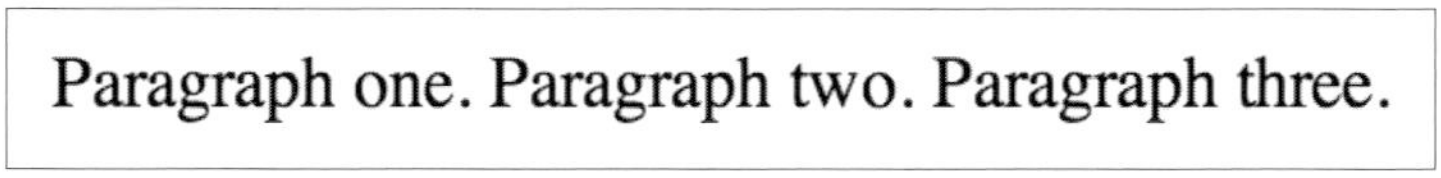

Figure 4.1 Three paragraphs displayed as `inline-block` elements, sitting one right next to the other in a horizontal line

The Space Between Inline-Block Elements

One important distinction with inline-block elements is that they are not always touching, or displayed directly against one another. Usually a small space will exist between two inline-block elements. This space, though perhaps annoying, is normal. We'll discuss why this space exists and how to remove it in the next lesson.

Lastly, using a value of none will completely hide an element and render the page as if that element doesn't exist. Any elements nested within this element will also be hidden.

```
1.  div {
2.    display: none;
3.  }
```

Knowing how elements are displayed and how to change their `display` is fairly important, as the `display` of an element has implications on how the box model is rendered. As we discuss the box model, we'll be sure to look at these different implications and how they can affect the presentation of an element.

What Is the Box Model?

According to the box model concept, every element on a page is a rectangular box and may have width, height, padding, borders, and margins (see **Figure 4.2**).

That's worth repeating: Every element on a page is a rectangular box.

Figure 4.2 When we look at each element individually, we can see how they are all rectangular, regardless of their presented shapes

Every element on every page conforms to the box model, so it's incredibly important. Let's take a look at it, along with a few new CSS properties, to better understand what we are working with.

Working with the Box Model

Every element is a rectangular box, and there are several properties that determine the size of that box. The core of the box is defined by the width and height of an element, which may be determined by the `display` property, by the contents of the element, or by specified `width` and `height` properties. `padding` and then `border` expand the dimensions of the box outward from the element's width and height. Lastly, any `margin` we have specified will follow the border.

Each part of the box model corresponds to a CSS property: `width`, `height`, `padding`, `border`, and `margin`.

Let's look these properties inside some code:

```
1.  div {
2.    border: 6px solid #949599;
3.    height: 100px;
```

```
4.    margin: 20px;
5.    padding: 20px;
6.    width: 400px;
7.  }
```

According to the box model, the total width of an element can be calculated using the following formula:

```
margin-right + border-right + padding-right + width + padding-left +
border-left + margin-left
```

In comparison, according to the box model, the total height of an element can be calculated using the following formula:

```
margin-top + border-top + padding-top + height + padding-bottom +
border-bottom + margin-bottom
```

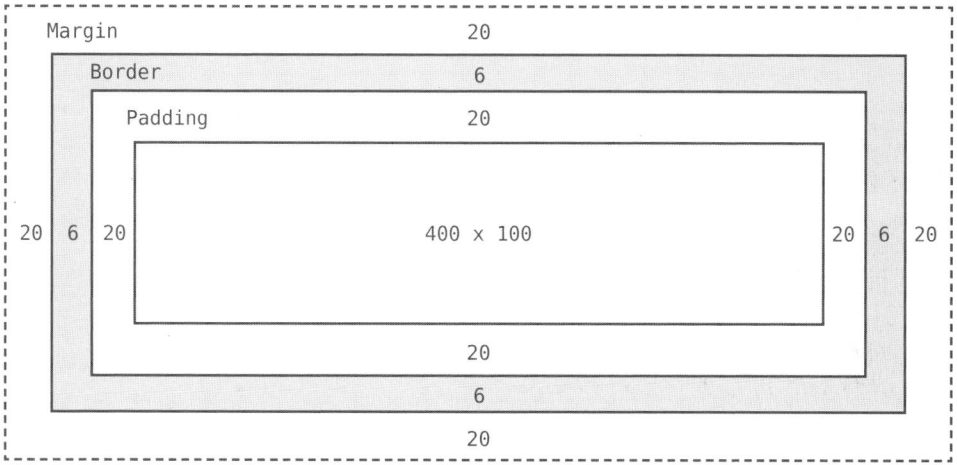

Figure 4.3 The box model broken down, including a base height and width plus paddings, borders, and margins

Using the formulas with the box shown in **Figure 4.3**, we can find the total height and width of our example.

- **Width:** 492px = 20px + 6px + 20px + 400px + 20px + 6px + 20px

- **Height:** 192px = 20px + 6px + 20px + 100px + 20px + 6px + 20px

The box model is without question one of the more confusing parts of HTML and CSS. We set a `width` property value of 400 pixels, but the actual width of our element is 492 pixels. By default the box model is additive; thus to determine the actual size of a box we need to take into account padding, borders, and margins for all four sides of the box. Our width not only includes the `width` property value, but also the size of the left and right padding, left and right borders, and left and right margins.

So far a lot of these properties might not make a whole lot of sense, and that's all right. To clarify things, let's take a close look at all of the properties—`width`, `height`, `padding`, `border`, and `margin`—that go into forming the box model.

Width & Height

Every element has default width and height. That width and height may be `0` pixels, but browsers, by default, will render every element with size. Depending on how an element is displayed, the default height and width may be adequate. If an element is key to the layout of a page, it may require specified `width` and `height` property values. In this case, the property values for non-inline elements may be specified.

Width

The default width of an element depends on its display value. Block-level elements have a default width of `100%`, consuming the entire horizontal space available. Inline and inline-block elements expand and contract horizontally to accommodate their content. Inline-level elements cannot have a fixed size, thus the `width` and `height` properties are only relevant to non-inline elements. To set a specific width for a non-inline element, use the `width` property:

```
1.  div {
2.    width: 400px;
3.  }
```

Height

The default height of an element is determined by its content. An element will expand and contract vertically as necessary to accommodate its content. To set a specific height for a non-inline element, use the `height` property:

```
1.  div {
2.    height: 100px;
3.  }
```

Sizing Inline-Level Elements

Please keep in mind that inline-level elements will not accept the `width` and `height` properties or any values tied to them. Block and inline-block elements will, however, accept the `width` and `height` properties and their corresponding values.

Margin & Padding

Depending on the element, browsers may apply default margins and padding to an element to help with legibility and clarity. We will generally see this with text-based elements. The default margins and padding for these elements may differ from browser to browser and element to element. In Lesson 1 we discussed using a CSS reset to tone all of these default values down to zero. Doing so allows us to work from the ground up and to specify our own values.

Margin

The `margin` property allows us to set the amount of space that surrounds an element. Margins for an element fall outside of any border and are completely transparent in color. Margins can be used to help position elements in a particular place on a page or to provide breathing room, keeping all other elements a safe distance away. Here's the `margin` property in action:

```
1.  div {
2.    margin: 20px;
3.  }
```

One oddity with the `margin` property is that vertical margins, `top` and `bottom`, are not accepted by inline-level elements. These vertical margins are, however, accepted by block-level and inline-block elements.

Padding

The `padding` property is very similar to the `margin` property; however, it falls inside of an element's border, should an element have a border. The `padding` property is used to provide spacing directly within an element. Here's the code:

```
1.  div {
2.    padding: 20px;
3.  }
```

The `padding` property, unlike the `margin` property, works vertically on inline-level elements. This vertical `padding` may blend into the line above or below the given element, but it will be displayed.

Margin & Padding on Inline-Level Elements

Inline-level elements are affected a bit differently than block and inline-block elements when it comes to margins and padding. Margins only work horizontally—`left` and `right`—on inline-level elements. Padding works on all four sides of inline-level elements; however, the `vertical` padding—the `top` and `bottom`—may bleed into the lines above and below an element.

Margins and padding work like normal for block and inline-block elements.

Margin & Padding Declarations

In CSS, there is more than one way to declare values for certain properties. We can use longhand, listing multiple properties and values one after the other, in which each value has its own property. Or we can use shorthand, listing multiple values with one property. Not all properties have a shorthand alternative, so we must make sure we are using the correct property and value structure.

The `margin` and `padding` properties come in both longhand and shorthand form. When using the shorthand `margin` property to set the same value for all four sides of an element, we specify one value:

```
1.  div {
2.    margin: 20px;
3.  }
```

To set one value for the `top` and `bottom` and another value for the left and right sides of an element, specify two values: `top` and `bottom` first, then `left` and `right`. Here we are placing margins of 10 pixels on the `top` and `bottom` of a `<div>` and margins of 20 pixels on the `left` and `right`:

```
1.    div {
2.      margin: 10px 20px;
3.    }
```

To set unique values for all four sides of an element, specify those values in the order of `top`, `right`, `bottom`, and `left`, moving clockwise. Here we are placing margins of 10 pixels on the `top` of a `<div>`, 20 pixels on the `right`, 0 pixels on the `bottom`, and 15 pixels on the `left`.

```
1.    div {
2.      margin: 10px 20px 0 15px;
3.    }
```

Using the `margin` or `padding` property alone, with any number of values, is considered shorthand. With longhand, we can set the value for one side at a time using unique properties. Each property name (in this case `margin` or `padding`) is followed by a dash and the side of the box to which the value is to be applied: `top`, `right`, `bottom`, or `left`. For example, the `padding-left` property accepts only one value and will set the `left` padding for that element; the `margin-top` property accepts only one value and will set the `top` margin for that element.

```
1.  div {
2.    margin-top: 10px;
3.    padding-left: 6px;
4.  }
```

When we wish to identify only one `margin` or `padding` value, it is best to use the long-hand properties. Doing so keeps our code explicit and helps us to avoid any confusion down the road. For example, did we really want to set the `top`, `right`, and `left` sides of the element to have margins of `0` pixels, or did we really only want to set the `bottom` margin to `10` pixels? Using longhand properties and values here helps to make our intentions clear. When dealing with three or more values, though, shorthand is incredibly helpful.

Margin & Padding Colors

The `margin` and `padding` properties are completely transparent and do not accept any color values. Being transparent, though, they show the background colors of relative elements. For margins, we see the background color of the parent element, and for padding, we see the background color of the element the `padding` is applied to.

Borders

Borders fall between the padding and margin, providing an outline around an element. The `border` property requires three values: `width`, `style`, and `color`. Shorthand values for the `border` property are stated in that order—`width`, `style`, `color`. In longhand, these three values can be broken up into the `border-width`, `border-style`, and `border-color` properties. These longhand properties are useful for changing, or overwriting, a single border value.

The `width` and `color` of borders can be defined using common CSS units of length and color, as discussed in Lesson 3.

Borders can have different appearances. The most common style values are `solid`, `double`, `dashed`, `dotted`, and `none`, but there are several others to choose from.

Here is the code for a 6-pixel-wide, solid, gray border that wraps around all four sides of a `<div>`:

```
1.  div {
2.    border: 6px solid #949599;
3.  }
```

Figure 4.4 Different border sizes and styles

Individual Border Sides

As with the `margin` and `padding` properties, borders can be placed on one side of an element at a time if we'd like. Doing so requires new properties: `border-top`, `border-right`, `border-bottom`, and `border-left`. The values for these properties are the same as those of the `border` property alone: `width`, `style`, and `color`. If we want, we can make a border appear only on the bottom of an element:

```
1.  div {
2.    border-bottom: 6px solid #949599;
3.  }
```

Additionally, styles for individual border sides may be controlled at an even finer level. For example, if we wish to change only the `width` of the bottom border we can use the following code:

```
1.  div {
2.    border-bottom-width: 12px;
3.  }
```

These highly specific longhand border properties include a series of hyphen-separated words starting with the `border` base, followed by the selected side—`top`, `right`, `bottom`, or `left`—and then `width`, `style`, or `color`, depending on the desired property.

Border Radius

While we're looking at borders and their different properties, we need to examine the `border-radius` property, which enables us to round the corners of an element.

The `border-radius` property accepts length units, including percentages and pixels, that identify the radius by which the corners of an element are to be rounded. A single value will round all four corners of an element equally; two values will round the `top-left`/`bottom-right` and `top-right`/`bottom-left` corners in that order; four values will round the `top-left`, `top-right`, `bottom-right`, and `bottom-left` corners in that order.

When considering the order in which multiple values are applied to the `border-radius` property (as well as the `margin` and `padding` properties), remember that they move in a clockwise fashion starting at the top left of an element.

```
1.  div {
2.    border-radius: 5px;
3.  }
```

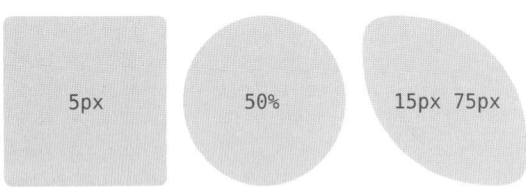

Figure 4.5
Different border-radius sizes

The `border-radius` property may also be broken out into longhand properties that allow us to change the radii of individual corners of an element. These longhand properties begin with `border`, continue with the corner's vertical location (`top` or `bottom`) and the corner's horizontal location (`left` or `right`), and then end with `radius`. For example, to change the top-right corner radius of a `<div>`, the `border-top-right-radius` property can be used.

```
1.  div {
2.    border-top-right—radius: 5px;
3.  }
```

Box Sizing

Until now the box model has been an additive design. If you set the `width` of an element to `400` pixels and then add `20` pixels of `padding` and a `border` of `10` pixels on every side, the actual full width of the element becomes `460` pixels. Remember, we need to add the `width`, `padding`, and `border` property values together to get the actual, full width of an element.

The box model may, however, be changed to support different calculations. CSS3 introduced the `box-sizing` property, which allows us to change exactly how the box model works and how an element's size is calculated. The property accepts three primary values—`content-box`, `padding-box`, and `border-box`—each of which has a slightly different impact on how the box size is calculated.

Content Box

The `content-box` value is the default value, leaving the box model as an additive design. If we don't use the `box-sizing` property, this will be the default value for all elements. The size of an element begins with the `width` and `height` properties, and then any `padding`, `border`, or `margin` property values are added on from there.

```
1.  div {
2.    -webkit-box-sizing: content-box;
3.      -moz-box-sizing: content-box;
4.           box-sizing: content-box;
5.  }
```

Browser-Specific Properties & Values

What are all those hyphens and letters on the `box-sizing` property?

As CSS3 was introduced, browsers gradually began to support different properties and values, including the `box-sizing` property, by way of vendor prefixes. As parts of the CSS3 specification are finalized and new browser versions are released, these vendor prefixes become less and less relevant. As time goes on, vendor prefixes are unlikely to be a problem; however, they still provide support for some of the older browsers that leveraged them. We may run across them from time to time, and we may even want to use them should we wish to support older browsers.

Vendor prefixes may be seen on both properties and values, all depending on the CSS specification. Here they are shown on the `box-sizing` property. Browser vendors were free to chose when to use a prefix and when not to. Thus, some properties and values require vendor prefixes for certain browser vendors but not for others.

Moving forward, when a property or value needs a vendor prefix, the prefix will only be used in the introduction of that property or value (in the interest of keeping our code digestible and concise). Do not forget to add the necessary vendor prefixes when you're actually writing the code.

For reference, the most common vendor prefixes are outlined here:

- Mozilla Firefox: `-moz-`
- Microsoft Internet Explorer: `-ms-`
- Webkit (Google Chrome and Apple Safari): `-webkit-`

Padding Box

The `padding-box` value alters the box model by including any `padding` property values within the `width` and `height` of an element. When using the `padding-box` value, if an element has a width of 400 pixels and a `padding` of 20 pixels around every side, the actual `width` will remain 400 pixels. As any `padding` values increase, the content size within an element shrinks proportionately.

If we add a `border` or `margin`, those values will be added to the `width` or `height` properties to calculate the full box size. For example, if we add a `border` of 10 pixels and a `padding` of 20 pixels around every side of the element with a `width` of 400 pixels, the actual full width will become 420 pixels.

```
1.  div {
2.    box-sizing: padding-box;
3.  }
```

Border Box

Lastly, the `border-box` value alters the box model so that any `border` or `padding` property values are included within the `width` and `height` of an element. When using the `border-box` value, if an element has a `width` of 400 pixels, a `padding` of 20 pixels around every side, and a `border` of 10 pixels around every side, the actual `width` will remain 400 pixels.

If we add a `margin`, those values will need to be added to calculate the full box size. No matter which `box-sizing` property value is used, any `margin` values will need to be added to calculate the full size of the element.

```
1.  div {
2.    box-sizing: border-box;
3.  }
```

Figure 4.6
Different box-sizing values allow the width of an element—and its box—to be calculated from different areas

Picking a Box Size

Generally speaking, the best `box-sizing` value to use is `border-box`. The `border-box` value makes our math much, much easier. If we want an element to be `400` pixels wide, it is, and it will remain `400` pixels wide no matter what padding or border values we add to it.

Additionally, we can easily mix length values. Say we want our box to be `40%` wide. Adding a `padding` of `20` pixels and a `border` of `10` pixels around every side of an element isn't difficult, and we can still guarantee that the actual `width` of our box will remain `40%` despite using pixel values elsewhere.

The only drawback to using the `box-sizing` property is that as part of the CSS3 specification, it isn't supported in every browser; it especially lacks support in older browsers. Fortunately this is becoming less and less relevant as new browsers are released. Chances are we're safe to use the `box-sizing` property, but should we notice any issues, it's worth looking into which browser those issues are occurring with.

Developer Tools

Most browsers have what are known as *Developer Tools*. These tools allow us to inspect an element on a page, see where that element lives within the HTML document, and see what CSS properties and values are being applied to it. Most of these tools also include a box model diagram to show the computed size of an element.

To see the Developer Tools in Google Chrome, click "View" within the menu bar and navigate to "Developer" and then "Developer Tools." This loads a drawer at the bottom of the browser window that provides a handful of tools for inspecting our code.

Clicking the magnifying glass at the bottom of this drawer enables us to hover over and then click on different elements on the page to review more information about them. After selecting an element, we'll see a handful of tabs on the right-hand side of the Elements panel within our Developer Tools. Selecting the "Computed" tab will show us a breakdown of the box model for our selected element.

Play around with the Developer Tools, be it in Google Chrome, Mozilla Firefox, Apple Safari, or other browsers; there is much to learn from looking at our code. I generally leave the Developer Tools open at all times when writing HTML and CSS. And I frequently inspect the code of other websites to see how they are built, too.

Figure 4.7 The Google Chrome Developer Tools, which help us to inspect the HTML and CSS on any page

The box model is one of the most confusing parts of learning how to write HTML and CSS. It is also one of the most powerful parts of HTML and CSS, and once we have it mastered, most everything else—like positioning content—will come to us fairly easily.

In Practice

Let's jump back into our Styles Conference website to center it on the page and add some more content.

1. Let's start by adjusting our box size to use the `border-box` version of the box model, which will make sizing all of our elements much easier. Within our `main.css` file, just below our reset, let's add a comment to identify the code for what will become our grid and help determine the layout of our website. We're putting this below our reset so that it falls in the proper position within the cascade.

   From there, we can use the universal selector, *, along with universal pseudo-elements, `*:before` and `*:after`, to select every imaginable element and change the `box-sizing` to `border-box`. Remember, we're going to want to include the necessary vendor prefixes for the `box-sizing` property, as it is a relatively new property.

   ```
   1.  /*
   2.  ========================================
   3.  Grid
   4.  ========================================
   5.  */
   6.
   7.  *,
   8.  *:before,
   ```

```
9.    *:after {
10.     -webkit-box-sizing: border-box;
11.        -moz-box-sizing: border-box;
12.             box-sizing: border-box;
13.  }
```

2. Next we'll want to create a class that will serve as a container for our elements. We can use this container class on different elements to set a common `width`, center the elements on the page, and apply some common horizontal `padding`.

    Just below our universal selector rule set, let's create a selector with a class of `container`. Within this selector let's set our `width` to 960 pixels, our `left` and `right` padding to 30 pixels, our `top` and `bottom` margins to 0, and our `left` and `right` margins to `auto`.

    Setting a `width` tells the browser definitively how wide any element with the class of `container` should be. Using a `left` and `right` margin of `auto` in conjunction with this `width` lets the browser automatically figure out equal `left` and `right` margins for the element, thus centering it on the page. Lastly, the `left` and `right` padding ensures that our content isn't sitting directly on the edge of the element and provides a little breathing room for the content.

```
1.    .container {
2.      margin: 0 auto;
3.      padding-left: 30px;
4.      padding-right: 30px;
5.      width: 960px;
6.    }
```

3. Now that we have a container class available to use, let's go ahead and apply the class of `container` throughout our HTML to the `<header>` and `<footer>` elements on each page, including the `index.html`, `speakers.html`, `schedule.html`, `venue.html`, and `register.html` files.

```
1.    <header class="container">...</header>
2.
3.    <footer class="container">...</footer>
```

4. While we're at it, let's go ahead and center the rest of the content on our pages. On the home page, our `index.html` file, let's add the class of `container` to each `<section>` element on the page, one for our hero section (the section that introduces our conference) and one for our teasers section.

```
1.    <section class="container">...</section>
```

Additionally, let's wrap all of the <h1> elements on each page with a <section> element with the class of container.

```
1.  <section class="container">
2.
3.    <h1>...</h1>
4.
5.  </section>
```

We'll come back and adjust these elements and classes later, but for now we're headed in the right direction.

5. Now that all of our content is centered, let's create some vertical spacing between elements. For starters let's place a 22-pixel bottom margin on a few of our heading and paragraph elements. We'll place and comment on these typography styles below our grid styles.

```
1.  /*
2.    =======================================
3.    Typography
4.    =======================================
5.  */
6.
7.  h1, h3, h4, h5, p {
8.    margin-bottom: 22px;
9.  }
```

We intentionally skipped <h2> and <h6> elements, as the design does not call for margins on <h2> elements and as we won't be using any <h6> elements at this time.

6. Let's also try our hand at creating a border and some rounded corners. We'll start by placing a button within the top <section> element on our home page, just below the header.

Previously we added an <a> element within this <section> element. Let's add the classes of btn and btn-alt to this anchor.

```
1.  <a class="btn btn-alt">...</a>
```

Now let's create some styles for those classes within our CSS. Below our typography rule set, let's create a new section of the CSS file for buttons.

To begin let's add the `btn` class and apply some common styles that can be shared across all buttons. We'll want all of our buttons to have a 5-pixel `border-radius`. They should be displayed as `inline-block` elements so we can add `padding` around all four sides without issue; we'll remove any `margin`.

```
1.   /*
2.      ========================================
3.      Buttons
4.      ========================================
5.   */
6.
7.   .btn {
8.     border-radius: 5px;
9.     display: inline-block;
10.    margin: 0;
11.  }
```

We'll also want to include styles specific to this button, which we'll do by using the `btn-alt` class. Here we'll add a 1-pixel, `solid`, gray border with 10 pixels of `padding` on the `top` and `bottom` of the button and 30 pixels of `padding` on the `left` and `right` of the button.

```
1.   .btn-alt {
2.     border: 1px solid #dfe2e5;
3.     padding: 10px 30px;
4.   }
```

Using both the `btn` and `btn-alt` classes on the same <a> element allows these styles to be layered on, rendering all of the styles on a single element.

7. Because we're working on the home page, let's also add a bit of `padding` to the <section> element that contains our <a> element with the classes of `btn` and `btn-alt`. We'll do so by adding a class attribute value of `hero` to the <section> element, alongside the `container` class attribute value, as this will be the leading section of our website.

```
1.   <section class="hero container">
2.     ...
3.   </section>
```

Next we'll want to create a new section within our CSS file for home page styles, and, once we're ready, we'll use the class of `hero` to apply `padding` around all four sides of the `<section>` element.

```
1.   /*
2.      ======================================
3.      Home
4.      ======================================
5.   */
6.
7.   .hero {
8.     padding: 22px 80px 66px 80px;
9.   }
```

Our website is starting to come together, especially the home page, as shown in **Figure 4.8**.

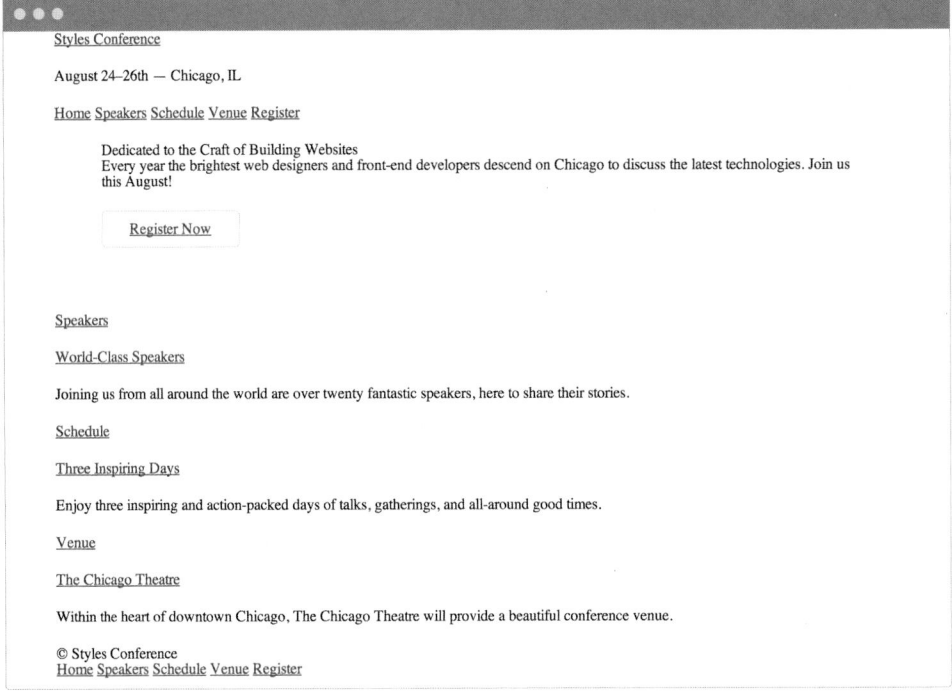

Figure 4.8 Our Styles Conference home page, taking shape after a few updates

The source code for the exercises within this lesson can be found at http://learn.shayhowe.com/html-css/opening-the-box-model/.

The Universal Selector

In the first step of this exercise we were introduced to the *universal selector*. In CSS the asterisk, *, is the universal selector, which selects every element. Rather than listing every single element imaginable, we can use the asterisk as a catch-all to select all elements for us.

The :before and :after pseudo-elements also mentioned in this step are elements that can be dynamically generated with CSS. We're not going to be using these elements within our project; however, when using the universal selector it's a good practice to also include these pseudo-elements in case they should ever appear.

Summary

Take a second and pat yourself on the back. I'll wait.

Learning all the different parts of the box model is no small feat. These concepts, although briefly introduced, take quite a bit of time to fully master, and we're on the right path toward doing so.

In brief, within this lesson we talked about the following:

- How different elements are displayed
- What the box model is and why it's important
- How to change the size, including the height and width, of elements
- How to add margin, padding, and borders to elements
- How to change the box sizing of elements and the effects this has on the box model

Now that we have a better understanding of how elements are displayed and sized, it's time to move into positioning these elements.

Lesson 5

Positioning Content

One of the best things about CSS is that it gives us the ability to position content and elements on a page in nearly any imaginable way, bringing structure to our designs and helping make content more digestible.

There are a few different types of positioning within CSS, and each has its own application. In this chapter we're going to take a look at a few different use cases—creating reusable layouts and uniquely positioning one-off elements—and describe a few ways to go about each.

Positioning with Floats

One way to position elements on a page is with the `float` property. The `float` property is pretty versatile and can be used in a number of different ways.

Essentially, the `float` property allows us to take an element, remove it from the normal flow of a page, and position it to the left or right of its parent element. All other elements on the page will then flow around the floated element. An `<img>` element floated to the side of a few paragraphs of text, for example, will allow the paragraphs to wrap around the image as necessary.

When the `float` property is used on multiple elements at the same time, it provides the ability to create a layout by floating elements directly next to or opposite each other, as seen in multiple-column layouts.

The `float` property accepts a few values; the two most popular values are `left` and `right`, which allow elements to be floated to the left or right of their parent element.

```
1.  img {
2.    float: left;
3.  }
```

Floats in Practice

Let's create a common page layout with a header at the top, two columns in the center, and a footer at the bottom (see **Figure 5.1**). Ideally this page would be marked up using the `<header>`, `<section>`, `<aside>`, and `<footer>` elements as discussed in Lesson 2, "Getting to Know HTML." Inside the `<body>` element, the HTML may look like this:

```
1.  <header>...</header>
2.  <section>...</section>
3.  <aside>...</aside>
4.  <footer>...</footer>
```

Figure 5.1 A common page layout without any floats

Here the <section> and <aside> elements, as block-level elements, will be stacked on top of one another by default. However, we want these elements to sit side by side. By floating the <section> to the left and the <aside> to the right, we can position them as two columns sitting opposite one another. Our CSS should look like this:

```
1.  section {
2.    float: left;
3.  }
4.
5.  aside {
6.    float: right;
7.  }
```

For reference, when an element is floated, it will float all the way to the edge of its parent element. If there isn't a parent element, the floated element will then float all the way to the edge of the page.

When we float an element, we take it out of the normal flow of the HTML document. This causes the width of that element to default to the width of the content within it. Sometimes, such as when we're creating columns for a reusable layout, this behavior is not desired. It can be corrected by adding a fixed width property value to each column. Additionally, to prevent floated elements from touching one another, causing the content of one to sit directly next to the content of the other, we can use the margin property to create space between elements.

Here, we are extending the previous code block, adding a `margin` and `width` to each column to better shape our desired outcome (**Figure 5.2**).

```
1.  section {
2.    float: left;
3.    margin: 0 1.5%;
4.    width: 63%;
5.  }
6.  aside {
7.    float: right;
8.    margin: 0 1.5%;
9.    width: 30%;
10. }
```

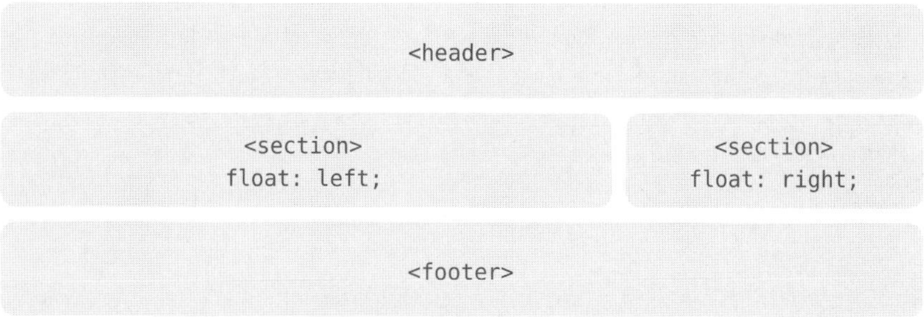

Figure 5.2 A two-column page layout using floats

Floats May Change an Element's Display Value

When floating an element, it is also important to recognize that an element is removed from the normal flow of a page, and that may change an element's default `display` value. The `float` property relies on an element having a `display` value of `block`, and may alter an element's default `display` value if it is not already displayed as a block-level element.

For example, an element with a `display` value of `inline`, such as the `<span>` inline-level element, ignores any `height` or `width` property values. However, should that inline-level element be floated, its `display` value will be changed to `block`, and it may then accept `height` or `width` property values.

As we float elements we must keep an eye on how their `display` property values are affected.

With two columns we can float one column to the left and another to the right, but with more columns we must change our approach. Say, for example, we'd like to have a row of three columns between our <header> and <footer> elements. If we drop our <aside> element and use three <section> elements, our HTML might look like this:

```
1.   <header>...</header>
2.   <section>...</section>
3.   <section>...</section>
4.   <section>...</section>
5.   <footer>...</footer>
```

To position these three <section> elements in a three-column row, instead of floating one column to the left and one column to the right, we'll float all three <section> elements to the left. We'll also need to adjust the width of the <section> elements to account for the additional columns and to get them to sit one next to the other (see **Figure 5.3**).

```
1.   section {
2.     float: left;
3.     margin: 0 1.5%;
4.     width: 30%;
5.   }
```

Here we have three columns, all with equal `width` and `margin` values and all floated to the `left`.

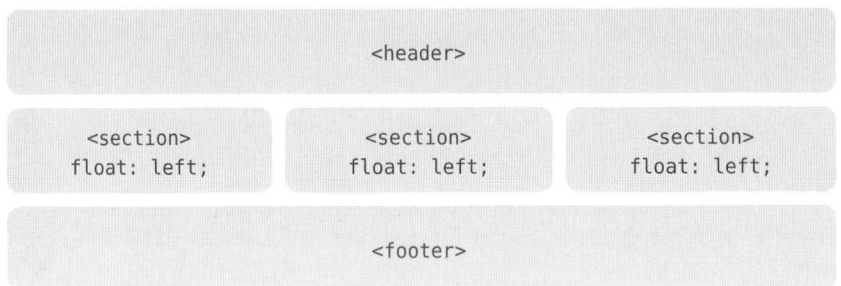

Figure 5.3 A three-column page layout using floats

Clearing & Containing Floats

The `float` property was originally designed to allow content to wrap around images. An image could be floated, and all of the content surrounding that image could then naturally flow around it. Although this works great for images, the float property was never actually intended to be used for layout and positioning purposes, and thus it comes with a few pitfalls.

One of those pitfalls is that occasionally the proper styles will not render on an element that it is sitting next to or is a parent element of a floated element. When an element is floated, it is taken out of the normal flow of the page, and, as a result, the styles of elements around that floated element can be negatively impacted.

Often `margin` and `padding` property values aren't interpreted correctly, causing them to blend into the floated element; other properties can be affected, too.

Another pitfall is that sometimes unwanted content begins to wrap around a floated element. Removing an element from the flow of the document allows all the elements around the floated element to wrap and consume any available space around the floated element, which is often undesired.

With our previous two-column example, after we floated the `<section>` and `<aside>` elements, and before we set a `width` property value on either of them, the content within the `<footer>` element would have wrapped in between the two floated elements above it, filling in any available space. Consequently, the `<footer>` element would have sat in the gutter between the `<section>` and `<aside>` elements, consuming the available space (see **Figure 5.4**).

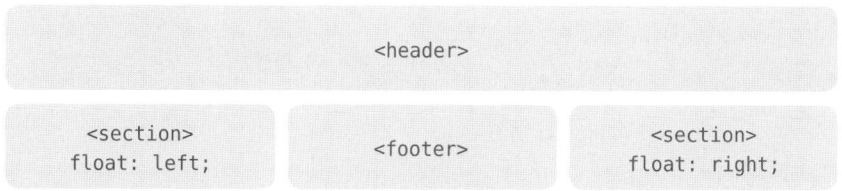

Figure 5.4 A two-column page layout without any identified column widths or cleared floats

To prevent content from wrapping around floated elements, we need to clear, or contain, those floats and return the page to its normal flow. We'll proceed by looking at how to clear floats, and then we'll take a look at how to contain floats.

Clearing Floats

Clearing floats is accomplished using the `clear` property, which accepts a few different values: the most commonly used values being `left`, `right`, and `both`.

```
1.  div {
2.    clear: left;
3.  }
```

The `left` value will clear left floats, while the `right` value will clear right floats. The `both` value, however, will clear both left and right floats and is often the most ideal value.

Going back to our previous example, if we use the `clear` property with the value of `both` on the `<footer>` element, we are able to clear the floats (see **Figure 5.5**). It is important that this `clear` be applied to an element appearing after the floated elements, not before, to return the page to its normal flow.

```
1.  footer {
2.    clear: both;
3.  }
```

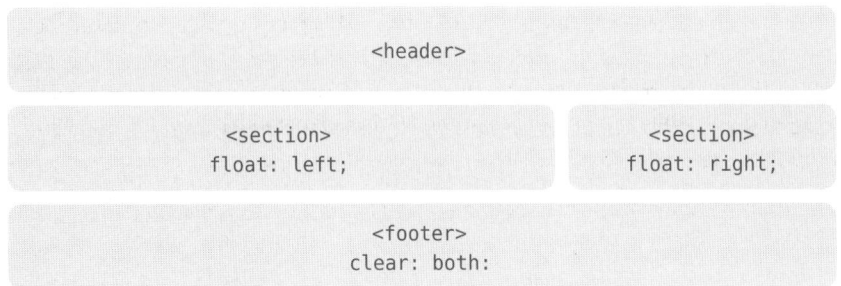

Figure 5.5 A two-column page layout with properly cleared floats

Containing Floats

Rather than clearing floats, another option is to contain the floats. The outcomes of containing floats versus those of clearing them are nearly the same; however, containing floats does help to ensure that all of our styles will be rendered properly.

To contain floats, the floated elements must reside within a parent element. The parent element will act as a container, leaving the flow of the document completely normal outside of it. The CSS for that parent element, represented by the `group` class below, is shown here:

```
1.  .group:before,
2.  .group:after {
3.    content: "";
4.    display: table;
5.  }
6.  .group:after {
7.    clear: both;
8.  }
9.  .group {
10.   clear: both;
11.   *zoom: 1;
12. }
```

There's quite a bit going on here, but essentially what the CSS is doing is clearing any floated elements within the element with the class of group and returning the flow of the document back to normal.

More specifically, the :before and :after pseudo-elements, as mentioned in the Lesson 4 exercise, are dynamically generated elements above and below the element with the class of group. Those elements do not include any content and are displayed as table-level elements, much like block-level elements. The dynamically generated element after the element with the class of group is clearing the floats within the element with the class of group, much like the clear from before. And lastly, the element with the class of group itself also clears any floats that may appear above it, in case a left or right float may exist. It also includes a little trickery to get older browsers to play nicely.

It is more code than the clear: both; declaration alone, but it can prove to be quite useful.

Looking at our two-column page layout from before, we could wrap the <section> and <aside> elements with a parent element (see **Figure 5.6**). That parent element then needs to contain the floats within itself. The code would look like this:

HTML

```
1.  <header>...</header>
2.  <div class="group">
3.    <section>...</section>
4.    <aside>...</aside>
5.  </div>
6.  <footer>...</footer>
```

CSS

```
1.  .group:before,
2.  .group:after {
3.    content: "";
4.    display: table;
5.  }
6.  .group:after {
7.    clear: both;
8.  }
9.  .group {
10.   clear: both;
11.   *zoom: 1;
12.  }
13. section {
14.   float: left;
15.   margin: 0 1.5%;
16.   width: 63%;
17. }
18. aside {
19.   float: right;
20.   margin: 0 21.5%;
21.   width: 30%;
22. }
```

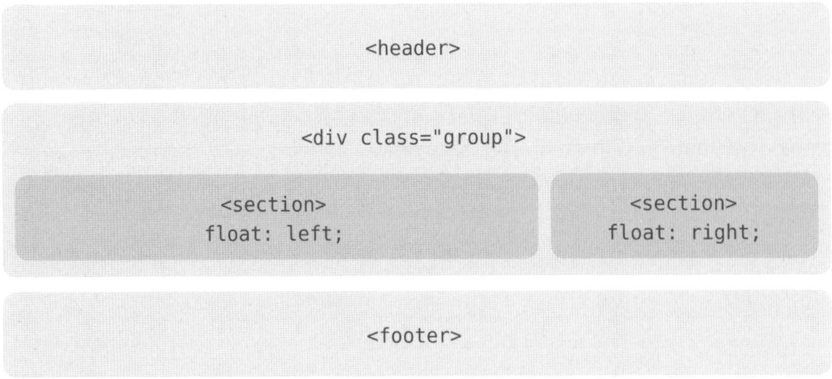

Figure 5.6 A two-column page layout with contained floats

The technique shown here for containing elements is know as a "clearfix" and can often be found in other websites with the class name of `clearfix` or `cf`. We've chosen to use the class name of `group`, though, as it is representing a group of elements, and better expresses the content.

As elements are floated, it is important to keep note of how they affect the flow of a page and to make sure the flow of a page is reset by either clearing or containing the floats as necessary. Failing to keep track of floats can cause quite a few headaches, especially as pages begin to have multiple rows of multiple columns.

In Practice

Let's return to the Styles Conference website to try floating some content.

1. First things first, before we begin floating any elements, let's provide a way to contain those floats by adding the clearfix to our CSS. Within the `main.css` file, just below our grid styles, let's add the clearfix under the class name `group`, just like before.

    ```
    1.  /*
    2.     =========================================
    3.     Clearfix
    4.     =========================================
    5.  */
    6.
    7.  .group:before,
    8.  .group:after {
    9.    content: "";
    10.   display: table;
    11. }
    12. .group:after {
    13.   clear: both;
    14. }
    15. .group {
    16.   clear: both;
    17.   *zoom: 1;
    18. }
    ```

2. Now that we can contain floats, let's float the primary <h1> within the <header> element to the left and allow all of the other content in the header to wrap to the right of it.

To do this, let's add a class of `logo` to the `<h1>` element. Then within our CSS, let's add a new section of styles for the primary header. In this section we'll select the `<h1>` element with the `logo` class and then `float` it to the left.

HTML

```
1.   <h1 class="logo">
2.     <a href="index.html">Styles Conference</a>
3.   </h1>
```

CSS

```
1.   /*
2.     ==========================================
3.     Primary header
4.     ==========================================
5.   */
6.
7.   .logo {
8.     float: left;
9.   }
```

3. While we're at it, let's add a little more detail to our logo. We'll begin by placing a `<br>` element, or line break, between the word "Styles" and the word "Conference" to force the text of our logo to sit on two lines.

    Within the CSS, let's add a border to the top of our logo and some vertical `padding` to give the logo breathing room.

HTML

```
1.   <h1 class="logo">
2.     <a href="index.html">Styles <br> Conference</a>
3.   </h1>
```

CSS

```
1.   .logo {
2.     border-top: 4px solid #648880;
3.     padding: 40px 0 22px 0;
4.     float: left;
5.   }
```

4. Because we floated the `<h1>` element, we'll want to contain that `float`. The closest parent element of the `<h1>` element is the `<header>` element, so we'll want to add the class of `group` to the `<header>` element. Doing this applies the clearfix styles we set up earlier to the `<header>` element.

```
1.    <header class="container group">
2.      ...
3.    </header>
```

5. The `<header>` element is taking shape, so let's take a look at the `<footer>` element. Much like we did with the `<header>` element, we'll float our copyright to the left within the `<small>` element and let all other elements wrap around it to the right.

   Unlike the `<header>` element, though, we're not going to use a class directly on the floated element. This time we're going to apply a class to the parent of the floated element and use a unique CSS selector to select the element and then float it.

   Let's start by adding the class of `primary-footer` to the `<footer>` element. Because we know we'll be floating an element within the `<footer>` element, we should also add the class of `group` while we're at it.

```
1.    <footer class="primary-footer container group">
2.      ...
3.    </footer>
```

6. Now that the class of `primary-footer` is on the `<footer>` element, we can use that class to prequalify the `<small>` element with CSS. We'll want to select and `float` the `<small>` element to the `left`. Let's not forget to create a new section within our `main.css` file for these primary footer styles.

```
1.    /*
2.      ========================================
3.      Primary footer
4.      ========================================
5.    */
6.
7.    .primary-footer small {
8.      float: left;
9.    }
```

To review, here we are selecting the `<small>` element, which must reside within an element with the class attribute value of `primary-footer`, such as our `<footer>` element, for example.

7. Lastly, let's put some `padding` on the top and bottom of the `<footer>` element to help separate it a little more from the rest of the page. We can do this directly by using the `primary-footer` class with a class selector.

```
1.  .primary-footer {
2.    padding-bottom: 44px;
3.    padding-top: 44px;
4.  }
```

With all of these changes to the `<header>` and `<footer>` elements, we have to be sure to make them on every page, not just the `index.html` page. Our current home page is shown in **Figure 5.7**.

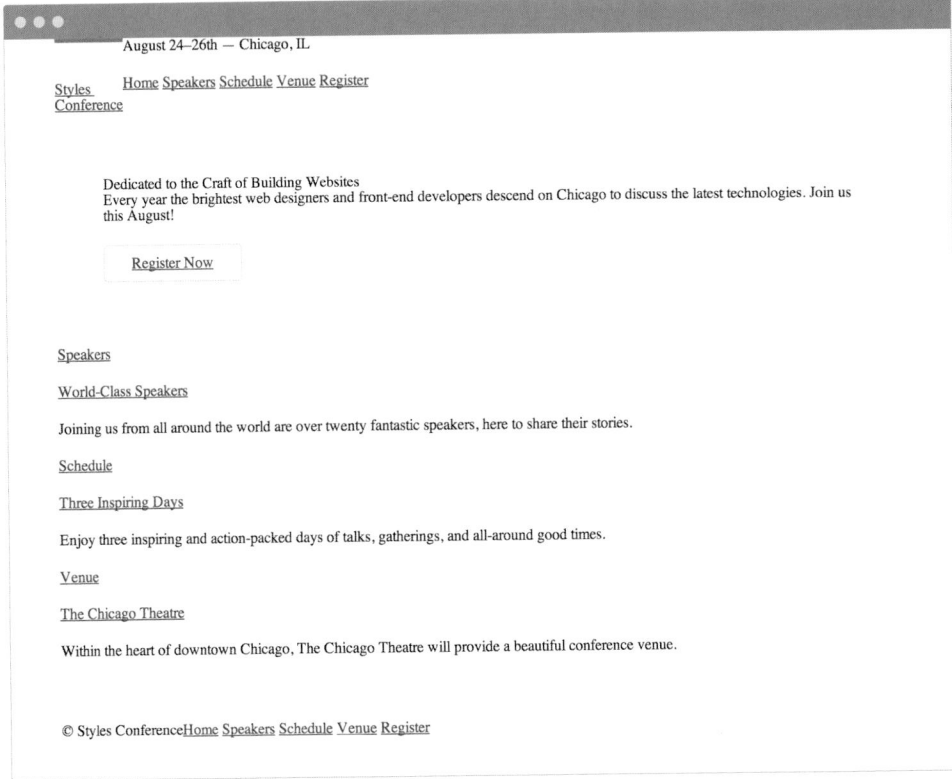

Figure 5.7 With a few floats, the `<header>` and `<footer>` elements on our Styles Conference home page are coming together

Positioning with Inline-Block

In addition to using floats, another way we can position content is by using the `display` property in conjunction with the `inline-block` value. The inline-block method, as we'll discuss, is primarily helpful for laying out pages or for placing elements next to one another within a line.

Recall that the `inline-block` value for the `display` property will display elements within a line while allowing them to accept all box model properties, including `height`, `width`, `padding`, `border`, and `margin`. Using inline-block elements allows us to take full advantage of the box model without having to worry about clearing any floats.

Inline-Block in Practice

Let's take a look at our three-column example from before. We'll start by keeping our HTML just as it is:

```
1.    <header>...</header>
2.    <section>...</section>
3.    <section>...</section>
4.    <section>...</section>
5.    <footer>...</footer>
```

Now instead of floating our three `<section>` elements, we'll change their display values to `inline-block`, leaving the `margin` and `width` properties from before alone. Our resulting CSS will look like this:

```
1.    section {
2.      display: inline-block;
3.      margin: 0 1.5%;
4.      width: 30%;
5.    }
```

Unfortunately, this code alone doesn't quite do the trick, and the last `<section>` element is pushed to a new row. Remember, because inline-block elements are displayed on the same line as one another, they include a single space between them. When the size of each single space is added to the `width` and horizontal `margin` values of all the elements in the row, the total width becomes too great, pushing the last `<section>` element to a new row. In order to display all of the `<section>` elements on the same row, the white space between each `<section>` element must be removed.

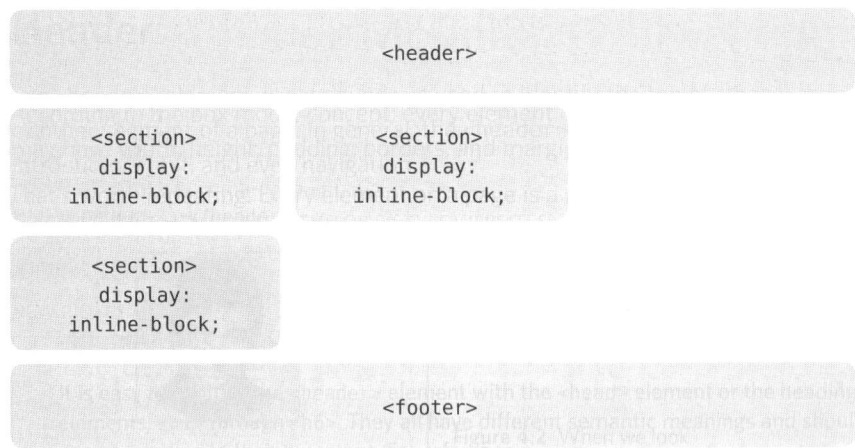

Figure 5.8 A three-column page layout using inline-block elements without removing any unnecessary white space

Removing Spaces Between Inline-Block Elements

There are a number of ways to remove the space between inline-block elements, and some are more complex than others. We are going to focus on two of the easiest ways, both of which happen inside HTML.

The first solution is to put each new `<section>` element's opening tag on the same line as the previous `<section>` element's closing tag. Rather than using a new line for each element, we'll end and begin elements on the same line. Our HTML could look like this:

```
1.   <header>...</header>
2.   <section>
3.     ...
4.   </section><section>
5.     ...
6.   </section><section>
7.     ...
8.   </section>
9.   <footer>...</footer>
```

Writing inline-block elements this way ensures that the space between inline-block elements within HTML doesn't exist; consequently, the space will not appear when the page is rendered (see **Figure 5.9**).

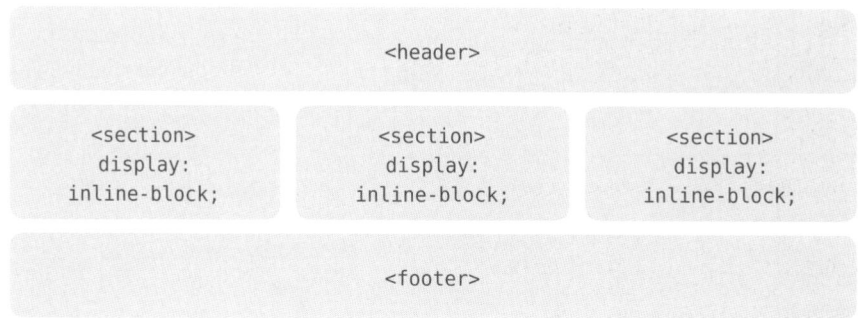

Figure 5.9 A three-column page layout using inline-block elements with properly removed white space

Another way to remove the white space between inline-block elements is to open an HTML comment directly after an inline-block element's closing tag. Then, close the HTML comment immediately before the next inline-block element's opening tag. Doing this allows inline-block elements to begin and end on separate lines of HTML and "comments out" any potential spaces between the elements. The resulting code would look like this:

```
1.   <header>...</header>
2.   <section>
3.     ...
4.   </section><!--
5.   --><section>
6.     ...
7.   </section><!--
8.   --><section>
9.     ...
10.  </section>
11.  <footer>...</footer>
```

Neither of these options is perfect, but they are helpful. I tend to favor using comments for better organization, but which option you choose is entirely up to you.

Creating Reusable Layouts

When building a website, it is always best to write modular styles that may be reused elsewhere, and reusable layouts are high on the list of reusable code. Layouts can be created using either floats or inline-block elements, but which works best and why?

Whether it's better to use floats or inline-block elements to lay out the structure of a page is open to debate. My approach is to use inline-block elements to create the grid—or layout—of a page and to then use floats when I want content to wrap around a given element (as floats were intended to do with images). Generally, I also find inline-block elements easier to work with.

That said, use whatever works best for you. If you are comfortable with one approach over the other, then go for it.

Currently there are new CSS specifications in the works—specifically `flex-` and `grid-`based properties—that will help address how to best lay out pages. Keep an eye out for these methods as they begin to surface.

In Practice

With a solid understanding of reusable layouts, the time has come to implement one in our Styles Conference website.

1. For the Styles Conference website, we'll create a three-column reusable layout using inline-block elements. We'll do so in a way that allows us to have three columns of equal width or two columns with the total width split between them, two-thirds in one and one-third in the other.

   To begin, we'll create classes that define the `width` of these columns. The two classes we'll create are `col-1-3`, for one-third, and `col-2-3`, for two-thirds. Within the grid section of our `main.css` file, let's go ahead and define these classes and their corresponding widths.

   ```
   1.  .col-1-3 {
   2.    width: 33.33%;
   3.  }
   4.  .col-2-3 {
   5.    width: 66.66%;
   6.  }
   ```

2. We'll want both of the columns to be displayed as inline-block elements. We'll need to make sure that their vertical alignment is set to the `top` of each column, too.

Let's create two new selectors that will share the `display` and `vertical-alignment` property styles.

```
1.  .col-1-3,
2.  .col-2-3 {
3.    display: inline-block;
4.    vertical-align: top;
5.  }
```

Looking at the CSS again, we've created two class selectors, `col-1-3` and `col-2-3`, that are separated with a comma. The comma at the end of the first selector signifies that another selector is to follow. The second selector is followed by the opening curly bracket, {, which signifies that style declarations are to follow. By comma-separating the selectors, we can bind the same styles to multiple selectors at one time.

3. We'll want to put some space in between each of the columns to help break up the content. We can accomplish this by putting horizontal `padding` on each of the columns.

This works well; however, when two columns are sitting next to one another, the width of the space between them will be double that of the space from the outside columns to the edge of the row. To balance this we'll place all of our columns within a grid and add the same `padding` from our columns to that grid.

Let's use a class name of `grid` to identify our grid, and then let's identify the same horizontal `padding` for our `grid`, `col-1-3`, and `col-2-3` classes. With commas separating our selectors again, our CSS looks like this:

```
1.  .grid,
2.  .col-1-3,
3.  .col-2-3 {
4.    padding-left: 15px;
5.    padding-right: 15px;
6.  }
```

4. When we're setting up the horizontal `padding`, we'll need to be careful. Remember, in the last lesson we created a container element, known by the class of `container`, to center all of our content on a page within a 960-pixel-wide element. Currently if we were to put an element with the class of `grid` inside an element with the class

of `container`, their horizontal paddings would add to one another, and our columns would not appear proportionate to the width of the rest of the page.

We don't want this to happen, so instead, we'll have to share some of the styles from the `container` rule set with the `grid` rule set. Specifically, we'll need to share the `width` property and values (to make sure our page stays fixed at 960 pixels wide) and the `margin` property and values (to center any element with the class of `grid` on the page).

We'll accomplish this by breaking up the old `container` rule set into the following:

```
1.   .container,
2.   .grid {
3.     margin: 0 auto;
4.     width: 960px;
5.   }
6.   .container {
7.     padding-left: 30px;
8.     padding-right: 30px;
9.   }
```

Now any element with the class of `container` or `grid` will be 960 pixels wide and centered on the page. Additionally, we've preserved the existing horizontal padding for any element with the class of `container` by moving it into a new, separate rule set.

5. All right—all of the heavy lifting needed to get our reusable grid styles into place is finished. Now it's time to work in our HTML and to see how these classes perform.

    We'll begin with the teasers on the home page, within our `index.html` file, aligning them into three columns. Currently, the teasers are wrapped in a `<section>` element with the class of `container`. We'll want to change that class from `container` to `grid` so that we can begin placing columns within it.

```
1.   <section class="grid">
2.     ...
3.   </section>
```

6. Next, we'll want to add a class of `col-1-3` to each of the `<section>` elements within the `<section>` element with the class of `grid`.

```
1.   <section class="grid">
2.
3.     <section class="col-1-3">
4.       ...
```

```
5.    </section>
6.
7.    <section class="col-1-3">
8.       ...
9.    </section>
10.
11.   <section class="col-1-3">
12.      ...
13.   </section>
14.
15. </section>
```

7. And lastly, because each of our columns is an inline-block element, we'll want to make sure we remove the empty white space between them. We'll use comments to do this, and we'll add a little bit of documentation noting each upcoming section while we're at it to better organize our code.

```
1.    <section class="grid">
2.
3.    <!-- Speakers -->
4.
5.    <section class="col-1-3">
6.       ...
7.    </section><!--
8.
9.    Schedule
10.
11.   --><section class="col-1-3">
12.      ...
13.   </section><!--
14.
15.   Venue
16.
17.   -->section class="col-1-3">
18.      ...
19.   </section>
20.
21. </section>
```

To review, on line 3 we leave a comment identifying the "Speakers" section to follow. At the end of line 7, we open a comment immediately after the closing `</section>` tag. Within that comment, on line 9 we identify the "Schedule" section to come. We then close the comment at the beginning of line 11, just before the opening `<section>` tag. This same comment structure reappears on lines 13 through 17 between the two `<section>` elements, right before the "Venue" section. In all, we've commented out any potential white space between the columns while also using those comments to identify our sections.

We now have a reusable three-column grid that supports multiple arrangements, using both one-third- and two-thirds-width columns. Our home page now has three columns, breaking up all the different teasers, as shown in **Figure 5.10**.

The source code for the exercises within this lesson can be found at http://learn.shayhowe.com/html-css/positioning-content/.

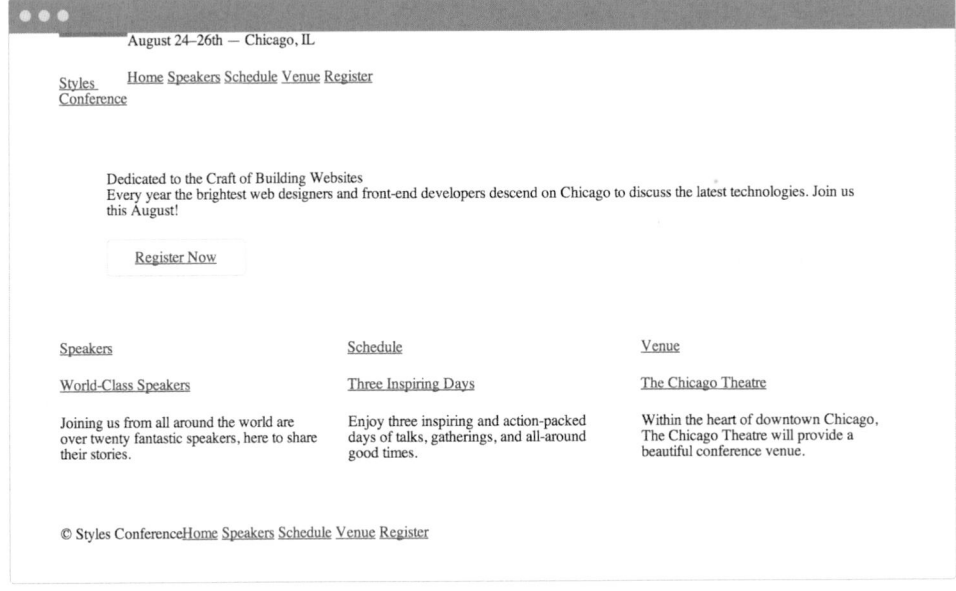

Figure 5.10 Our Styles Conference home page now includes a three-column layout

Uniquely Positioning Elements

Every now and then we'll want to precisely position an element, but floats or inline-block elements won't do the trick. Floats, which remove an element from the flow of a page, often produce unwanted results as surrounding elements flow around the floated element. Inline-block elements, unless we're creating columns, can be fairly awkward to get into the proper position. For these situations we can use the `position` property in connection with box offset properties.

The `position` property identifies *how* an element is positioned on a page and whether or not it will appear within the normal flow of a document. This is used in conjunction with the box offset properties—`top`, `right`, `bottom`, and `left`—which identify exactly *where* an element will be positioned by moving elements in a number of different directions.

By default every element has a `position` value of `static`, which means that it exists in the normal flow of a document and it doesn't accept any box offset properties. The `static` value is most commonly overwritten with a `relative` or `absolute` value, which we'll examine next.

Relative Positioning

The `relative` value for the `position` property allows elements to appear within the normal flow a page, leaving space for an element as intended while not allowing other elements to flow around it; however, it also allows an element's display position to be modified with the box offset properties. For example, consider the following HTML and CSS (see **Figure 5.11**):

HTML

```
1.   <div>...</div>
2.   <div class="offset">...</div>
3.   <div>...</div>
```

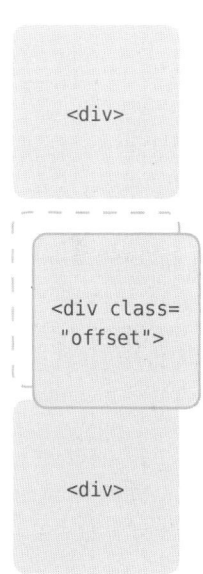

Figure 5.11
A relatively positioned element including left and top box offset properties

CSS

```
1.  div {
2.    border: 1px solid #949599;
3.    height: 200px;
4.    width: 200px;
5.  }
6.  .offset {
7.    left: 20px;
8.    position: relative;
9.    top: 20px;
10. }
```

Here the second `<div>` element, the element with the class of `offset`, has a `position` value of `relative` and two box offset properties, `left` and `top`. This preserves the original position of the element, and other elements are not allowed to move into this space. Additionally, the box offset properties reposition the element, pushing it 20 pixels from the `left` and 20 pixels from the `top` of its original location.

With relatively positioned elements, it's important to know that the box offset properties identify where an element will be moved from given its original position. Thus, the `left` property with a value of 20 pixels will actually push the element towards the right, from the left, 20 pixels. The `top` property with a value of 20 pixels, then, will push an element towards the bottom, from the top, 20 pixels.

When we position the element using the box offset properties, the element overlaps the element below it rather than moving that element down as the `margin` or `padding` properties would.

Absolute Positioning

The `absolute` value for the `position` property is different from the `relative` value in that an element with a `position` value of `absolute` will not appear within the normal flow of a document, and the original space and position of the absolutely positioned element will not be preserved.

Additionally, absolutely positioned elements are moved in relation to their closest relatively positioned parent element. Should a relatively positioned parent element not exist, the absolutely positioned element will be positioned in relation to the <body> element. That's quite a bit of information; let's take a look at how this works inside some code (see **Figure 5.12**):

HTML

```
1.  <section>
2.    <div class="offset">...</div>
3.  </section>
```

CSS

```
1.  section {
2.    position: relative;
3.  }
4.  div {
5.    position: absolute;
6.    right: 20px;
7.    top: 20px;
8.  }
```

```
<section>
position: relative;

<div class="offset>
position: absolute;
right: 20px;
top: 20px;
```

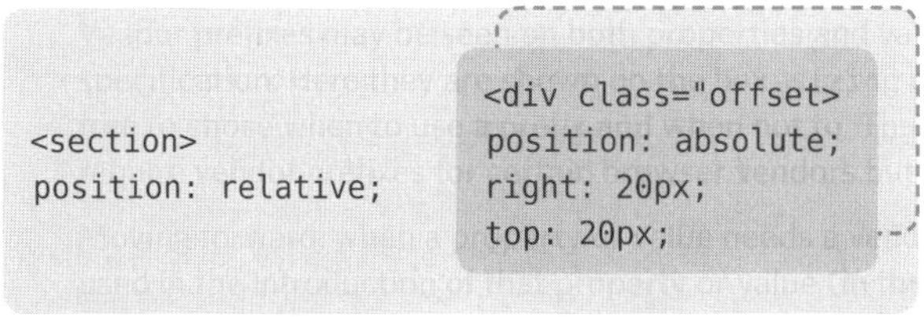

Figure 5.12 An absolutely positioned element including right and top box offset properties

In this example the <section> element is relatively positioned but doesn't include any box offset properties. Consequently its position doesn't change. The <div> element with a class of offset includes a position value of absolute. Because the <section> element is the closest relatively positioned parent element to the <div> element, the <div> element will be positioned in relation to the <section> element.

With relatively positioned elements, the box offset properties identify in which direction an element would be moved in relation to itself. With absolutely positioned elements, the box offset properties identify in which direction an element will be moved in relation to its closest relatively positioned parent element.

As a result of the `right` and `top` box offset properties, the `<div>` element will appear `20` pixels from the `right` and `20` pixels from the `top` of the `<section>`.

Because the `<div>` element is absolutely positioned, it does not sit within the normal flow of the page and will overlap any surrounding elements. Additionally, the original position of the `<div>` is not preserved, and other elements are able to occupy that space.

Typically, most positioning can be handled without the use of the `position` property and box offset properties, but in certain cases they can be extremely helpful.

Summary

Learning how to position content within HTML and CSS is a huge step toward mastering the two languages. Add to this the box model, and we're well on our way to becoming front-end developers.

To review, within this lesson we covered the following:

- What floats are and how to use them to position content
- How to clear and contain floated elements
- How to position content with inline-block elements
- How to remove the white space between inline-block elements
- How to uniquely position content with relatively and absolutely positioned elements

We're adding new skills with each lesson, so let's keep going. Next up, typography!

Lesson 6

Working with Typography

The field of web typography has grown substantially over time. There are a couple of different reasons for its rise in popularity; one widely acknowledged reason is the development of a system for embedding our own web fonts on a website.

In the past we were limited to a small number of typefaces that we could use on a website. These typefaces were the most commonly installed fonts on computers, so they were the most likely to render properly on-screen. If a font wasn't installed on a computer, it wouldn't render on the website either. Now, with the ability to embed fonts, we have a much larger palette of typefaces to choose from, including those that we add to a website.

While the ability to embed fonts gives us access to countless new typefaces, it's also important for us to know the basic principles of typography. In this lesson we're going to take a look at some of these basic principles and how to apply them to our web pages using HTML and CSS.

Typeface vs. Font

The terms "typeface" and "font" are often interchanged, causing confusion. Here is a breakdown of exactly what each term means.

A *typeface* is what we see. It is the artistic impression of how text looks, feels, and reads.

A *font* is a file that contains a typeface. Using a font on a computer allows the computer to access the typeface.

One way to help clarify the difference between a typeface and a font is to compare them to a song and an MP3. A typeface is very similar to a song in that it is a work of art. It is created by an artist or artists and is open to public interpretation. A font, on the other hand, is very similar to an MP3 in that it is not the artistic impression itself, but only a method of delivering the artistic value.

Adding Color to Text

Typically one of the first decisions we'll make when building a website is choosing the primary typeface and text color to be used. While there are a number of other properties that can be changed—size, weight, and so on—the typeface and text color generally have the largest impact on the look and legibility of a page. Getting rid of the browser defaults and using our own typeface and text color immediately begins setting the tone of our page.

The only property we need to set the color of text is the `color` property. The `color` property accepts one color value, but in many different formats. These formats, as we discussed in Lesson 3, "Getting to Know CSS," include keywords, hexadecimal values, and RGB, RGBa, HSL, and HSLa values. Hexadecimal values are the most prevalent, as they provide the most control with the least amount of effort.

Let's take a look at the CSS required to change the color of all the text within the <html> element on a page:

```
1.  html {
2.    color: #555;
3.  }
```

Changing Font Properties

CSS offers a lot of different properties for editing the look and feel of text on a page. These properties fit into two categories: font-based properties and text-based properties. Most of these properties will be prefaced with either `font-*` or `text-*`. To begin we'll discuss the font-based properties.

Font Family

The `font-family` property is used to declare which font—as well as which fallback or substitute fonts—should be used to display text. The value of the `font-family` property contains multiple font names, all comma separated.

The first declared font, starting from the left, is the primary font choice. Should the first font be unavailable, alternative fonts are declared after it in order of preference from left to right.

Font names consisting of two or more words need to be wrapped in quotation marks. Additionally, the last font should be a keyword value, which will use the system default font for the specified type, most commonly either `sans-serif` or `serif`.

The `font-family` property in action looks like this:

```
1.  body {
2.    font-family: "Helvetica Neue", Helvetica, Arial, sans-serif;
3.  }
```

In this case, `Helvetica Neue` is the preferred font to display. If this font is unavailable or not installed on a given device, the next font in the list—Helvetica—will be used, and so on.

Font Size

The `font-size` property provides the ability to set the size of text using common length values, including pixels, em units, percentages, points, or `font-size` keywords.

Here the CSS is setting a `font-size` of 14 pixels on the <body> element:

```
1.  body {
2.    font-size: 14px;
3.  }
```

Font Style

To change text to italics, or to prevent text from being italicized, we'll use the `font-style` property. The `font-style` property accepts four keyword values: `normal`, `italic`, `oblique`, and `inherit`. Of these four, the most commonly used are `italic` (sets text to italic) and `normal` (returns text to its normal style).

The following CSS sets all elements with a class of `special` to include a `font-style` of `italic`:

```
1.  .special {
2.    font-style: italic;
3.  }
```

Font Variant

It doesn't happen often, but occasionally text will need to be set in small capitals, also known as small caps. For this specific case we'll use the `font-variant` property. The `font-variant` property accepts three values: `normal`, `small-caps`, and `inherit`. The most typically seen values are `normal` and `small-caps`, which are used to switch typefaces between normal and small caps variants.

To switch all elements with a class of `firm`, we'll use a `font-variant` of `small-caps`:

```
1.  .firm {
2.    font-variant: small-caps;
3.  }
```

Font Weight

Occasionally, we'll want to style text as bold or to change the specific weight of a typeface. For these cases we'll use the `font-weight` property. The `font-weight` property accepts either keyword or numeric values.

Keyword values include `normal`, `bold`, `bolder`, `lighter`, and `inherit`. Of these keyword values, it is recommended to primarily use `normal` and `bold` to change text from normal to bold and vice versa. Rather than using the keyword values `bolder` or `lighter`, it's better to use a numeric value for more specific control.

In practice, here's the CSS to set the `font-weight` to `bold` for any element with the class of `daring`:

```
1.  .daring {
2.    font-weight: bold;
3.  }
```

The numeric values 100, 200, 300, 400, 500, 600, 700, 800, and 900 pertain specifically to typefaces that have multiple weights. The order of these weights starts with the thinnest weight, 100, and scales up to the thickest weight, 900. For reference, the keyword value of `normal` maps to 400 and the keyword `bold` maps to 700; thus, any numeric value below 400 will be fairly thin, and any value above 700 will be fairly thick.

Changing the `font-weight` to 600 for any element with the class of `daring` now renders that text as semibold—not quite as thick as the `bold` keyword value from before:

```
1.  .daring {
2.    font-weight: 600;
3.  }
```

Typeface Weights

Before using a numeric value, we need to check and see whether the typeface we are using comes in the weight we'd like to use. Attempting to use a weight that's not available for a given typeface will cause those styles to default to the closest value.

For example, the Times New Roman typeface comes in two weights: `normal`, or 400, and `bold`, or 700. Attempting to use a weight of 900 will default the typeface to the closest related weight, 700 in this case.

Line Height

Line height, the distance between two lines of text (often referred to as leading) is declared using the `line-height` property. The `line-height` property accepts all general length values, which we covered in Lesson 3, "Getting to Know CSS."

The best practice for legibility is to set the `line-height` to around one and a half times our `font-size` property value. This could be quickly accomplished by setting the `line-height` to 150%, or just 1.5. However, if we're working with a baseline grid, having a little more control over our `line-height` using pixels may be preferable.

Looking at the CSS, we're setting a `line-height` of 22 pixels within the <body> element, thus placing 22 pixels between each line of text:

```
1.  body {
2.    line-height: 22px;
3.  }
```

Line height may also be used to vertically center a single line of text within an element. Using the same property value for the `line-height` and `height` properties will vertically center the text:

```
1.  .btn {
2.    height: 22px;
3.    line-height: 22px;
4.  }
```

This technique may be seen with buttons, alert messages, and other single-line text blocks.

Shorthand Font Properties

All of the `font`-based properties listed earlier may be combined and rolled into one `font` property and shorthand value. The `font` property can accept multiple `font`-based property values. The order of these property values should be as follows, from left to right: `font-style`, `font-variant`, `font-weight`, `font-size`, `line-height`, and `font-family`.

As a shorthand value, these property values are listed from left to right without the use of commas (except for font names, as the `font-family` property value uses commas). A forward slash, /, separator is needed between the `font-size` and `line-height` property values.

When using this shorthand value, every property value is optional *except* the `font-size` and `font-family` property values. That said, we can include only the `font-size` and `font-family` property values in the shorthand value if we wish.

```
1.  html {
2.    font: italic small-caps bold 14px/22px "Helvetica Neue",
        Helvetica, Arial, sans-serif;
3.  }
```

Font Properties All Together

Let's take a look at an example that uses all these `font`-based properties together. The following HTML and CSS demonstrates the different possibilities when styling text; the final result of this code can be seen in **Figure 6.1**.

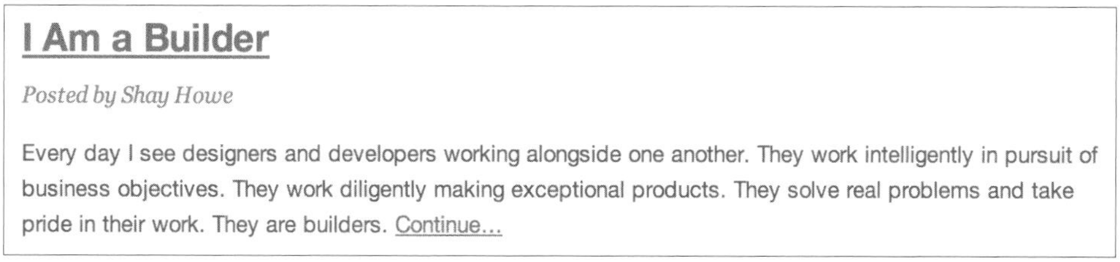

I Am a Builder

Posted by Shay Howe

Every day I see designers and developers working alongside one another. They work intelligently in pursuit of business objectives. They work diligently making exceptional products. They solve real problems and take pride in their work. They are builders. Continue...

Figure 6.1 A sample blog post teaser using font-based properties

HTML

```
1.   <h2><a href="#">I Am a Builder</a></h2>
2.
3.   <p class="byline">Posted by Shay Howe</p>
4.
5.   <p>Every day I see designers and developers working alongside one another.
     They work intelligently in pursuit of business objectives. They work
     diligently making exceptional products. They solve real problems and take
     pride in their work. They are builders. <a href="#">Continue&#8230;</a></p>
```

CSS

```
1.   h2,
2.   p {
3.     color: #555;
4.     font: 13px/20px "Helvetica Neue", Helvetica, Arial, sans-serif;
5.   }
6.   a {
7.     color: #648880;
8.   }
9.   a:hover {
10.    color: #293f50;
```

continues

```
11.  }
12.  h2 {
13.     font-size: 22px;
14.     font-weight: bold;
15.     margin-bottom: 6px;
16.  }
17.  .byline {
18.     color: #8c8c8c;
19.     font-family: Georgia, Times, "Times New Roman", serif;
20.     font-style: italic;
21.  }
```

CSS Pseudo-Classes

The demonstration here uses the `:hover` CSS pseudo-class, something we've never seen before. For reference, pseudo-classes are keywords that may be added to the end of a selector to style an element when it's in a unique state.

The `:hover` pseudo-class styles an element when a user hovers over that element. When used with the `<a>` element, as shown here, all `<a>` elements will receive unique styles when they are hovered over. Now our `<a>` elements will change color upon being hovered over.

In Practice

Diving back into our Styles Conference website, let's start adding some font-based properties.

1.   We'll begin by updating the font on all of our text. To do this, we'll apply styles to our `<body>` element. We'll start with a color, and we'll also add in `font-weight`, `font-size`, `line-height`, and `font-family` values by way of the `font` property and shorthand values.

     In an attempt to keep our `main.css` file as organized as possible, let's create a new section for these custom styles, placing it just below our reset and above our grid styles.

We need to add the following:

```
1.   /*
2.      ========================================
3.      Custom styles
4.      ========================================
5.   */
6.
7.   body {
8.     color: #888;
9.     font: 300 16px/22px "Open Sans", "Helvetica Neue", Helvetica,
          Arial, sans-serif;
10.  }
```

2. In Lesson 4, "Opening the Box Model," we began adding some typographic styles, specifically adding a bottom `margin` to a few different levels of headings and paragraphs. Within the same section of the `main.css` file, let's add a color to the level-one through level-four headings.

```
1.   h1, h2, h3, h4 {
2.     color: #648880;
3.   }
```

While we're at it, let's also add in font sizes for these different heading levels. Our <h1> and <h2> elements will use fairly large `font-size` values; consequently, we'll also want to increase their `line-height` values to keep the text within these elements legible. For reference, we'll make their `line-height` values 44 pixels, double the value of the base `line-height` set within the <body> element rule set.

```
1.   h1 {
2.     font-size: 36px;
3.     line-height: 44px;
4.   }
5.   h2 {
6.     font-size: 24px;
7.     line-height: 44px;
8.   }
9.   h3 {
10.    font-size: 21px;
11.  }
```

continues

```
12. h4 {
13.    font-size: 18px;
14. }
```

3. Our <h5> elements are going to be a little more unique than the rest of our headings. Accordingly, we're going to change their styles a bit.

We'll use a different `color` property value and a slightly smaller `font-size` for these elements, and we're going to change the `font-weight` to 400, or `normal`.

By default, browsers render headings with a `font-weight` of `bold`. Our headings, however, are currently all set to a `font-weight` of 300. Our reset at the top of our `main.css` file changed the `font-weight` to `normal`, and then our `font-weight` of 300 within the <body> element rule set changed all headings to a `font-weight` of 300.

The `font-weight` of 400 on the <h5> element will actually make it slightly thicker than the rest of our other headings and text.

```
1. h5 {
2.    color: #a9b2b9;
3.    font-size: 14px;
4.    font-weight: 400;
5. }
```

4. Our reset at the beginning of our style sheet also reset the browser default styles for the <strong>, <cite>, and <em> elements, which we'll want to add back in. For our <strong> elements we'll want to set a `font-weight` of 400, which actually equates to `normal`, not `bold`, as the typeface we're using is thicker than most typefaces. Then, for our <cite> and <em> elements we'll want to set a `font-style` of `italic`.

```
1. strong {
2.    font-weight: 400;
3. }
4. cite,
5. em {
6.    font-style: italic;
7. }
```

5. We're on a roll, so let's keep going by adding some styles to our anchor elements. Currently they are the browser default blue. Let's make them the same color as our <h1> through <h4> heading elements. Additionally, let's use the :hover pseudo-class to change the color to a light gray when a user hovers over an anchor.

```
1.  /*
2.  ======================================
3.  Links
4.  ======================================
5.  */
6.
7.  a {
8.    color: #648880;
9.  }
10. a:hover {
11.   color: #a9b2b9;
12. }
```

6. Now let's take a look at our <header> element and update our styles there. We'll begin updating our logo by adding the font-size and line-height properties within the logo rule set. Adding to the existing border-top, float, and padding properties, the new rule set should look like this:

```
1.  .logo {
2.    border-top: 4px solid #648880;
3.    float: left;
4.    font-size: 48px;
5.    line-height: 44px;
6.    padding: 40px 0 22px 0;
7.  }
```

7. Because we've bumped up the size of the logo quite a bit, let's add a `margin` to the `<h3>` element within the `<header>` element to balance it. We'll do so by placing a class attribute value of `tagline` on the `<h3>` element and then using that class within our CSS to apply the proper margins.

Let's not forget that the changes to the `<h3>` element need to happen on every page.

HTML

```
1.  <h3 class="tagline">August &ndash;26th &mdash; Chicago, IL</h3>
```

CSS

```
1.  .tagline {
2.    margin: 66px 0 22px 0;
3.  }
```

8. After the `<h3>` element with the class attribute value of `tagline` comes the `<nav>` element. Let's add a `class` attribute value of `primary-nav` to the `<nav>` element and add `font-size` and `font-weight` properties to make the navigation stand out against the rest of the header.

HTML

```
1.  <nav class="primary-nav">
2.    ...
3.  </nav>
```

CSS

```
1.  .primary-nav {
2.    font-size: 14px;
3.    font-weight: 400;
4.  }
```

9. With the `<header>` element in slightly better shape, let's also take a look at our `<footer>` element. Using the `primary-footer` class, let's change the `color` and `font-size` for all the text within the `<footer>` element. Additionally, let's bump up the `font-weight` of the `<small>` element to 400.

Including the existing styles, the styles for our primary footer section should look like this:

```
1.   .primary-footer {
2.     color: #648880;
3.     font-size: 14px;
4.     padding-bottom: 44px;
5.     padding-top: 44px;
6.   }
7.   .primary-footer small {
8.     float: left;
9.     font-weight: 400;
10.  }
```

10. Let's update our home page a bit, too. We'll start with the hero section, increasing the overall `line-height` of the section to 44 pixels. We'll also make the text within this section larger, increasing the <h2> element's `font-size` to 36 pixels and the <p> element's `font-size` to 24 pixels.

We can make all of these changes by using the existing `hero` class selector and creating new selectors for the <h2> and <p> elements. Our styles for the hero section will now break down in this way:

```
1.   .hero {
2.     line-height: 44px;
3.     padding: 22px 80px 66px 80px;
4.   }
5.   .hero h2 {
6.     font-size: 36px;
7.   }
8.   .hero p {
9.     font-size: 24px;
10.  }
```

11. Lastly, we have one small issue to fix on our home page. Previously we gave all of our anchor elements a light gray color value when a user hovers over them. This works great, except for within the three teasers on our home page where the anchor element wraps both <h3> and <h5> elements. Because the <h3> and <h5> elements have their own `color` definition, they are not affected by the `:hover` pseudo-class styles from before.

Fortunately we can fix this, although it's going to require a fairly complicated selector. We'll begin by adding a `class` attribute value of `teaser` to all three columns on the home page. We'll use this class as a qualifying selector shortly.

```
1.   <section class="grid">
2.
3.     <!-- Speakers -->
4.
5.     <section class="teaser col-1-3">
6.       <a href="speakers.html">
7.         <h5>Speakers</h5>
8.         <h3>World-Class Speakers</h3>
9.       </a>
10.      <p>Joining us from all around the world are over twenty
             fantastic speakers, here to share their stories.</p>
11.    </section>
12.
13.    ...
14.
15.  </section>
```

With a qualifying class in place, we're ready to do some CSS heavy lifting and create a fairly complex selector. We'll begin our selector with the `teaser` class, as we only want to target elements within an element with the class of `teaser`. From there we want to apply styles to elements that reside within anchor elements that are being hovered over; thus we'll add the `a` type selector along with the `:hover` pseudo-class. Lastly, we'll add the `h3` type selector to select the actual <h3> elements we wish to apply styles to.

Altogether, our selector and styles for these <h3> elements will look like this:

```
1.   .teaser a:hover h3 {
2.     color: #a9b2b9;
3.   }
```

Whew, that was quite a bit. The good news is that our Styles Conference home page is starting to look really nice and is showing a bit of personality (see **Figure 6.2**).

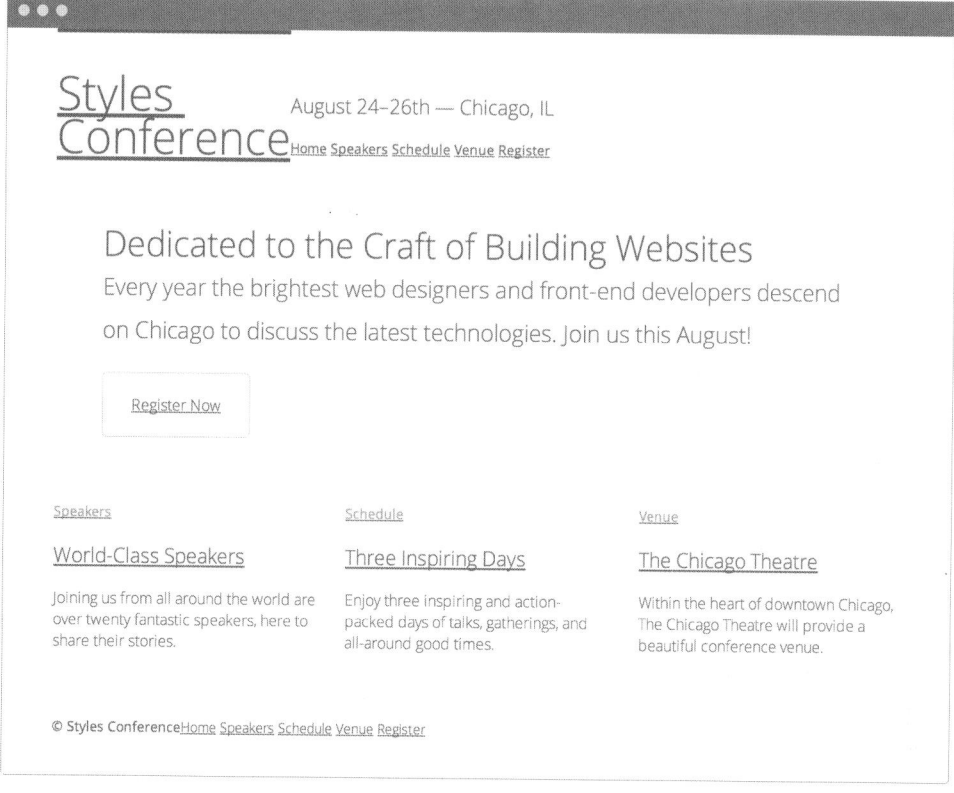

Figure 6.2 Our Styles Conference website has received quite a bit of love from a handful of font-based properties

Applying Text Properties

Knowing how to set the family, size, style, variant, weight, and line height of a font is only half the battle. Additionally we can decide how to align, decorate, indent, transform, and space text. Let's start with text alignment.

Text Align

Aligning text is an important part of building a rhythm and flow on a page; we do this using the `text-align` property. The `text-align` property has five values: `left`, `right`, `center`, `justify`, and `inherit`. All of these values are fairly straightforward; as expected, they align text to the left, right, or center, or they justify text.

The following CSS sets all paragraph text to be center aligned:

```
1.  p {
2.    text-align: center;
3.  }
```

The `text-align` property, however, should not be confused with the `float` property. The `text-align` values `left` and `right` will align text within an element to the left or right, whereas the `float` values `left` and `right` will move the entire element. Sometimes the `text-align` property will give us the desired outcome, and other times we may need to use the `float` property.

Text Decoration

The `text-decoration` property provides a handful of ways to spruce up text. It accepts the keyword values of `none`, `underline`, `overline`, `line-through`, and `inherit`. Use of the `text-decoration` property varies, but the most popular use is to underline links, which is a default browser style.

Here the CSS styles any element with the class of `note` with a `text-decoration` of `underline`:

```
1.  .note {
2.    text-decoration: underline;
3.  }
```

Multiple `text-decoration` values may be applied to an element at once by space-separating each keyword within the value.

Text Indent

The `text-indent` property can be used to indent the first line of text within an element, as is commonly seen in printed publications. All common length values are available for this property, including pixels, points, percentages, and so on. Positive values will indent text inward, while negative values will indent text outward.

Here, the CSS indents the text for all `<p>` elements inward by `20` pixels:

```
1.  p {
2.    text-indent: 20px;
3.  }
```

Text Shadow

The `text-shadow` property allows us to add a shadow or multiple shadows to text. The property generally takes four values, all listed one after the other from left to right. The first three values are lengths, and the last value is a color.

Within the three length values, the first value determines the shadow's horizontal offset, the second value determines the shadow's vertical offset, and the third value determines the shadow's blur radius. The fourth, and last, value is the shadow's color, which can be any of the color values used within the `color` property.

The `text-shadow` property here is casting a `30%` opaque black shadow 3 pixels towards the right, 6 pixels down, and blurred 2 pixels off all `<p>` element text:

```
1.  p {
2.    text-shadow: 3px 6px 2px rgba(0, 0, 0, .3);
3.  }
```

Using negative length values for the horizontal and vertical offsets allows us to move shadows toward the left and the top.

Multiple text shadows can also be chained together using comma-separated values, adding more than one shadow to the text. Using numerous shadows allows us to place them above and below the text, or in any variation we desire.

Box Shadow

The text-shadow property places a shadow specifically on the text of an element. If we'd like to place a shadow on the element as a whole, we can use the box-shadow property. The box-shadow property works just like the text-shadow property, accepting values for horizontal and vertical offsets, a blur, and a color.

The box-shadow property also accepts an optional fourth length value, before the color value, for the spread of a shadow. As a positive length value, the spread will expand the shadow larger than the size of the element it's applied to, and as a negative length value the spread will shrink the shadow to be smaller than the size of the element it's applied to.

Lastly, the box-shadow property may include an optional inset value at the beginning of the value to place the shadow inside an element as opposed to outside the element.

Text Transform

Similar to the font-variant property, there is the text-transform property. While the font-variant property looks for an alternate variant of a typeface, the text-transform property will change the text inline without the need for an alternate typeface. The text-transform property accepts five values: none, capitalize, uppercase, lowercase, and inherit.

The capitalize value will capitalize the first letter of each word, the uppercase value will capitalize every letter, and the lowercase value will make every letter lowercase. Using none will return any of these inherited values back to the original text style.

The following CSS sets all <p> element text to appear in all uppercase letters:

```
1.  p {
2.    text-transform: uppercase;
3.  }
```

Letter Spacing

Using the `letter-spacing` property, we can adjust the space (or tracking) between the letters on a page. A positive length value will push letters farther apart from one another, while a negative length value will pull letters closer together. The keyword value `none` will return the space between letters back to its normal size.

Using a relative length value with the `letter-spacing` property will help ensure that we maintain the correct spacing between letters as the `font-size` of the text is changed. It is, however, always a good idea to double-check our work.

With the CSS here, all of the letters within our <p> elements will appear `.5 em` closer together:

```
1.  p {
2.    letter-spacing: -.5em;
3.  }
```

Word Spacing

Much like the `letter-spacing` property, we can also adjust the space between words within an element using the `word-spacing` property. The `word-spacing` property accepts the same length values and keywords as the `letter-spacing` property. Instead of spacing letters apart, though, the `word-spacing` property applies those values between words.

Here every word within a <p> element will be spaced `.25 em` apart.

```
1.  p {
2.    word-spacing: .25em;
3.  }
```

Text Properties All Together

Let's revisit our blog teaser demonstration from before, this time adding in a few `text`-based properties on top of our `font`-based properties. The result can be seen in **Figure 6.3**.

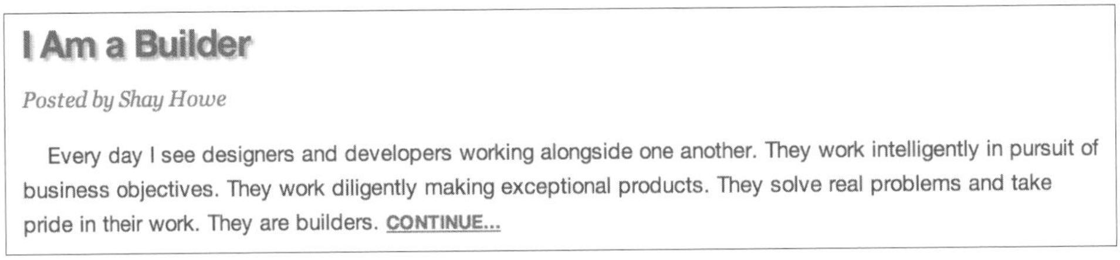

I Am a Builder

Posted by Shay Howe

Every day I see designers and developers working alongside one another. They work intelligently in pursuit of business objectives. They work diligently making exceptional products. They solve real problems and take pride in their work. They are builders. CONTINUE...

Figure 6.3 A sample blog post teaser using `font`-based and `text`-based properties

HTML

```
1.  <h2><a href="#">I Am a Builder</a></h2>
2.
3.  <p class="byline">Posted by Shay Howe</p>
4.
5.  <p class="intro">Every day I see designers and developers working
    alongside one another. They work intelligently in pursuit of
    business objectives. They work diligently making exceptional
    products. They solve real problems and take pride in their work.
    They are builders. <a href="#">Continue&#8230;</a></p>
```

CSS

```
1.  h2,
2.  p {
3.    color: #555;
4.    font: 13px/20px "Helvetica Neue", Helvetica, Arial, sans-serif;
5.  }
6.  a {
7.    color: #648880;
8.  }
9.  a:hover {
10.   color: #293f50;
11. }
```

```
12. h2 {
13.   font-size: 22px;
14.   font-weight: bold;
15.   letter-spacing: -.02em;
16.   margin-bottom: 6px;
17. }
18. h2 a {
19.   text-decoration: none;
20.   text-shadow: 2px 2px 1px rgba(0, 0, 0, .2);
21. }
22. .byline {
23.   color: #8c8c8c;
24.   font-family: Georgia, Times, "Times New Roman", serif;
25.   font-style: italic;
26. }
27. .intro {
28.   text-indent: 15px;
29. }
30. .intro a {
31.   font-size: 11px;
32.   font-weight: bold;
33.   text-decoration: underline;
34.   text-transform: uppercase;
35. }
```

In Practice

With `text`-based properties under our belts, let's jump back into our Styles Conference website and put them to work.

1. Currently every link on the page is underlined, which is the default style for anchor elements. This style is a little overbearing at times, though, so we're going to change it up a bit.

   Adding to our links section within our `main.css` file, we'll begin by removing the underline from all anchor elements by way of the `text-decoration` property. Next, we'll select all anchor elements that appear within a paragraph element and give them a bottom `border`.

We could use the `text-decoration` property instead of the `border-bottom` property to underline all the links within each paragraph; however, by using the `border-bottom` property we have more control over the underline's appearance. Here, for example, the underline will be a different color than the text itself.

Our links section, which includes our previous hover styles, should look like this:

```
1.  a {
2.    color: #648880;
3.    text-decoration: none;
4.  }
5.  a:hover {
6.    color: #a9b2b9;
7.  }
8.  p a {
9.    border-bottom: 1px solid #dfe2e5;
10. }
```

2. Going back to our <h5> elements from before, which have slightly different styles than the rest of the headings, let's make them all uppercase using the `text-transform` property. Our new <h5> element styles should look like this:

```
1.  h5 {
2.    color: #a9b2b9;
3.    font-size: 14px;
4.    font-weight: 400;
5.    text-transform: uppercase;
6.  }
```

3. Let's revisit our <header> element to apply additional styles to our navigation menu (to which we previously added the `primary-nav` class attribute value). After the existing `font-size` and `font-weight` properties, let's add some slight `letter-spacing` and change our text to all uppercase via the `text-transform` property.

Our styles for the <nav> element with the `primary-nav` class attribute value should now look like this:

```
1.  .primary-nav {
2.    font-size: 14px;
3.    font-weight: 400;
4.    letter-spacing: .5px;
5.    text-transform: uppercase;
6.  }
```

4. Previously, we floated our logo to the left within the <header> element. Now our tagline sits directly to the right of the logo; however, we'd like it to appear all the way to the right of the <header> element, flush right.

We need to add the text-align property with a value of right to the <h3> element with the class attribute value of tagline to get the tagline to sit all the way to the right.

When added to the existing margin property, our new styles for the <h3> element with the class attribute value of tagline will look like this:

```
1.  .tagline {
2.    margin: 66px 0 22px 0;
3.    text-align: right;
4.  }
```

5. We'd also like our navigation menus, both in the <header> and <footer> elements, to sit flush right. Because both the <header> and <footer> elements have child elements that are floated to the left, we can use the same approach as we did with our tagline.

The floated elements within the <header> and <footer> elements are taken out of the normal flow of the page, and this causes other elements to wrap around them. In this specific case, our navigation menus are the elements wrapping around the floated elements.

Because we'll be sharing the same styles across both navigation menus, we'll give them each the class of nav. Our <header> element will now look like this:

```
1.  <header class="container group">
2.
3.    <h1 class="logo">...</h1>
4.
5.    <h3 class="tagline">...</h3>
6.
7.    <nav class="nav primary-nav">
8.      ...
9.    </nav>
10.
11. </header>
```

And our `<footer>` element will now look like this:

```
1.   <footer class="primary-footer container group">
2.
3.     <small>...</small>
4.
5.     <nav class="nav">
6.       ...
7.     </nav>
8.
9.   </footer>
```

Let's not forget, changes to our `<header>` and `<footer>` elements need to be made on every page.

6. With the `nav` class in place on both navigation menus, let's create a new section within our `main.css` file to add shared navigation styles. We'll begin by adding the `text-align` property with a value of `right` to a `nav` class rule set. We'll expand these styles later on, but this will serve as a great foundation.

```
1.   /*
2.     ========================================
3.     Navigation
4.     ========================================
5.   */
6.
7.   .nav {
8.     text-align: right;
9.   }
```

7. While we're adding the `text-align` property to a few different elements, let's also add the `text-align` property with a value of `center` to our `hero` class selector rule set. For reference, these styles, including our existing `line-height` and `padding` properties, are located within the home page section of our `main.css` file.

```
1.   .hero {
2.     line-height: 44px;
3.     padding: 22px 80px 66px 80px;
4.     text-align: center;
5.   }
```

Our Styles Conference now has some serious style. (Bad joke, sorry.) Seriously, though, all of our styles are coming along quite well, and our website is progressing, as shown in Figure 6.4.

Figure 6.4 Our Styles Conference website is coming along quite well after adding a few text-based properties

Using Web-Safe Fonts

By default there are a few fonts that are pre-installed on every computer, tablet, smartphone, or other web-browsing-capable device. Because they've been installed on every device, we can use these fonts freely within our websites, knowing that no matter what device is browsing our site, the font will render properly. These fonts have become known as "web-safe fonts." There are only a handful of them, and the safest of the web-safe fonts are listed here:

- Arial
- Courier New, Courier
- Garamond
- Georgia
- Lucida Sans, Lucida Grande, Lucida
- Palatino Linotype
- Tahoma
- Times New Roman, Times
- Trebuchet
- Verdana

Embedding Web Fonts

We also have the ability to upload fonts to a server and include them on a website via the CSS `@font-face` at-rule. This capability has done wonders for online typography. Now, more than ever, typography is coming to life online.

Embedding our own web fonts looks a bit like the following CSS. First, we use the `@font-face` at-rule to identify our font's name, via the `font-family` property, as well as the source of our font (the path to the font file containing our chosen font), via the `src` property. From there we are able to use this font by including its name within any `font-family` property value. See **Figure 6.5**.

```
1.  @font-face {
2.    font-family: "Lobster";
3.    src: local("Lobster"), url("lobster.woff") format("woff");
4.  }
5.  body {
6.    font-family: "Lobster", "Comic Sans", cursive;
7.  }
```

I Am a Builder

Posted by Shay Howe

Every day I see designers and developers working alongside one another. They work intelligently in pursuit of business objectives. They work diligently making exceptional products. They solve real problems and take pride in their work. They are builders. CONTINUE...

Figure 6.5 By using a web font, we are able to use a typeface that would otherwise be unavailable

Having the ability to embed any typeface on a website does not mean we legally have the authority to do so. Typefaces are works of art, and posting them on our server may allow others to easily steal them. The authority to use a typeface depends on the licensing we've been warranted.

Fortunately, the value of using new typefaces online has been recognized, and companies have begun developing ways to license and include new fonts on websites. Some of these companies, like Typekit and Fontdeck, work off a subscription model for licensing fonts, while others, like Google Fonts, license the fonts for free. Before uploading any fonts, let's make sure we have permission to do so.

In Practice

To add a little character to our Styles Conference website, let's try using a Google Font on our website.

1. Let's head over to the Google Fonts website (www.google.com/fonts) and search for the font we'd like to use: Lato. Once we've found it, let's proceed with adding it to our collection and following the steps on their website to use the font.

   When the time comes to choose which font weights we'd like to use, let's make sure to select 300 and 400, as we've already been using those within our CSS. Let's also add 100 to the collection for another variation, too.

   Google will give us an additional `<link>` element to include in the `<head>` element of all of our pages. We'll place this new `<link>` element directly below our existing `<link>` element. The new element will include the proper style sheet reference to Google, which will take care of including a new CSS file with the proper `@font-face` at-rule necessary for us to use the Lato font.

   With the addition of the new `<link>` element, our `<head>` element will look like this:

```
1.  <head>
2.    <meta charset="utf-8">
3.    <title>Styles Conference</title>
4.    <link rel="stylesheet" href="assets/stylesheets/main.css">
5.    <link rel="stylesheet"
      href="http://fonts.googleapis.com/css?family=Lato:100,300,400">
6.  </head>
```

2. Once we have added the new `<link>` element to all of our pages, we are ready to begin using the Lato font. We'll do so by adding it to our primary font stack within the `font` property inside our `<body>` element styles.

Let's add Lato to the beginning of our font stack to make it `"Lato"`, `"Open Sans"`, `"Helvetica Neue"`, `Helvetica`, `Arial`, `sans-serif`.

Although `Lato` is a single word, because it is an embedded web font we'll want to surround it with quotation marks within any CSS reference. Our new `<body>` element styles will look like this:

```
1.  body {
2.    color: #888;
3.    font: 300 16px/22px "Lato", "Open Sans", "Helvetica Neue",
      Helvetica, Arial, sans-serif;
4.  }
```

3. Lato should now be up and running, visible in all of our text across the Styles Conference website. Let's take a closer look at our logo and update it a bit.

Within our `logo` class selector rule set, we'll begin by adding the `font-weight` property with a value of `100` to make the text fairly thin. We'll also use the `text-transform` property with a value of `uppercase` to make all of the letters uppercase, as well as the `letter-spacing` property with a value of `.5` pixels to add a tiny bit of space between each letter within the logo.

Altogether the styles for our logo will look like this:

```
1.  .logo {
2.    border-top: 4px solid #648880;
3.    float: left;
4.    font-size: 48px;
5.    font-weight: 100;
6.    letter-spacing: .5px;
7.    line-height: 44px;
8.    padding: 40px 0 22px 0;
9.    text-transform: uppercase;
10. }
```

4. Because we have a `font-weight` property value of `100` available, let's also set the paragraph element within our hero section to that weight. We can use the existing selector to do so, and the new rule set will look like this:

```
1.  .hero p {
2.    font-size: 24px;
3.    font-weight: 100;
4.  }
```

Our Styles Conference website has taken quite a few large steps this lesson, and the look and feel of our website is starting to really shine (see **Figure 6.6**).

The source code for the exercises within this lesson can be found at http://learn.shayhowe.com/html-css/working-with-typography/.

Figure 6.6 Our Styles Conference home page after adding the Lato Google web font

Including Citations & Quotes

Writing online sometimes involves citing different sources or quotations. All of the different citation and quotation cases can be covered semantically in HTML using the `<cite>`, `<q>`, and `<blockquote>` elements. Because they are usually distinguished from regular text in appearance, we'll discuss them here in the typography lesson.

Knowing when to use which element and attribute to properly mark up citations and quotes takes a bit of practice. In general, follow these rules:

- `<cite>`: Used to reference a creative work, author, or resource
- `<q>`: Used for short, inline quotations
- `<blockquote>`: Used for longer external quotations

Citing a Creative Work

The `<cite>` inline element is used in HTML to specifically cite a creative work; the element must include either the title of the work, the author's name, or a URL reference to the work. By default, content wrapped within the `<cite>` element will appear in italics within the browser.

For additional reference, it helps to include a hyperlink to the original source of the citation when relevant.

Here the book *Steve Jobs,* by Walter Isaacson, is referenced within the `<cite>` element (see **Figure 6.7**). Inside the citation is also a hyperlink to the book.

```
1.   <p>The book <cite><a href="http://www.amazon.com/Steve-Jobs-Walter-
     Isaacson/dp/1451648537">Steve Jobs</a></cite> is truly inspirational.</p>
```

The book *Steve Jobs* is truly inspirational.

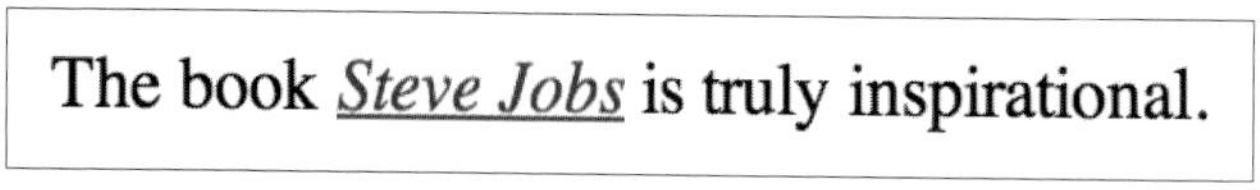

Figure 6.7 A citation of the book *Steve Jobs* using the `<cite>` element

Dialogue & Prose Quotation

Quite often, dialogue or prose is quoted inline, within other text. For this purpose, the <q> (or quote) inline element should be applied. The <q> element semantically indicates quoted dialogue or prose and shouldn't be used for any other purposes.

By default, the browser will insert the proper quotation marks for us and will even change the quotation marks based on the language identified within the lang global attribute.

Here's an example:

```
1.  <p>Steve Jobs once said, <q>One home run is much better than two
    doubles.</q></p>
```

Dialogue & Prose Citation

An optional attribute to include on the <q> element is the cite attribute. The cite attribute acts as a citation reference to the quote in the form of a URL. This attribute doesn't alter the appearance of the element; it simply adds value for screen readers and other devices. Because the attribute isn't viewable within the browser, it's also helpful to provide a hyperlink to this source next to the actual quotation.

Here's an example, which can also be seen in **Figure 6.8**:

```
1.  <p><a href="http://www.businessweek.com/magazine/content/
    06_06/b3970001.htm">Steve Jobs</a> once said, <q
    cite="http://www.businessweek.com/magazine/content/06_06/b3970001.htm">
    One home run is much better than two doubles.</q></p>
```

Steve Jobs once said, "One home run is much better than two doubles."

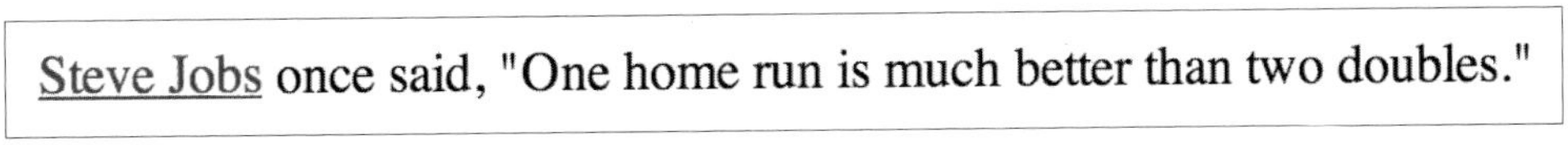

Figure 6.8 An inline quotation by Steve Jobs referenced from *Businessweek*

External Quotation

To quote a large block of text that comes from an external source and spans several lines, we'll use the `<blockquote>` element. The `<blockquote>` is a block-level element that may have other block-level elements nested inside it, including headings and paragraphs.

Here's an example that uses the `<blockquote>` element:

```
1.  <blockquote>
2.    <p>&#8220;In most people&#8217;s vocabularies, design is a
        veneer. It&#8217;s interior decorating. It&#8217;s the fabric of
        the curtains, of the sofa. But to me, nothing could be further
        from the meaning of design. Design is the fundamental soul of a
        human-made creation that ends up expressing itself in successive
        outer layers of the product.&#8221;</p>
3.  </blockquote>
```

External Citation

Longer quotes used within the `<blockquote>` element will often include a citation. This citation may comprise both the `cite` attribute and the `<cite>` element.

The `cite` attribute can be included on the `<blockquote>` element—in the same way that it was used on the `<q>` element earlier—to provide a citation reference to the quote in the form of a URL. The `<cite>` element then can fall after the actual quote itself to specify the original source of the quote, if relevant.

The HTML here outlines an extended quote from Steve Jobs that originally appeared in *Fortune* magazine. The quotation is marked up using the `<blockquote>` element with a cite attribute to specify where the quote originally appeared. In the `<blockquote>` element, the `<cite>` element, along with an `<a>` element, provides an additional citation and reference for the quote that is visible to users (see **Figure 6.9**).

```
1.  <blockquote cite="http://money.cnn.com/magazines/fortune/
        fortune_archive/2000/01/24/272277/index.htm">
2.    <p>&#8220;In most people&#8217;s vocabularies, design is a
        veneer. It&#8217;s interior decorating. It&#8217;s the fabric of
        the curtains, of the sofa. But to me, nothing could be further
        from the meaning of design. Design is the fundamental soul of a
        human-made creation that ends up expressing itself in successive
        outer layers of the product.&#8221;</p>
```

```
3.    <p><cite>&#8212; Steve Jobs in <a href="http://money.cnn.com/
      magazines/fortune/fortune_archive/2000/01/24/272277/index.htm">
      Fortune Magazine</a></cite></p>
4.    </blockquote>
```

"In most people's vocabularies, design is a veneer. It's interior decorating. It's the fabric of the curtains, of the sofa. But to me, nothing could be further from the meaning of design. Design is the fundamental soul of a human-made creation that ends up expressing itself in successive outer layers of the product."

— *Steve Jobs in Fortune Magazine*

Figure 6.9 An extended quote from Steve Jobs that originally appeared in *Fortune Magazine*

Summary

Learning how to style text is exciting, as our content can begin to convey some emotion. We can also start to play around with the hierarchy of our content, making our website more legible and digestible.

To quickly recap, within this lesson we discussed the following:

- Adding color to our text to enhance it
- Applying `font`-based properties, including `font-family`, `font-size`, `font-style`, `font-weight`, and more
- Applying `text`-based properties, including `text-align`, `text-decoration`, `text-indent`, `text-shadow`, and more
- The history behind web-safe fonts and how to embed our own web fonts
- How to properly mark up citations and quotations

Sharpening up our text and dabbling a bit with typography has brought our design along quite a way. Next, we'll bring a little more color to our website by going over backgrounds and gradients.

Lesson 7

Setting Backgrounds & Gradients

Backgrounds have a significant impact on the design of a website. They help create a site's look and feel, establish groupings, and assign priority, and they have a considerable influence on a website's usability.

Within CSS, element backgrounds can be a solid color, an image, a gradient, or a combination of these. As we decide how to implement these backgrounds, we should keep in mind that every background contributes to the overall appearance of our website.

In this lesson we're going to take a look at how to assign different types of backgrounds, including gradients, to elements; we'll also play around with a handful of CSS3 properties specific to backgrounds.

Adding a Background Color

The quickest way to add a background to an element is to add a single-color background using the `background` or `background-color` property. The `background` property accepts colors and images in shorthand form, while the `background-color` property is used strictly for setting solid background colors. Either property will work, and which one you decide to use depends on your preference as well as the case for which you're using it.

```
1.  div {
2.    background-color: #b2b2b2;
3.  }
```

When adding a background color, we have a few options for the values we can use. As with other color values, we can pick from keywords, hexadecimal codes, and RGB, RGBa, HSL, and HSLa values. Most commonly we'll see hexadecimal values; however, we may occasionally want to use RGBa or HSLa values for transparencies.

Transparent Backgrounds

When using an RGBa or HSLa value as a transparent background color, it's a good idea to provide a fallback color, too, because not all browsers recognize RGBa or HSLa values. And when a browser comes across a value it doesn't recognize, it will ignore it.

Fortunately, there is an easy way to provide a fallback background. CSS cascades from the top of a file to the bottom of a file; thus, we can use two `background-color` properties within a single rule set. The first `background-color` property will use a "safe" background color, such as a hexadecimal value, and the second `background-color` property will use an RGBa or HSLa value. Here, if a browser understands the RGBa or HSLa value it will render it, and if it doesn't, it will fall back to the hexadecimal value above it.

```
1.  div {
2.    background-color: #b2b2b2;
3.    background-color: rgba(0, 0, 0, .3);
4.  }
```

Adding a Background Image

Besides adding a background color to an element, we can also add a background image. Background images work similarly to background colors; however, they offer a few additional properties to finesse the images. As before, we can use the `background` property with a shorthand value, or we can use the `background-image` property outright. No matter which property we use, there must be an image source identified using a `url()` function.

The `url()` function value will be the background image's path, and the familiar rules for creating hyperlink paths apply here. Keep an eye out for different directories, and be sure to show exactly where the image resides. The path will be placed inside parentheses and quoted.

```
1.  div {
2.    background-image: url("alert.png");
3.  }
```

Adding a background image solely using a `url` value can provide undesirable results, as by default the background image will repeat horizontally and vertically from the top left of the given element to fill up the element's background. Thankfully we can use the `background-repeat` and `background-position` properties to control how or even whether the image repeats.

Background Repeat

By default, a background image will repeat indefinitely, both vertically and horizontally, unless otherwise specified. The `background-repeat` property may be used to change the direction in which a background image is repeated, if repeated at all.

```
1.  div {
2.    background-image: url("alert.png");
3.    background-repeat: no-repeat;
4.  }
```

The `background-repeat` property accepts four different values: `repeat`, `repeat-x`, `repeat-y`, and `no-repeat`. The `repeat` value is the default value and will repeat a background image both vertically and horizontally.

The `repeat-x` value will repeat the background image horizontally, while the `repeat-y` value will repeat the background image vertically. Lastly, the `no-repeat` value will tell the browser to display the background image once—that is, do not repeat it at all.

Background Position

By default, background images are positioned at the left top corner of an element. However, by using the `background-position` property, we can control exactly where the background image is placed relative to that corner.

```
1.  div {
2.    background-image: url("alert.png");
3.    background-position: 20px 10px;
4.    background-repeat: no-repeat;
5.  }
```

The `background-position` property requires two values: a horizontal offset (the first value) and a vertical offset (the second value). If only one value is specified, that value is used for both the horizontal and the vertical offsets.

Because we're moving the background image from the left top corner of the element, length values specifically will be in relation to that corner.

To set a `background-position` value, we can use the `top`, `right`, `bottom`, and `left` keywords, pixels, percentages, or any length measurement. Keywords and percentages work very similarly (see **Figure 7.1**). The keyword value `left top` is identical to the percentage value `0 0`, which will keep an image positioned at the left top corner of the element. The keyword value `right bottom` is identical to the percentage value `100% 100%`, which will position an image in the right bottom corner of the element.

Figure 7.1 Background images are positioned from the left top corner of an element

One advantage of percentages over keywords is the ability to center a background image by using `50%` as a value. To center the background image at the top of an element, we can use the value `50% 0`. Using pixels for a `background-position` value is also common, as pixels give us precise control over where our background will be positioned.

Shorthand Background Image Values

The background-color, background-image, background-position, and background-repeat properties may be rolled up into a shorthand value for the background property alone. The order of these properties as a shorthand background property value may vary, however it commonly falls as background-color, background-image, background-position, and then background-repeat.

```
1.  div {
2.    background: #b2b2b2 url("alert.png") 20px 10px no-repeat;
3.  }
```

Background Image Example

In the following example, we'll use the background property with a shorthand value that includes background-color, background-image, background-position, and background-repeat values.

Please take note that there is both a relative value and an absolute value within the background-position value. The first value, 20 pixels, is the horizontal value, positioning the background-image 20 pixels from the left of the element. The second value, 50%, is the vertical value, which vertically centers the background-image.

A few other properties and values are also included within the alert-success class rule set to further style the alert message (see Figure 7.2).

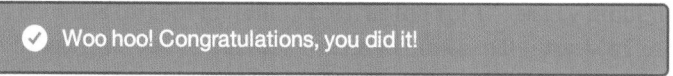

Figure 7.2 A success alert message including a background color and image

HTML

```
1.  <div class="alert-success">
2.    Woo hoo! Congratulations, you did it!
3.  </div>
```

CSS

```
1.  .alert-success {
2.    background: #67b11c url("tick.png") 20px 50% no-repeat;
```

```
3.     border: 2px solid #467813;
4.     border-radius: 5px;
5.     color: #fff;
6.     font-family: "Helvetica Neue", Helvetica, Arial, sans-serif;
7.     padding: 15px 20px 15px 50px;
8.   }
```

In Practice

Returning to our Styles Conference website, let's add some background colors. While we do that, we'll change a few other styles to keep all of our styles working together and to keep all of our content legible.

1. We'll begin by taking a big step and applying a blue background to the <body> element alongside the existing `color` and `font` properties. All of the styles for the <body> element rule set now include the following:

    ```
    1.  body {
    2.    background: #293f50;
    3.    color: #888;
    4.    font: 300 16px/22px "Lato", "Open Sans", "Helvetica Neue",
          Helvetica, Arial, sans-serif;
    5.  }
    ```

    We've placed a blue `background` on the <body> element purposely, as our website will have a few different rows of `background` colors, and the most frequent `background` color will be blue.

2. Now that every page on our Styles Conference website includes a blue `background`, let's clean up a few areas that will keep that blue background. Specifically, our <header> and <footer> elements will remain blue, as will the hero section on the home page.

    Within our <header> and <footer> elements let's make all of our link colors start as white and then, when hovered over, turn the same green as our headings.

    We'll begin with our <header> element. In order to select all <a> elements within the <header> element, we'll add a class of `primary-header` to the <header> element (in addition to the existing `container` and `group` classes). Don't forget, we'll need to add this class to the <header> elements across all of our pages.

    ```
    1.  <header class="primary-header container group">
    2.    ...
    3.  </header>
    ```

With the `primary-header` class in place on the `<header>` element, and the existing `primary-footer` class in place on the `<footer>` element, we can add two new rule sets to the bottom of the links section within our `main.css` file.

The first rule set will select all `<a>` elements within an element with the class attribute value of `primary-header` or `primary-footer` and set their color to white, as defined by comma separating two individual selectors that share the same property and value. The second rule set will select the same `<a>` elements as before but will change their color to green when a user hovers over them.

```
1.  .primary-header a,
2.  .primary-footer a {
3.    color: #fff;
4.  }
5.  .primary-header a:hover,
6.  .primary-footer a:hover {
7.    color: #648880;
8.  }
```

3. While we're making some of our text white, let's make the text within the hero section of our home page white also, as it will remain on a blue `background`. We have the existing `hero` class rule set available to add styles to, so let's add our white text `color` there. In all, our `hero` class rule set should include the following:

```
1.  .hero {
2.    color: #fff;
3.    line-height: 44px;
4.    padding: 22px 80px 66px 80px;
5.    text-align: center;
6.  }
```

4. Also within the hero section of our home page, let's clean up some of the button styles. We'll begin by adding some new properties to our `btn` class rule set, within the buttons section of our `main.css` file.

Specifically, let's set the button text `color` to white, make sure our `cursor` is always a `pointer`, increase the `font-weight`, add a small amount of `letter-spacing`, and change our `text-transform` to `uppercase`.

In all, our new `btn` class rule set should look like this:

```
1.  .btn {
2.    border-radius: 5px;
3.    color: #fff;
4.    cursor: pointer;
```

```
 5.    display: inline-block;
 6.    font-weight: 400;
 7.    letter-spacing: .5px;
 8.    margin: 0;
 9.    text-transform: uppercase;
10.  }
```

We'll also clean up some of the alternate button styles by way of the btn-alt class rule set. Specifically, let's make the buttons' borders white and add hover styles including a white background and blue text color.

With all of the additions, our new btn-alt class rule set should look like this:

```
1.    .btn-alt {
2.      border: 1px solid #fff;
3.      padding: 10px 30px;
4.    }
5.    .btn-alt:hover {
6.      background: #fff;
7.      color: #648880;
8.    }
```

5. Now that we have all of the areas with blue backgrounds cleaned up, let's add styles for the rows that have white backgrounds. Let's create a new section within our main. css file for rows, just below the clearfix section. Within this new rows section, let's create a new class selector named row.

Within our new row class rule set, let's add a white background, a minimum width of 960 pixels (to make sure our row elements are always larger than the width of our container or grid elements), and some vertical padding. Altogether our new row section within our main.css file should look like this:

```
 1.    /*
 2.    ====================================
 3.    Rows
 4.    ====================================
 5.    */
 6.
 7.    .row {
 8.      background: #fff;
 9.      min-width: 960px;
10.      padding: 66px 0 44px 0;
11.    }
```

6. With our row class styles in place, let's add a row with a white background to our home page. We'll do this on our teasers section. Currently this area has a <section> element with the class of grid wrapping three additional <section> elements with the classes of teaser and col-1-3.

To add a white background to this section, we're going to wrap all of these elements in an element with the class of row.

Because we'll want the entire teasers section wrapped in a <section> element, we're going to add a new <section> element with the class of row that surrounds the existing <section> element with the class of grid.

Having two <section> elements wrapping the exact same content diminishes semantic value. To correct this we'll change the second <section> element, the one with the class of grid, to a <div> element. After all, at this point this element is only adding styles, not semantic meaning, and is appropriate as a <div> element.

The structure of our new teasers element should look like this:

```
1.   <section class="row">
2.     <div class="grid">
3.
4.       <!-- Speakers -->
5.
6.       <section class="teaser col-1-3">
7.         ...
8.       </section><!--
9.
10.      Schedule
11.
12.      --><section class="teaser col-1-3">
13.        ...
14.      </section><!--
15.
16.      Venue
17.
18.      --><section class="teaser col-1-3">
19.        ...
20.      </section>
21.
22.    </div>
23.  </section>
```

It is amazing how a few background colors can affect the design of a website. Our Styles Conference website is coming along quite nicely, and our home page, as shown in **Figure 7.3**, is proof.

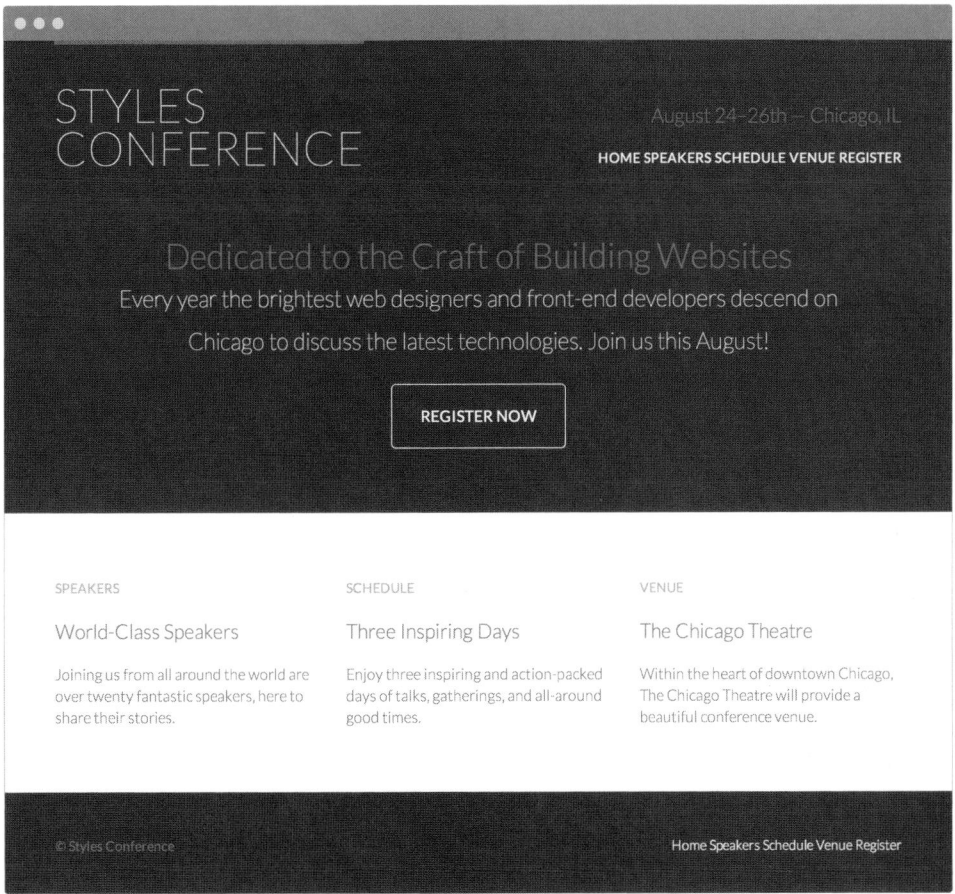

Figure 7.3 Our Styles Conference website home page after adding some background colors

Designing Gradient Backgrounds

Gradient backgrounds were introduced with CSS3, and designers and front-end developers everywhere rejoiced. Although gradient backgrounds do not work in legacy browsers, they are supported by all modern browsers.

Within CSS, gradient backgrounds are treated as background images. We can create a gradient using the `background` or `background-image` properties, just like a regular background image. The property value for a gradient background varies depending on what type of gradient we'd like, linear or radial.

Gradient Background Vendor Prefixes

In Lesson 4, "Opening the Box Model," we discussed adding vendor prefixes to new CSS properties or values so that browsers can support recently developed CSS features. Gradient background values were one of the values that required the use of vendor prefixes. Fortunately, most browsers have since eliminated the need for a vendor prefix in order to render a gradient background; however, it is still worth outlining vendor prefixes to ensure the best support.

At first, as we begin discussing linear gradient backgrounds, we'll include each of the different vendor prefixes. After that, in the interest of brevity, we'll omit the different prefixes as we continue to discuss gradient backgrounds, including radial gradient backgrounds.

Linear Gradient Background

For years designers and developers have been cutting up gradient image files, created using image-processing software, and using them as linear gradient backgrounds on elements. The process worked, but it took a while to implement and was very inflexible. Fortunately those days are gone, and linear gradient backgrounds can now be specified within CSS. If a color needs changing, there is no need to reproduce and recut an image and upload it to the server. Now all we need to do is change a quick value within CSS (see **Figure 7.4**). Beautiful.

```
1.  div {
2.    background: #466368;
3.    background: -webkit-linear-gradient(#648880, #293f50);
```

```
4.    background:    -moz-linear-gradient(#648880, #293f50);
5.    background:       linear-gradient(#648880, #293f50);
6.  }
```

Figure 7.4 A linear gradient background transitioning from the top to the bottom of an element

Linear gradients are identified by using the `linear-gradient()` function within the `background` or `background-image` property. The `linear-gradient()` function must include two color values, the first of which will be the beginning color value and the second of which will be the ending color value. The browser will then handle the transition between the two colors.

Before any gradient backgrounds are identified, we'll also put in a default `background` property with a solid color. The solid color is to be used as a fallback should a browser not support gradient backgrounds.

Changing the Direction of a Gradient Background

By default, linear gradient backgrounds move from the top to the bottom of an element, transitioning smoothly between the first color value and the second. This direction, however, may be changed with the use of keywords or a degree value stated before any color values.

For example, should we want a gradient to move from the left of an element to the right, we can use the keyword value `to right` to identify the direction in which the linear gradient should progress. Keyword values may also be combined. If we want the gradient to move from the left top to the right bottom of an element, we can use the keyword value of `to right bottom` (see **Figure 7.5**).

```
1.  div {
2.      background: #466368;
3.      background: linear-gradient(to right bottom, #648880, #293f50);
4.  }
```

Figure 7.5 A linear gradient background transitioning from the left top to the right bottom of an element

When we use a diagonal gradient on an element that isn't exactly square, the background gradient will not proceed directly from one corner to the other. Instead, the gradient will identify the absolute center of the element, place anchors in the perpendicular corners from where it should progress, and then move to the general direction of the corner stated within the value. These corners the gradient moves towards are called "magic corners," as they are not absolute. Eric Meyer has done a wonderful job of outlining this syntax in his article "Linear Gradient Keywords" at http://meyerweb.com/eric/thoughts/2012/04/26/lineargradient-keywords/.

Besides keywords, degree values are also acceptable. If we want our gradient to move to the left top of an element, we can use the degree value of 315deg, or if we want our gradient to move to the right bottom of an element, we can use the degree value of 135deg. This same concept can be applied for any degree value, 0 through 360.

Radial Gradient Background

While the linear gradient is perfect for a gradient moving from one direction to another, often the need for a radial gradient arises (see **Figure 7.6**). Radial background gradients work just like linear gradients and share many of the same values. For radial gradients, instead of using the `linear-gradient()` function within the `background` or `background-image` property, we'll use the `radial-gradient()` function.

```
1.  div {
2.    background: #466368;
3.    background: radial-gradient(#648880, #293f50);
4.  }
```

Figure 7.6 A radial gradient background transitioning from the center of an element to the outside of an element

Radial gradients work from the inside to the outside of an element. Thus, the first color identified within the `radial-gradient()` function will sit in the absolute center of the element, and the second color will sit on the outside of an element. The browser will then create the transition between the two colors.

One of the primary differences between radial gradients and linear gradients is that radial gradients can be quite complex, with values for location, size, radius, and so forth. We'll cover the basics, but please feel free to delve further into radial gradients, as they provide much more power than is outlined here.

CSS3 Gradient Background Generator

Working with CSS3 gradients by hand can be quite difficult at times, especially if you are new to them. Fortunately, a few CSS3 gradient generators (http://ie.microsoft.com/testdrive/graphics/cssgradientbackgroundmaker/default.html) have popped up. Each generator works a little differently, and some provide more options than others. If you're interested, I recommend doing some research to find the right generator for your needs.

Gradient Color Stops

At a minimum, gradient backgrounds will transition from one color to another; however, we may add multiple colors to a gradient and have the browser transition between all of them (see **Figure 7.7**). To do this we'll add color stops to the given gradient function, with commas separating each color stop from the next.

```
1.  div {
2.    background: #648880;
3.    background: linear-gradient(to right, #f6f1d3, #648880, #293f50);
4.  }
```

Figure 7.7 A linear gradient background including three colors transitioning from the left to the right of an element

By default, the browser will position every color stop an equal distance from the next and will transition between them accordingly. If more control over how colors are positioned is desired, a location along the gradient may be identified for each color stop. The location should be declared as a length value and should fall after the color value (see Figure 7.8).

```
1.  div {
2.    background: #648880;
3.    background: linear-gradient(to right, #f6f1d3, #648880 85%, #293f50);
4.  }
```

Figure 7.8 A linear gradient background, including three colors and their unique locations, transitioning from the left to the right of an element

Unless specified otherwise, the first color stop will be positioned at 0%, and the last color stop will be positioned at 100%.

Gradient Background Example

Using the same success alert message from before, we'll swap out the old background image for a linear gradient background image.

For this we'll include two `background` properties. The first `background` property specifies a solid color hexadecimal value, which serves as a fallback should a browser not support linear gradient backgrounds. The second `background` property includes the `linear-gradient()` function, which identifies a green gradient background that transitions from the top of the element to the bottom of the element (**see Figure 7.9**).

> **Woo hoo! Congratulations, you did it!**

Figure 7.9 A success alert message including a linear gradient background image

HTML

```
1.  <div class="alert-success">
2.    Woo hoo! Congratulations, you did it!
3.  </div>
```

CSS

```
1.  .alert-success {
2.    background: #67b11c;
3.    background: linear-gradient(#72c41f, #5c9e19);
4.    border: 2px solid #467813;
5.    border-radius: 5px;
6.    color: #fff;
7.    font-family: "Helvetica Neue", Helvetica, Arial, sans-serif;
8.    padding: 15px 20px;
9.  }
```

In Practice

With gradient backgrounds now in the mix, let's create a new row for our Styles Conference website, this time using a gradient.

1. We'll create a new row with a gradient background by using the class of row-alt. Because the new row will share the same min-width property and value as the row class selector, we'll combine these two selectors.

    ```
    1.  .row,
    2.  .row-alt {
    3.    min-width: 960px;
    4.  }
    ```

    Next we'll want to create new rule sets to apply styles specifically to the row-alt class selector. These new styles will include a gradient background that starts with green and transitions to yellow, from left to right.

Using the linear-gradient() function with the appropriate values and vendor prefixes, we'll add the gradient background to the row-alt class rule set. We'll also include a single background color before the gradient background as a fallback, just in case a browser doesn't support gradient backgrounds.

Lastly, we'll also add in some vertical padding.

Our updated row section now looks like this:

```
1.   .row,
2.   .row-alt {
3.     min-width: 960px;
4.   }
5.   .row {
6.     background: #fff;
7.     padding: 66px 0 44px 0;
8.   }
9.   .row-alt {
10.    background: #cbe2c1;
11.    background: -webkit-linear-gradient(to right, #a1d3b0, #f6f1d3);
12.    background:    -moz-linear-gradient(to right, #a1d3b0, #f6f1d3);
13.    background:         linear-gradient(to right, #a1d3b0, #f6f1d3);
14.    padding: 44px 0 22px 0;
15.  }
```

2. With our row-alt styles in place, let's put them to use on all of our interior pages. Currently, all of our interior pages have a <section> element with a class of container. Then, inside each <section> element is an <h1> element containing the heading of the page.

    We're going to alter these <section> elements much like we did the teaser <section> element on our home page. We'll wrap each <section> element with a class of container in a <section> element with the class of row-alt. We'll then change each <section> element with a class of container to a <div> element for better semantic alignment.

    Each of our interior pages should now include the following:

```
1.   <section class="row-alt">
2.     <div class="container">
3.
4.       <h1>...</h1>
5.
6.     </div>
7.   </section>
```

3. Because we are updating our interior pages, let's make their introductions, or leads, a little more appealing. We'll begin by adding a paragraph introducing each page just below the `<h1>` element in each `<section>` element with a class of `row-alt`. Our `speakers.html` page, for example, may now include the following lead section:

```
1.   <section class="row-alt">
2.     <div class="container">
3.
4.       <h1>Speakers</h1>
5.
6.       <p>We&#8217;re happy to welcome over twenty speakers to present
           on the industry&#8217;s latest technologies. Prepare for an
           inspiration extravaganza.</p>
7.
8.     </div>
9.   </section>
```

4. In addition to inserting the paragraph, let's also change some of the styles within the lead section. To do this, we'll add a class of `lead` to the `<div>` element that already has a class of `container`; this can be found nested directly inside the `<section>` element with a class of `row-alt`. Our lead section for each interior page will now look like this:

```
1.   <section class="row-alt">
2.     <div class="lead container">
3.
4.       ...
5.
6.     </div>
7.   </section>
```

5. Once the `lead` class is in place, we'll center all of the text within these `<div>` elements. We'll also increase the `font-size` and `line-height` of any paragraphs within these `<div>` elements.

   We'll create a new section for leads within our `main.css` file, just below the typography section, and add the following styles:

```
1.   /*
2.   ========================================
3.   Leads
4.   ========================================
```

```
5.  */
6.
7.  .lead {
8.    text-align: center;
9.  }
10. .lead p {
11.   font-size: 21px;
12.   line-height: 33px;
13. }
```

The interior pages of our Styles Conference website have now received some long-overdue love in the form of gradient `background` rows and leads (see **Figure 7.10**). Make sure to review the code for all of the interior pages to see their newly enhanced content, headings, and paragraphs.

Figure 7.10 The Speakers page of our Styles Conference website, complete with a gradient background row

The source code for the exercises within this lesson can be found at http://learn.shayhowe.com/html-css/setting-backgrounds-and-gradients/.

Using Multiple Background Images

For the longest time, elements were allowed to have only one background image at a time, which created quite a few constraints when designing a page. Fortunately, with CSS3, we can now use more than one background image on an element by comma-separating multiple background values within a `background` or `background-image` property.

The background image value that comes first will be the foremost background image, and the background image that's listed last will be the rearmost background image. Any value between the first and the last will reside within the middle ground accordingly. Here's an example of the CSS for a `<div>` element that uses three background images:

```
1.  div {
2.    background:
        url("foreground.png") 0 0 no-repeat,
        url("middle-ground.png") 0 0 no-repeat,
        url("background.png") 0 0 no-repeat;
3.  }
```

The preceding code uses a shorthand value for the background property, chaining multiple background image values together. These shorthand values may also be broken up into comma-separated values across the `background-image`, `background-position`, and `background-repeat` properties.

Multiple Background Images Example

Let's go back to the success alert message once more to combine both the tick background image and the linear gradient background image.

In order to do so, we'll include two values within the second background property. The first value, the foremost image, will be the tick image (see **Figure 7.11**). The second value, the rearmost image, will be the linear gradient. The two values are comma separated.

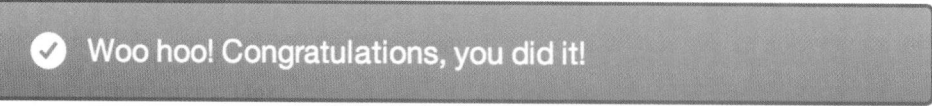

Figure 7.11 A success alert message with multiple background images including a tick image and a linear gradient

HTML

```
1.  <div class="alert-success">
2.    Woo hoo! Congratulations, you did it!
3.  </div>
```

CSS

```
1.  .alert-success {
2.    background: #67b11c;
3.    background: url("tick.png") 20px 50% no-repeat, linear-
         gradient(#72c41f, #5c9e19);
4.    border: 2px solid #467813;
5.    border-radius: 5px;
6.    color: #fff;
7.    font-family: "Helvetica Neue", Helvetica, Arial, sans-serif;
8.    padding: 15px 20px 15px 50px;
9.  }
```

Exploring New Background Properties

Along with gradient backgrounds and multiple background images, CSS3 also introduced three new CSS properties: background-size, background-clip, and background-origin. The background-size property allows us to change the size of a background image, while the background-clip and background-origin properties allow us to control where a background image is cropped and where a background image is contained within the element (inside the border or inside the padding, for example).

CSS3 Background Size

The background-size property allows us to specify a size for a background image. The property accepts a few different values, including length and keyword values.

When using length values, we can specify a width and a height value by using two space-separated values. The first value will set the width of the background image, while the second value will set the height of the background image. It's important to note that percentage values are in relation to the element's size, not the background image's original size.

Consequently, setting a `background-size` property with a `100%` width will make the background image occupy the full width of the element. If a second value isn't identified after the width, the height value will be automatically set to preserve the aspect ratio of the background image.

The keyword value `auto` may be used as either the width or height value to preserve the aspect ratio of the background image. For example, if we want to set the height of the background image to be `75%` of the height of the element while maintaining the image's aspect ratio, we can use a `background-size` property value of `auto 75%` (see **Figure 7.12**).

```
1.  div {
2.    background: url("shay.jpg") 0 0 no-repeat;
3.    background-size: auto 75%;
4.    border: 1px dashed #949599;
5.    height: 240px;
6.    width: 200px;
7.  }
```

Figure 7.12 A background image occupying 75% of an element's height with the image's width automatically adjusted to preserve its original aspect ratio

Cover & Contain Keyword Values

In addition to length `background-size` property values, there are also `cover` and `contain` keyword values available to the `background-size` property.

The `cover` keyword value specifies that the background image will be resized to completely cover an element's width and height. The background image's original aspect ratio will be preserved, yet the image will stretch or shrink as necessary to cover the entire element. Often when using the `cover` keyword value, part of the background image is cut off in order for the image to occupy the full available space of the element.

The `contain` keyword value, on the other hand, specifies that the background image will be resized to reside entirely contained within an element's width and height. In doing so the background image's original aspect ratio will be preserved, but the image will stretch or shrink as necessary to remain within the width and height of the element. In contrast with the `cover` keyword value, the `contain` keyword value will always show the full background image; however, oftentimes it will not occupy the full available space of the element.

Both the `cover` and `contain` keyword values may result in slightly distorted background images, particularly when the images are stretched beyond their original dimensions. We'll want to keep an eye out for this when using these values, to make sure the resulting styles are satisfactory.

CSS3 Background Clip & Background Origin

The `background-clip` property specifies the surface area a background image will cover, and the `background-origin` property specifies where the `background-position` should originate. The introduction of these two new properties corresponds with the introduction of three new keyword values: `border-box` (see **Figure 7.13**), `padding-box` (see **Figure 7.14**), and `content-box` (see **Figure 7.15**). Each of these three values may be used for the `background-clip` and `background-origin` properties.

```
1.  div {
2.    background: url("shay.jpg") 0 0 no-repeat;
3.    background-clip: padding-box;
4.    background-origin: border-box;
5.  }
```

The `background-clip` property value is set to `border-box` by default, allowing a background image to extend into the same area as any border. Meanwhile, the `background-origin` property value is set to `padding-box` by default, allowing the beginning of a background image to extend into the padding of an element.

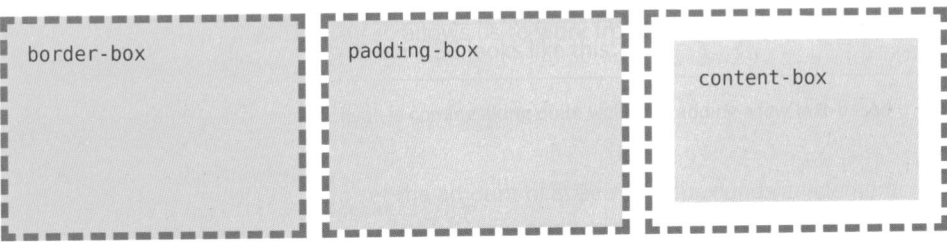

Figure 7.13 The `border-box` value extends the background into the `border` of an element

Figure 7.14 The `padding-box` value extends the background into the `padding` of an element, but the background is contained within any `border`

Figure 7.15 The `content-box` value contains the background within the `border` and `padding` of an element

We first discussed these keyword values when we covered the box-sizing property back in Lesson 4, "Opening the Box Model." The values themselves haven't changed in meaning, but their functions do change with the use of the different background properties.

Summary

Adding backgrounds and gradients to our pages allows us to bring color to the forefront of our designs. These features also help to define how content is grouped and to improve the layout of our pages as a whole.

To review, this lesson covered the following:

- How to add background colors and images to elements
- CSS gradients, both linear and radial, and how to customize them
- How to apply multiple background images to a single element
- New CSS3 properties that allow us to change the size, surface area, and origin of background images

Adding background colors, gradients, and images brings forth quite a few possibilities to enhance the overall design of our websites. Soon we'll discuss how to semantically add images (aside from background images) and other media to our pages. But before that, let's take a look at how to semantically create lists.

Lesson 8

Creating Lists

Lists are a part of everyday life. To-do lists determine what to get done. Navigational routes provide turn-by-turn lists of directions. Recipes provide lists of ingredients and lists of instructions. With a list for nearly everything, it's easy to understand why they are also popular online.

When we want to use a list on a website, HTML provides three different types to choose from: unordered, ordered, and description lists. Choosing which type of list to use—or whether to use a list at all—comes down to the content and the most semantically appropriate option for displaying that content.

In addition to the three different types of lists available within HTML, there are multiple ways to style these lists with CSS. For example, we can choose what type of marker to use on a list. The marker could be square, round, numeric, alphabetical, or perhaps nonexistent. Also, we can decide if a list should be displayed vertically or horizontally. All of these choices play significant roles in the styling of our web pages.

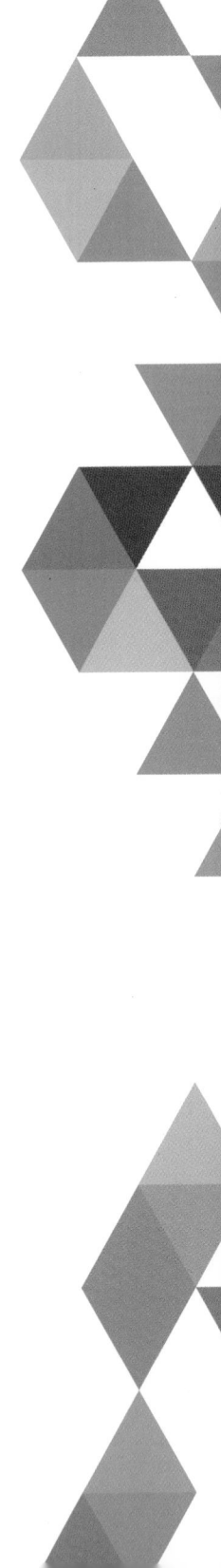

Unordered Lists

An unordered list is simply a list of related items whose order does not matter. Creating an unordered list in HTML is accomplished using the unordered list block-level element, `<ul>` (see **Figure 8.1**). Each item within an unordered list is individually marked up using the list item element, `<li>`.

By default, most browsers add a vertical `margin` and left `padding` to the `<ul>` element and precede each `<li>` element with a solid dot. This solid dot is called the list item marker, and it can be changed using CSS.

```
1.  <ul>
2.    <li>Orange</li>
3.    <li>Green</li>
4.    <li>Blue</li>
5.  </ul>
```

- Orange
- Green
- Blue

Figure 8.1 An unordered list with three list items whose order doesn't matter

Ordered Lists

The ordered list element, `<ol>`, works very much like the unordered list element; individual list items are created in the same manner (see **Figure 8.2**). The main difference between an ordered list and an unordered list is that with an ordered list, the order in which items are presented is important.

Because the order matters, instead of using a dot as the default list item marker, an ordered list uses numbers.

```
1.  <ol>
2.    <li>Head north on N Halsted St</li>
3.    <li>Turn right on W Diversey Pkwy</li>
4.    <li>Turn left on N Orchard St</li>
5.  </ol>
```

Ordered lists also have unique attributes available to them including `start` and `reversed`.

1. Head north on N Halsted St
2. Turn right on W Diversey Pkwy
3. Turn left on N Orchard St

Figure 8.2 An ordered list with three list items whose order does matter

Start Attribute

The start attribute defines the number from which an ordered list should start (see **Figure 8.3**). By default, ordered lists start at 1. However, there may be cases where a list should start at 30 or another number. When we use the start attribute on the <ol> element, we can identify exactly which number an ordered list should begin counting from.

The start attribute accepts only integer values, even though ordered lists may use different numbering systems, such as roman numerals.

```
1.  <ol start="30">
2.    <li>Head north on N Halsted St</li>
3.    <li>Turn right on W Diversey Pkwy</li>
4.    <li>Turn left on N Orchard St</li>
5.  </ol>
```

30. Head north on N Halsted St
31. Turn right on W Diversey Pkwy
32. Turn left on N Orchard St

Figure 8.3 An ordered list with three list items and a start attribute value of 30

Reversed Attribute

The reversed attribute, when used on the <ol> element, allows a list to appear in reverse order. An ordered list of five items numbered 1 to 5 may be reversed and ordered from 5 to 1 (see **Figure 8.4**).

The reversed attribute is a Boolean attribute, and as such it doesn't accept any value. It is either true or false. False is the default value; the value becomes true when the attribute name reversed appears on the <ol> element.

```
1.  <ol reversed>
2.    <li>Head north on N Halsted St</li>
3.    <li>Turn right on W Diversey Pkwy</li>
4.    <li>Turn left on N Orchard St</li>
5.  </ol>
```

3. Head north on N Halsted St
2. Turn right on W Diversey Pkwy
1. Turn left on N Orchard St

Figure 8.4 An ordered list with three list items and the reversed attribute

Value Attribute

The value attribute may be used on an individual `<li>` element within an ordered list to change its value within the list. The number of any list item appearing below a list item with a value attribute will be recalculated accordingly.

As an example, if the second list item has a value attribute value of 9, the number on that list item marker will appear as if it is the ninth item (**see Figure 8.5**). All subsequent list items will be numbered upwards from 9.

```
1.  <ol>
2.    <li>Head north on N Halsted St</li>
3.    <li value="9">Turn right on W Diversey Pkwy</li>
4.    <li>Turn left on N Orchard St</li>
5.  </ol>
```

```
 1. Head north on N Halsted St
 9. Turn right on W Diversey Pkwy
10. Turn left on N Orchard St
```

Figure 8.5 An ordered list with three list items, in which the second list item has a value attribute value of 9

Description Lists

Another type of list seen online (but not as often as unordered or ordered lists) is the description list. Description lists are used to outline multiple terms and their descriptions, as in a glossary, for example.

Creating a description list in HTML is accomplished using the description list block-level element, `<dl>`. Instead of using a `<li>` element to mark up list items, the description list requires two block-level elements: the description term element, `<dt>`, and the description element, `<dd>`.

A description list may contain numerous terms and descriptions, one after the other (see **Figure 8.6**). Additionally, a description list may have multiple terms per description, as well as multiple descriptions per term. A single term may have multiple meanings and warrant multiple descriptions. Conversely, a single description may be suitable for multiple terms.

When adding a description list, the <dt> element must come before the <dd> element. The definition term and the description that directly follows it correspond to one another; thus, the order of these elements is important.

By default, the <dl> element will include vertical margins, just like the <ul> and <ol> elements. Additionally, the <dd> element includes a left margin by default.

```
1.  <dl>
2.    <dt>study</dt>
3.    <dd>The devotion of time and attention to acquiring knowledge
      on an academic subject, especially by means of books</dd>
4.    <dt>design</dt>
5.    <dd>A plan or drawing produced to show the look and function or
      workings of a building, garment, or other object before it is
      built or made</dd>
6.    <dd>Purpose, planning, or intention that exists or is thought to
      exist behind an action, fact, or material object</dd>
7.    <dt>business</dt>
8.    <dt>work</dt>
9.    <dd>A person's regular occupation, profession, or trade</dd>
10. </dl>
```

study
    The devotion of time and attention to acquiring knowledge on an
    academic subject, especially by means of books
design
    A plan or drawing produced to show the look and function or
    workings of a building, garment, or other object before it is built or
    made
    Purpose, planning, or intention that exists or is thought to exist behind
    an action, fact, or material object
business
work
    A person's regular occupation, profession, or trade

Figure 8.6 A description list with multiple terms and descriptions

Nesting Lists

One feature that makes lists extremely powerful is their ability to be nested. Every list may be placed within another list; they can be nested continually. But the potential to nest lists indefinitely doesn't provide free rein to do so. Lists should still be reserved specifically for where they hold the most semantic value.

One trick with nesting lists is to know where to begin and end each list and list item. Speaking specifically about unordered and ordered lists, as that is where most nesting will occur, the only element that may reside directly within the `<ul>` and `<ol>` elements is the `<li>` element. To repeat, the only element we can place as a direct child of the `<ul>` and `<ol>` elements is the `<li>` element.

That said, once inside the `<li>` element, the standard set of elements may be added, including any `<ul>` or `<ol>` elements.

To nest a list rather than closing a list item, begin a new list (see **Figure 8.7**). Once the nested list is complete and closed, close the wrapping list item and continue on with the original list.

```
1.   <ol>
2.      <li>Walk the dog</li>
3.      <li>Fold laundry</li>
4.      <li>
5.        Go to the grocery and buy:
6.        <ul>
7.          <li>Milk</li>
8.          <li>Bread</li>
9.          <li>Cheese</li>
10.       </ul>
11.     </li>
12.     <li>Mow the lawn</li>
13.     <li>Make dinner</li>
14.  </ol>
```

1. Walk the dog
2. Fold laundry
3. Go to the grocery and buy:
   - Milk
   - Bread
   - Cheese
4. Mow the lawn
5. Make dinner

Figure 8.7 An ordered list with a nested unordered list

Because nesting lists can be a little tricky—and unwanted styles will appear if it's done incorrectly—let's quickly review. The `<ul>` and `<ol>` elements may contain only `<li>` elements. The `<li>` element may contain any normal element as desired; however, the `<li>` element has to be a direct child of either a `<ul>` or `<ol>` element.

It's also worth noting that as lists are nested inside of other lists, their list item markers will change according to how deeply the list is nested. In the previous example, the unordered list nested within the ordered list uses hollow circles instead of solid discs as the list item marker. This change happens because the unordered list is nested one level into the ordered list.

Fortunately we have control over how these list item markers appear at any level, which we'll take a look at next.

List Item Styling

Unordered and ordered lists use list item markers by default. For unordered lists these are typically solid dots, while ordered lists typically use numbers. With CSS the style and position of these list item markers may be adjusted.

List Style Type Property

The list-style-type property is used to set the content of a list item marker (see **Figure 8.8**). The available values range from squares and decimal numbers all the way to Armenian numbering, and the style may be placed on either the <ul>, <ol>, or <li> elements within CSS.

Any list-style-type property value can be added to either unordered or ordered lists. With this in mind, it is possible to use a numeric list item marker on an unordered list and a nonnumeric marker on an ordered list.

HTML

```
1.  <ul>
2.    <li>Orange</li>
3.    <li>Green</li>
4.    <li>Blue</li>
5.  </ul>
```

CSS

```
1.  ul {
2.    list-style-type: square;
3.  }
```

- Orange
- Green
- Blue

Figure 8.8 An unordered list with a list-style-type property value of square

List Style Type Values

As previously mentioned, the `list-style-type` property comes with a handful of different values. The following list outlines these values as well as their corresponding content.

LIST STYLE TYPE VALUE	CONTENT
none	No list item
disc	A filled circle
circle	A hollow circle
square	A filled square
decimal	Decimal numbers
decimal-leading-zero	Decimal numbers padded by initial zeros
lower-roman	Lowercase roman numerals
upper-roman	Uppercase roman numerals
lower-greek	Lowercase classical Greek
lower-alpha / lower-latin	Lowercase ASCII letters
upper-alpha / upper-latin	Uppercase ASCII letters
armenian	Traditional Armenian numbering
georgian	Traditional Georgian numbering

Using an Image as a List Item Marker

There may come a time when the default `list-style-type` property values are not enough, and we want to customize our own list item marker. Doing so is most commonly accomplished by placing a background image on each `<li>` element within a list (see **Figure 8.9**).

The process includes removing any default `list-style-type` property value and adding a background image and padding to the `<li>` element.

In detail, the `list-style-type` property value of none will remove existing list item markers. The `background` property will identify a background image, along with its position and repeat value, if necessary. And the `padding` property will provide space to the left of the text for the background image.

HTML

```
1.  <ul>
2.    <li>Orange</li>
3.    <li>Green</li>
4.    <li>Blue</li>
5.  </ul>
```

> Orange
> Green
> Blue

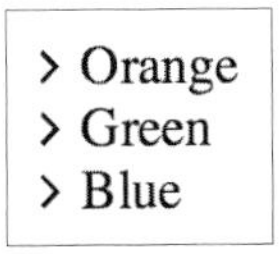

Figure 8.9 An unordered list with a custom list item marker by way of a background image

CSS

```
1.  li {
2.    background: url("arrow.png") 0 50% no-repeat;
3.    list-style-type: none;
4.    padding-left: 12px;
5.  }
```

List Style Position Property

By default the list item marker is to the left of the content within the `<li>` element. This list style positioning is described as `outside`, meaning all of the content will appear directly to the right, outside of the list item marker. Using the `list-style-position` property, we can change the default value of `outside` to `inside` or `inherit`.

The `outside` property value places the list item marker to the left of the `<li>` element and doesn't allow any content to wrap below the list item marker. The `inside` property value (which is rarely seen or used) places the list item marker in line with the first line of the `<li>` element and allows other content to wrap below it as needed (see **Figure 8.10**).

HTML

```
1.  <ul>
2.    <li>Cupcakes...</li>
3.    <li>Sprinkles...</li>
4.  </ul>
```

CSS

```
1.  ul {
2.    list-style-position: inside;
3.  }
```

- Cupcakes – One of the best desserts known to ever exist, especially when topped with cream cheese frosting
- Sprinkles – One of the most popular toppings for cupcakes, adding that extra bit of decoration and sugar

Figure 8.10 An unordered list with a `list-style-position` property value of `inside`

Shorthand List Style Property

The list style properties discussed thus far, `list-style-type` and `list-style-position`, can be combined into one shorthand `list-style` property value. When using the `list-style` property, we can use one or all list style property values at a time. The order of these shorthand values should be `list-style-type` followed by `list-style-position`.

```
1.  ul {
2.    list-style: circle inside;
3.  }
4.  ol {
5.    list-style: lower-roman;
6.  }
```

Horizontally Displaying List

Occasionally we may want to display lists horizontally rather than vertically. Perhaps we want to divide a list into multiple columns, to build a navigational list, or to put a few list items in a single row. Depending on the content and desired appearance, there are a few different ways to display lists as a single line, such as by making the `display` property value of `<li>` elements `inline` or `inline-block` or by floating them.

Displaying List

The quickest way to display a list on a single line is to give the `<li>` elements a `display` property value of `inline` or `inline-block`. Doing so places all the `<li>` elements within a single line, with a single space between each list item.

If the spaces between each of the `<li>` elements are troublesome, they may be removed using the same techniques we discussed in Lesson 5, "Positioning Content."

More often than not, we'll use the `inline-block` property value rather than the `inline` property value. The `inline-block` property value allows us to easily add vertical margins and other spacing to the `<li>` elements, whereas the `inline` property value does not.

When changing the `display` property value to `inline` or `inline-block`, the list item marker, be it a bullet, number, or other style, is removed (see **Figure 8.11**).

HTML

```
1.  <ul>
2.    <li>Orange</li>
3.    <li>Green</li>
4.    <li>Blue</li>
5.  </ul>
```

CSS

```
1.  li {
2.    display: inline-block;
3.    margin: 0 10px;
4.  }
```

| Orange   Green   Blue |

Figure 8.11 An unordered list with each `<li>` element displayed with an `inline-block` property value

Floating List

Changing the `display` property value to `inline` or `inline-block` is quick; however, it removes the list item marker. If the list item marker is needed, floating each `<li>` element is a better option than changing the `display` property.

Setting all `<li>` elements' `float` property to `left` will horizontally align all `<li>` elements directly next to each other without any space between them. When we float each `<li>` element, the list item marker is displayed by default and will actually sit on top of the `<li>` element next to it. To prevent the list item marker from being displayed on top of other `<li>` elements, a horizontal `margin` or `padding` should be added (see **Figure 8.12**).

HTML

```
1.  <ul>
2.    <li>Orange</li>
3.    <li>Green</li>
4.    <li>Blue</li>
5.  </ul>
```

CSS

```
1.  li {
2.    float: left;
3.    margin: 0 20px;
4.  }
```

| ▪ Orange   ▪ Green   ▪ Blue |

Figure 8.12 An unordered list with each `<li>` element floated to the `left`

As when floating any element, this breaks the flow of the page. We must remember to clear our floats—most commonly with the clearfix technique—and return the page back to its normal flow.

Navigational List Example

We'll often develop, and find, navigation menus using unordered lists. These lists are commonly laid out as horizontal lists, using either of the two techniques previously mentioned. Here is an example of a horizontal navigation menu marked up using an unordered list with <li> elements displayed as inline-block elements (see Figure 8.13).

Figure 8.13 A navigation menu marked up using an unordered list

HTML

```
1.  <nav class="navigation">
2.    <ul>
3.      <li><a href="#">Profile</a></li><!--
4.      --><li><a href="#">Settings</a></li><!--
5.      --><li><a href="#">Notifications</a></li><!--
6.      --><li><a href="#">Logout</a></li>
7.    </ul>
8.  </nav>
```

CSS

```
1.  .navigation ul {
2.    font: bold 11px "Helvetica Neue", Helvetica, Arial, sans-serif;
3.    margin: 0;
4.    padding: 0;
5.    text-transform: uppercase;
6.  }
7.  .navigation li {
8.    display: inline-block;
9.  }
10. .navigation a {
```

```
11.    background: #395870;
12.    background: linear-gradient(#49708f, #293f50);
13.    border-right: 1px solid rgba(0, 0, 0, .3);
14.    color: #fff;
15.    padding: 12px 20px;
16.    text-decoration: none;
17. }
18. .navigation a:hover {
19.    background: #314b60;
20.    box-shadow: inset 0 0 10px 1px rgba(0, 0, 0, .3);
21. }
22. .navigation li:first-child a {
23.    border-radius: 4px 0 0 4px;
24. }
25. .navigation li:last-child a {
26.    border-right: 0;
27.    border-radius: 0 4px 4px 0;
28. }
```

In Practice

Now that we know how to build lists within HTML and CSS, let's loop back to our Styles Conference website and see where we might be able to use lists.

1. Currently the navigation menus within the `<header>` and `<footer>` elements on our pages consist of a handful of anchor elements. These anchor elements could be better organized in an unordered list.

    Using an unordered list (via the `<ul>` element) and list items (via the `<li>` element) will give structure to our navigation menus. These new elements, however, will display our navigation menus vertically.

    We're going to want to change the `display` value of our `<li>` elements to `inline-block` to get all of them to align in a horizontal row. When we do that, though, we'll also need to account for the blank space left between each `<li>` element. Thinking back to Lesson 5, "Positioning Content," we know that opening an HTML comment at the end of a `<li>` element and closing an HTML comment at the beginning of a `<li>` element will remove this space.

Keeping this in mind, the markup for the navigation menu within our `<header>` element will now look like this:

```
1.  <nav class="nav primary-nav">
2.    <ul>
3.      <li><a href="index.html">Home</a></li><!--
4.      --><li><a href="speakers.html">Speakers</a></li><!--
5.      --><li><a href="schedule.html">Schedule</a></li><!--
6.      --><li><a href="venue.html">Venue</a></li><!--
7.      --><li><a href="register.html">Register</a></li>
8.    </ul>
9.  </nav>
```

Along these same lines, the markup for the navigation menu within our `<footer>` element will now look like this:

```
1.  <nav class="nav">
2.    <ul>
3.      <li><a href="index.html">Home</a></li><!--
4.      --><li><a href="speakers.html">Speakers</a></li><!--
5.      --><li><a href="schedule.html">Schedule</a></li><!--
6.      --><li><a href="venue.html">Venue</a></li><!--
7.      --><li><a href="register.html">Register</a></li>
8.    </ul>
9.  </nav>
```

Let's not forget to make these changes in all of our HTML files.

2. With the unordered list in place, let's make sure the list items align horizontally, and let's clean up their styles a bit. We'll use the existing nav class to help target our new styles.

We'll begin by setting all of the `<li>` elements within any element with the class attribute value of nav to be displayed `inline-block`, to include some horizontal margins, and to be vertically aligned to the top of the element.

Additionally, we'll use the `:last-child` pseudo-class selector to identify the last `<li>` element and reset its right margin to 0. Doing so ensures that any horizontal space between the `<li>` element and the edge of its parent element is removed.

Within our `main.css` file, below our existing navigation styles, let's add the following CSS:

```
1.  .nav li {
2.    display: inline-block;
3.    margin: 0 10px;
4.    vertical-align: top;
5.  }
6.  .nav li:last-child {
7.    margin-right: 0;
8.  }
```

You may be wondering why our unordered list didn't include any list item markers or default styles. These styles were removed by the reset at the top of our style sheet. If we look at the reset, we'll see our `<ol>`, `<ul>`, and `<li>` elements all include a `margin` and `padding` of `0`, and our `<ol>` and `<ul>` elements have a `list-style` value of none.

3. Our navigation menus aren't the only places we'll be using lists. We'll also use them on some of our internal pages, including the Speakers page. Let's add some speakers to our conference.

Within our `speakers.html` file just below our lead section, let's create a new section where we'll present all of our speakers. Reusing some existing styles, we'll use a `<section>` element with a `class` attribute value of `row` to wrap all of our speakers and apply a white background and padding behind them. Inside the `<section>` element, we'll add a `<div>` element with a `class` attribute value of `grid` to center our speakers on the page and allow us to use multiple columns in doing so.

So far our HTML below the lead section looks like this:

```
1.  <section class="row">
2.    <div class="grid">
3.
4.    </div>
5.  </section>
```

4. Inside the grid every speaker will be marked up with his or her own `<section>` element, which will include two columns. The first column will span two-thirds of the `<section>` element and will be marked up using a `<div>` element. The second column will span the remaining one-third of the `<section>` element and will be marked up using an `<aside>` element, as its content is secondary to the speaker and his or her specific talk.

Using our existing col-2-3 and col-1-3 classes, the outline for a speaker section will look like this:

```
1.   <section id="shay-howe">
2.
3.     <div class="col-2-3">
4.       ...
5.     </div><!--
6.
7.     --><aside class="col-1-3">
8.       ...
9.     </aside>
10.
11.  </section>
```

There are a few items to notice here. First, each <section> element for each speaker includes an ID attribute with the speaker's name as the attribute value. Later, when we create the schedule for our conference, these ID attributes will serve as anchors, allowing us to link from the schedule to a speaker's profile.

Additionally, the closing tag of the <div> element is followed by the opening of an HTML comment, and the opening tag of the <aside> element is preceded by the closing of an HTML comment. Because the column-based classes will display these elements as inline-block elements, we are removing the blank space that will appear between them.

5. Inside the two-thirds column, marked up with the <div> element, we'll use a few headings and paragraphs to show the speaker's name, the title and abstract of the talk, and a short biography.

Including this content, a speaker section will look like this:

```
1.   <section id="shay-howe">
2.
3.     <div class="col-2-3">
4.
5.       <h2>Shay Howe</h2>
6.       <h5>Less Is More: How Constraints Cultivate Growth</h5>
7.
8.       <p>By setting constraints, we force ourselves...</p>
9.
10.      <h5>About Shay</h5>
11.
```

```
12.      <p>As a designer and front-end developer, Shay...</p>
13.
14.    </div><!--
15.
16.    --><aside class="col-1-3">
17.      ...
18.    </aside>
19.
20.  </section>
```

6. Within the one-third column, marked up with an <aside> element, we're going to add a <div> element with a class attribute value of speaker-info. We'll use a <div> element because we'll be adding styles to this element soon.

Before getting into any styles, though, let's add an unordered list within the <div> element that includes as list items some relevant links for the speaker.

Now our HTML for a speaker will look like this:

```
1.  <section id="shay-howe">
2.
3.    <div class="col-2-3">
4.
5.      <h2>Shay Howe</h2>
6.      <h5>Less Is More: How Constraints Cultivate Growth</h5>
7.
8.      <p>By setting constraints, we force ourselves...</p>
9.
10.     <h5>About Shay</h5>
11.
12.     <p>As a designer and front-end developer, Shay...</p>
13.
14.   </div><!--
15.
16.   --><aside class="col-1-3">
17.     <div class="speaker-info">
18.
19.       <ul>
20.         <li><a href=
              "https://twitter.com/shayhowe">@shayhowe</a></li>
```

continues

```
21.          <li><a href=
                "http://learn.shayhowe.com/">learn.shayhowe.com</a></li>
22.        </ul>
23.
24.      </div>
25.    </aside>
26.
27. </section>
```

7. With the <div> element with a class attribute value of speaker-info ready, we can add some styles to it.

We'll begin by adding a new section within our main.css file for the Speaker page styles. From there, let's add a 1-pixel solid gray border with a 5-pixel radius around any element that includes the class attribute value of speaker-info.

Next, let's add a top margin of 88 pixels to position the element on the same vertical line as the first paragraph of the talk description, and let's also add 22 pixels of vertical padding inside the element to provide room for the nested unordered list.

Lastly, let's center all of the text within the element.

In all, our CSS for the speaker-info class rule set looks like this:

```
1.  /*
2.    =======================================
3.    Speakers
4.    =======================================
5.  */
6.
7.  .speaker-info {
8.    border: 1px solid #dfe2e5;
9.    border-radius: 5px;
10.   margin-top: 88px;
11.   padding: 22px 0;
12.   text-align: center;
13. }
```

Let's take a minute to review why we're using a <div> element here and the corresponding styles.

We're placing a <div> element inside the <aside> element with the class attribute value of col-1-3 because we'll want the padding inherited from the col-1-3 class to be outside of the `border` on the `<div>` element. Before long we'll be including an image within the `<div>` element, alongside the unordered list; therefore we created a `<div>` element as opposed to applying these styles directly to the `<ul>` element.

8. As we add more and more speakers to the page, we'll want to ensure that they remain an equal distance apart vertically. To do so, we'll create a `speaker` class rule set which includes a bottom `margin` of 44 pixels, like this:

```
1.  .speaker {
2.    margin-bottom: 44px;
3.  }
```

We can then apply this class to the `<section>` element for each speaker, provided it isn't the last speaker. We'll omit this class on the last speaker, as we don't want to create any unnecessary margins before our `<footer>` element. With more than one speaker, our layout will look like this:

```
1.  <section class="row">
2.    <div class="grid">
3.
4.      <section class="speaker" id="chris-mills">
5.
6.        <div class="col-2-3">
7.          ...
8.        </div><!--
9.
10.       --><aside class="col-1-3">
11.         ...
12.       </aside>
13.
14.     </section>
15.
16.     <section id="shay-howe">
17.
18.       <div class="col-2-3">
19.         ...
20.       </div><!--
21.
22.       --><aside class="col-1-3">
23.         ...
```

continues

```
24.        </aside>
25.
26.      </section>
27.
28.    </div>
29.  </section>
```

Notice how the first speaker `<section>` element, for Chris Mills, includes the class attribute value of `speaker`, which vertically separates it from the speaker `<section>` element for myself, Shay Howe. The last speaker `<section>` element, again for myself, doesn't include a class attribute value of `speaker` in order to keep it a proper distance from the `<footer>` element.

Our navigation menus are now complete, and the Speakers page is taking shape (see **Figure 8.14**).

The source code for the exercises within this lesson can be found at http://learn.shayhowe.com/html-css/creating-lists.

Summary

Lists are used quite commonly in HTML, often in places that might not be obvious or apparent. The key is to use them as semantically as possible and to leverage them where they best fit.

Let's recap. Within this lesson we covered the following:

- How to create unordered, ordered, and description lists
- How to properly nest lists inside of other lists
- How to change the list item marker style and position
- How to use a background image instead of a list item marker
- How to horizontally display or float lists

Now that we know how to add lists to our pages, let's add media to our pages, too. In the next chapter we'll dive into embeddable media such as images, audio, and video.

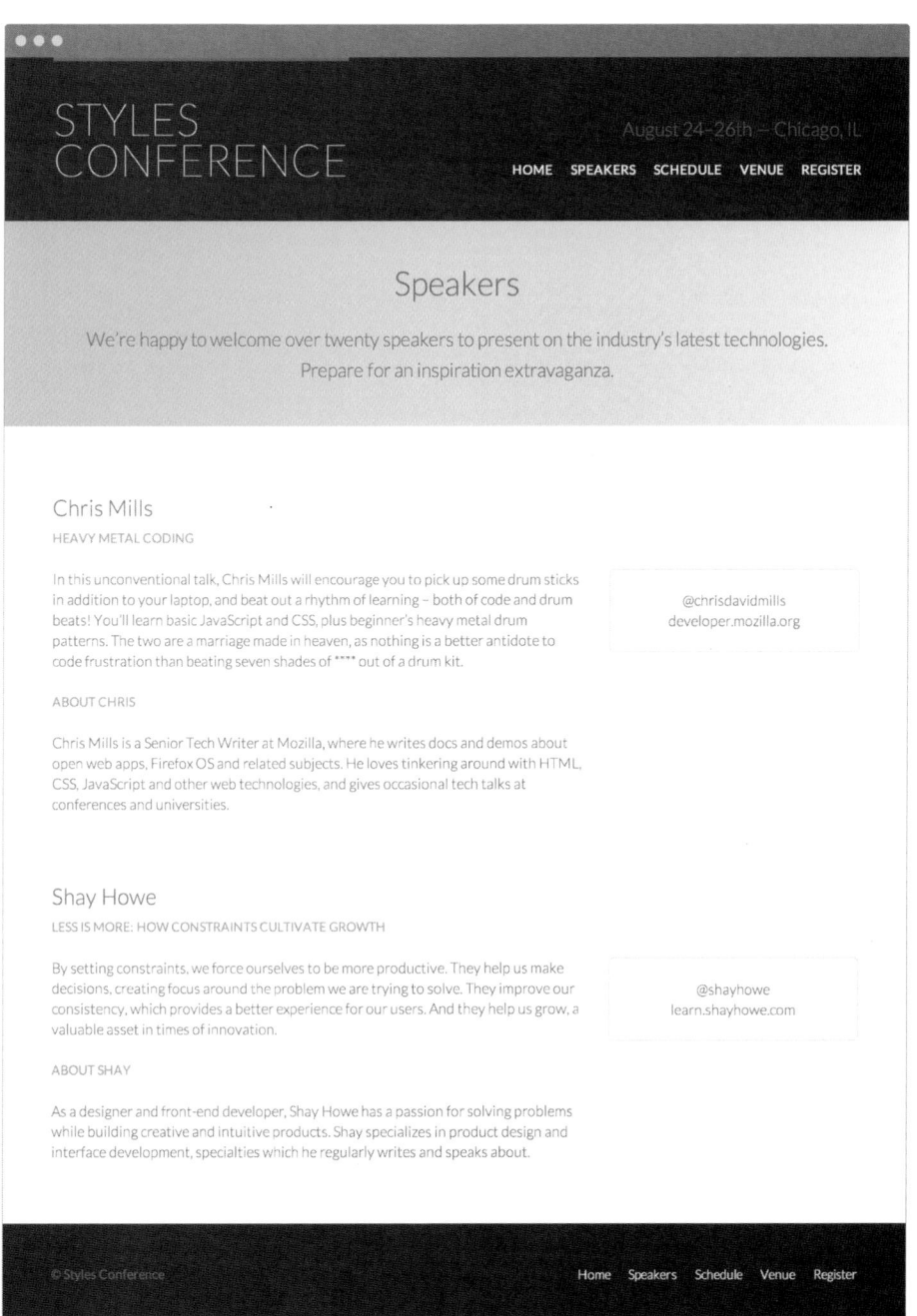

Figure 8.14 Our Speakers page after updating our navigation menus and adding speakers

Lesson 9

Adding Media

We browse the Internet in search of interesting and informative content, which we usually find in the form of plain text. To accompany this plain text, HTML provides ways to embed rich media in the form of images, audio tracks, and videos, as well as to embed content from another web page in the form of an inline frame.

The ability to include images, audio tracks, videos, and inline frames within websites has been around for some time. Browser support for images and inline frames has generally been pretty good. And while the ability to add audio tracks and videos to a website has been around for years, the process has been fairly cumbersome. Fortunately, this process has improved and is much easier with support directly from HTML.

Today, we can freely use images, audio, video, and inline frames knowing that this content is supported across all major browsers.

Adding Images

To add images to a page, we use the `<img>` inline element. The `<img>` element is a self-containing, or empty, element, which means that it doesn't wrap any other content and it exists as a single tag. For the `<img>` element to work, a `src` attribute and value must be included to specify the source of the image (see **Figure 9.1**). The `src` attribute value is a URL, typically relative to the server where a website is hosted.

In conjunction with the `src` attribute, the `alt` (alternative text) attribute, which describes the contents of an image, should be applied. The `alt` attribute value is picked up by search engines and assistive technologies to help convey the purpose of an image. The `alt` text will be displayed in place of the image if for some reason the image is not available (see **Figure 9.2**).

```
1.   <img src="dog.jpg" alt="A black, brown, and white dog wearing a kerchief">
```

Figure 9.1 An image embedded within HTML

A black, brown, and white dog wearing a kerchief

Figure 9.2 The alternate text, "A black, brown, and white dog wearing a kerchief," shown in place of a missing image

Supported Image Formats

Images come in a variety of different file formats, and each browser may support (or not support) different formats. By and large, the most commonly supported formats online are `gif`, `jpg`, and `png` images. Of these, the most widely used formats today are `jpg` and `png`. The `jpg` format provides quality images with high color counts while maintaining a decent file size, ideal for faster load times. The `png` format is great for images with transparencies or low color counts. We most commonly see `jpg` images used for photographs and `png` images used for icons or background patterns.

Sizing Images

It is important to identify the size of an image in order to tell the browser how large the image should be before the page even loads; thus the browser can reserve space for the image and render the page faster. There are a few different ways to size images so that they work well on a page. One option is to use the `width` and `height` attributes directly within the `<img>` tag in HTML.

Additionally, images may be sized using the `width` and `height` properties in CSS. When both the HTML attributes and CSS properties are used, the CSS attributes will take precedence over the HTML attributes.

Specifying either a width or height will cause the other dimension to adjust automatically to maintain the aspect ratio of the image. As an example, if we want an image to be 200 pixels tall but are less specifically concerned about how wide it is, we can set the `height` to `200` pixels, and the width of the image will adjust accordingly. Setting both a `width` and `height` will work also; however, doing so may break the aspect ratio of an image, causing it to appear distorted (see **Figure 9.3**).

Figure 9.3 An image with defined width and height that cause it to be distorted

```
1.    img {
2.      height: 200px;
3.      width: 200px;
4.    }
```

While using the `width` and `height` attributes directly in HTML provides some semantic value by noting an image's original size, it can be difficult to manage numerous images that all need to be the same size. In this event, it's common practice to use CSS to resize the images.

Positioning Images

We can use a number of different approaches to position images on a web page. By default images are positioned as inline-level elements; however, their positions may be changed using CSS, specifically the `float`, `display`, and box model properties, including `padding`, `border`, and `margin`.

Inline Positioning Images

The `<img>` element is by default an inline-level element. Adding an image without any styles to a page will position that image within the same line as the content that surrounds it (see **Figure 9.4**). Additionally, the height of the line in which an image appears will be changed to match the height of the image, which can create large vertical gaps within that line.

1.  ```
    <p>Gatsby is a black, brown, and white hound mix puppy who loves
    howling at fire trucks and collecting belly rubs. <img src=
    "dog.jpg" alt="A black, brown, and white dog wearing a kerchief">
    Although he spends most of his time sleeping he is also quick to
    chase any birds who enter his vision.</p>
    ```

Gatsby is a black, brown, and white hound mix puppy who loves howling at fire trucks and collecting

belly rubs. Although he spends most of his time sleeping he is also quick to chase any birds who enter his vision.

Figure 9.4 An image displayed inline within a paragraph

Leaving images untouched in their default positioning isn't too common. More often than not, images are displayed as block-level elements or are floated flush to one side.
    ```

Block Positioning Images

Adding the `display` property to an image and setting its value to `block` forces the image to be a block-level element (see **Figure 9.5**). This makes the image appear on its own line, allowing the surrounding content to be positioned above and below the image.

```
1.    img {
2.      display: block;
3.    }
```

Gatsby is a black, brown, and white hound mix puppy who loves howling at fire trucks and collecting belly rubs.

Although he spends most of his time sleeping he is also quick to chase any birds who enter his vision.

Figure 9.5 An image displayed as a block within a paragraph

Positioning Images Flush Left or Right

Sometimes displaying an image as `inline` or `block`, or perhaps even `inline-block`, isn't ideal. We may want the image to appear on the left or right side of its containing element, while all of the other content wraps around the image as necessary. To do this, we use the `float` property with a value of either `left` or `right`.

Remembering back to Lesson 5, "Positioning Content," we recall that the `float` property was originally intended to position images to the left or right of a containing element. Now we'll use it for that original purpose.

Floating an image is a start; however, all other content will align directly against it. To provide spacing around an image, we'll use the `margin` property (see **Figure 9.6**). Additionally, we can use the `padding`, `border`, and `background` properties to build a frame for the image, if desired.

```
1.    img {
2.      background: #e8eae9;
3.      border: 1px solid #c6c9cc;
4.      float: right;
```

```
5.    margin: 8px 0 0 20px;
6.    padding: 4px;
7.  }
```

> Gatsby is a black, brown, and white hound mix puppy who loves howling at fire trucks and collecting belly rubs. Although he spends most of his time sleeping he is also quick to chase any birds who enter his vision.
>
>

Figure 9.6 An image styled to appear within a frame and floated to the right of its containing element

When to Use an Image Element vs. a Background Image

There are two primary ways to add images to a web page. One way, as covered here, is to use the `<img>` element within HTML. Another way is to use the `background` or `background-image` property within CSS to assign a background image to an element. Either option will do the job; however, they each have specific use cases.

The `<img>` element within HTML is the preferred option when the image being used holds semantic value and its content is relevant to the content of the page.

The `background` or `background-image` property within CSS is the preferred option when the image being used is part of the design or user interface of the page. As such, it's not directly relevant to the content of the page.

The `<img>` element is quite popular, and when it was originally added to the HTML specification it forever changed the way websites were built.

In Practice

Now that we know how to add and position images on a page, let's take a look at our Styles Conference website and see where we can add a few images.

1. Let's begin by adding some images to our home page. Specifically, we'll add an image within each of the teaser sections promoting a few of our pages.

Before we jump into the code, though, let's create a new folder named "images" within our "assets" folder. Then, within the "images" folder, let's create another folder named "home" specifically for our home page images. Within the "home" folder we'll add three images: `speakers.jpg`, `schedule.jpg`, and `venue.jpg`. (For reference, these images may be found on http://learn.shayhowe.com/html-css/adding-media.)

Then, inside our `index.html` file, each teaser section has an `<a>` element wrapping both an `<h3>` and an `<h5>` element. Let's move the `<h5>` element above the `<a>` element and replace it with an `<img>` element. The `src` attribute value for each `<img>` element will correspond to the folder structure and filename we set up, and the `alt` attribute value will describe the contents of each image.

The HTML for our first teaser, for the Speakers page, will look like this:

```
1.  <section class="teaser col-1-3">
2.    <h5>Speakers</h5>
3.    <a href="speakers.html">
4.      <img src="assets/images/home/speakers.jpg" alt="Professional
          Speaker">
5.      <h3>World-Class Speakers</h3>
6.    </a>
7.    <p>Joining us from all around the world are over twenty fantastic
          speakers, here to share their stories.</p>
8.  </section>
```

Let's continue this pattern for both the Schedule and Venue page teasers, too.

2. Now that we've added a few images to our home page, we'll need to clean up their styles a bit and make sure they properly fit into the layout of our page.

Since images are inline-level elements by default, let's change our images within the teaser sections to block-level elements. Let's also set their maximum `width` to `100%` to ensure they don't exceed the width of their respective columns. Changing this `width` value is important as it allows our images to adjust with the width of the columns as necessary.

Lastly, let's round the corners of the images slightly and apply 22 pixels of bottom `margin` to the images, providing a little breathing room.

Once we add these new styles to our existing home page styles (using the `teaser` class as a qualifying selector for the `<img>` elements), our CSS will look like this:

```
1.  .teaser img {
2.    border-radius: 5px;
```

```
3.    display: block;
4.    margin-bottom: 22px;
5.    max-width: 100%
6.  }
```

3. Next up, let's add images of all of the speakers to the Speakers page. We'll begin by creating a "speakers" folder within our "images" folder and placing images of all of the speakers there.

   Within the `speakers.html` file, let's add an `<img>` element within each of the speaker information `<aside>` elements. Let's place each `<img>` element inside the `<div>` element with the `class` attribute value of `speaker-info`, just above the `<ul>` element.

   The `src` attribute value of each image will correspond to the "speakers" folder we set up and the speaker's name; the `alt` attribute value will be the speaker's name.

   The `<aside>` element for myself, as a speaker, will look like this:

```
1.   <aside class="col-1-3">
2.     <div class="speaker-info">
3.
4.       <img src="assets/images/speakers/shay-howe.jpg"
           alt="Shay Howe">
5.
6.       <ul>
7.         <li><a href="https://twitter.com/shayhowe">@shayhowe</a></li>
8.         <li><a href="http://learn.shayhowe.com/">
             learn.shayhowe.com</a></li>
9.       </ul>
10.
11.    </div>
12.  </aside>
```

   This same pattern for adding an image should then be applied to all other speakers.

4. As we did with the images on our home page, we'll want to apply some styles to the images on the Speakers page.

   Let's begin by applying the `border-radius` property with a value of 50%, turning our images into circles. From there, let's set a fixed `height` of 130 pixels to each image and set them to be vertically aligned to the `top` of the line they reside within.

   With the `height` and vertical alignment in place, let's apply vertical margins to the images. Using a negative 66-pixel `margin` on the top of the images, we'll pull them slightly out of the `<aside>` element and make them vertically centered with the top `border` of the `<div>` element with a `class` attribute value of `speaker-info`. Then, applying a 22-pixel `margin` on the bottom of the image provides space between the image and the `<ul>` element below it.

When we add these new styles to our existing Speakers page styles (using the `speaker-info` class as a qualifying selector for the `<img>` elements), our CSS will look like this:

```
1.   .speaker-info img {
2.     border-radius: 50%;
3.     height: 130px;
4.     margin: -66px 0 22px 0;
5.     vertical-align: top;
6.   }
```

5. Since we are using an aggressive negative `margin` on the `<img>` element within the `<div>` element with a `class` attribute value of `speaker-info`, we need to remove the `padding` on the top of that `<div>` element.

Previously we were using the `padding` property with a value of `22px 0`, thus placing 22 pixels of `padding` on the top and bottom and `0` pixels of `padding` on the left and right of the `<div>` element. Let's swap this property and value out for the `padding-bottom` property, as that's the only `padding` we need to identify, and use a value of 22 pixels.

The new `speaker-info` class rule set looks like this:

```
1.   .speaker-info {
2.     border: 1px solid #dfe2e5;
3.     border-radius: 5px;
4.     margin-top: 88px;
5.     padding-bottom: 22px;
6.     text-align: center;
7.   }
```

Now both our home and Speaker pages are looking pretty sharp, as shown in **Figures 9.7** and **9.8**, respectively.

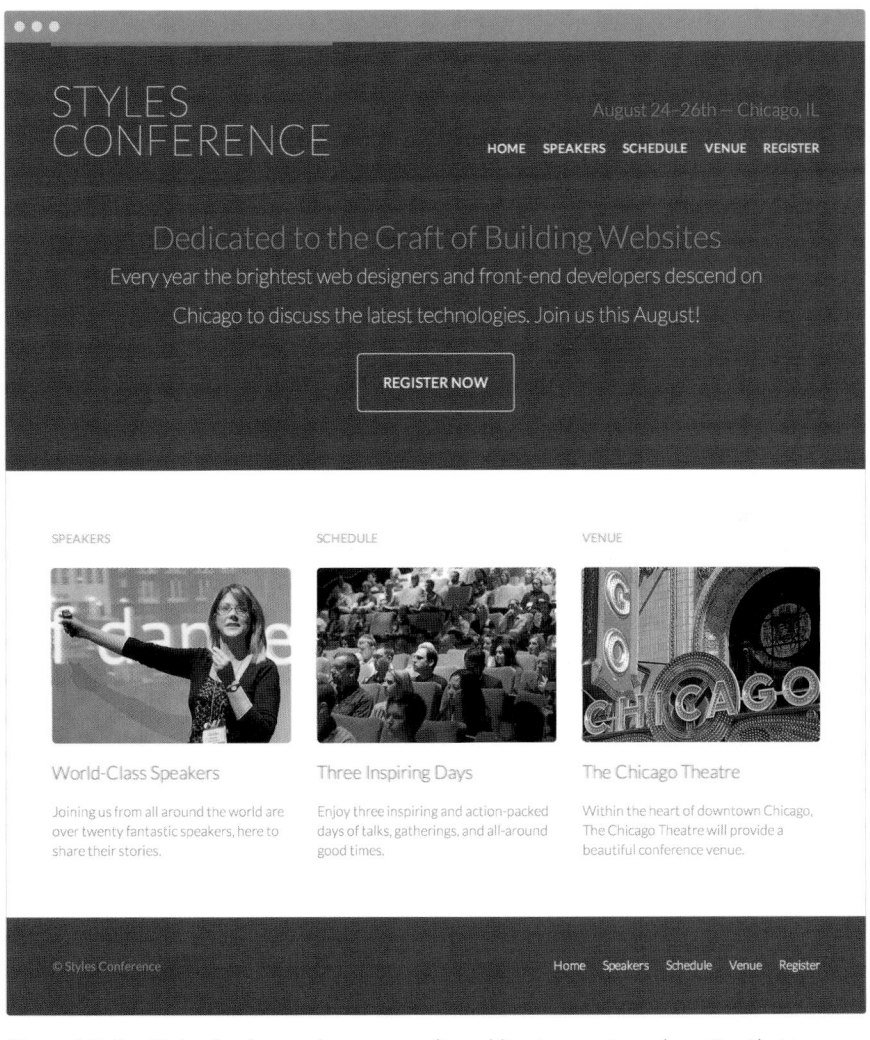

Figure 9.7 Our Styles Conference home page after adding images to each section that teases another page

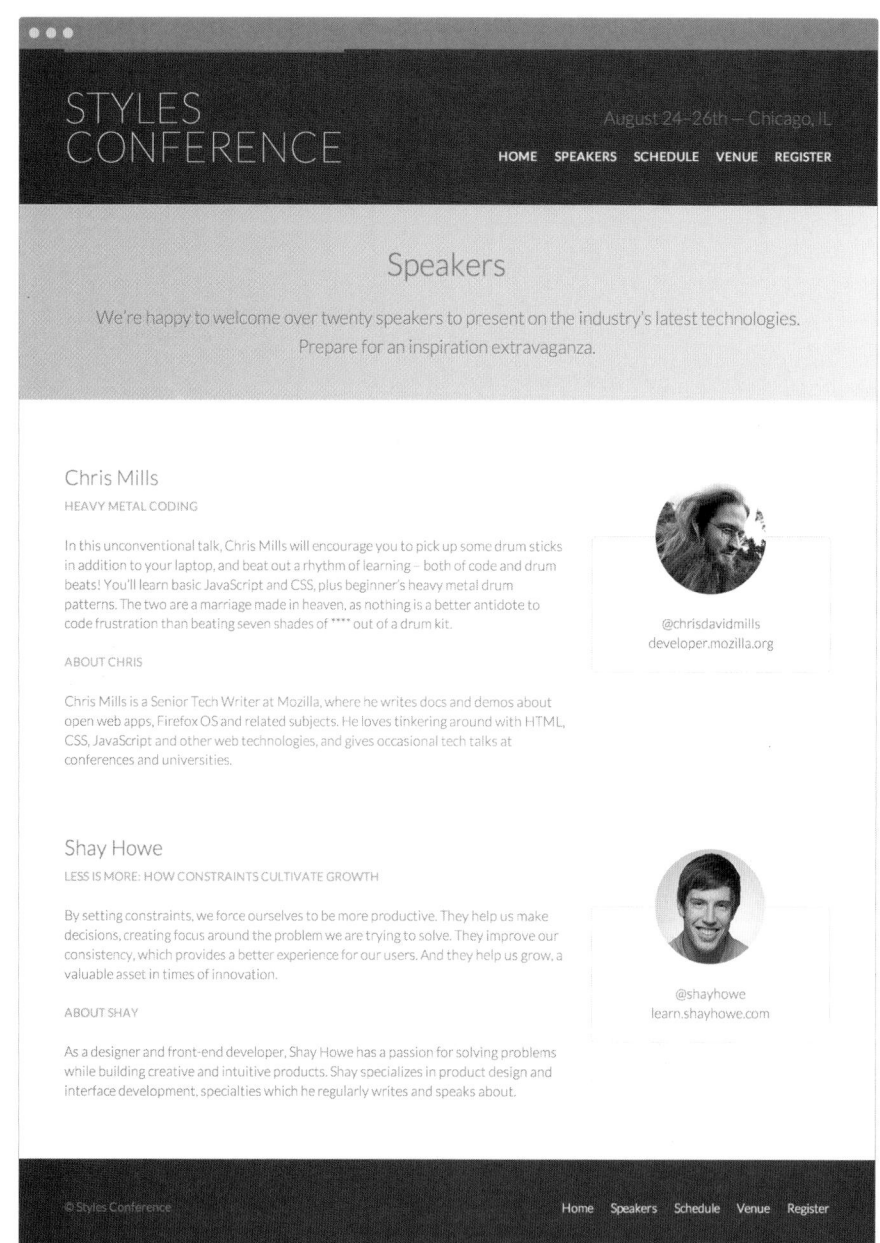

Figure 9.8 Our Styles Conference Speakers page after adding images for each of the speakers

Adding Audio

HTML5 provides a quick and easy way to add audio files to a website by way of the `<audio>` element. As with the `<img>` element, the `<audio>` element accepts a source URL specified by the `src` attribute. Unlike the `<img>` element, though, the `<audio>` element requires both opening and closing tags, which we'll discuss soon.

```
1.   <audio src="jazz.ogg"></audio>
```

Audio Attributes

Several other attributes may accompany the `src` attribute on the `<audio>` element; the most popular include `autoplay`, `controls`, `loop`, and `preload`.

The `autoplay`, `controls`, and `loop` attributes are all Boolean attributes. As Boolean attributes, they don't require a stated value. Instead, when each is present on the `<audio>` element its value will be set to `true`, and the `<audio>` element will behave accordingly.

By default, the `<audio>` element isn't displayed on a page. If the `autoplay` Boolean attribute is present on the `<audio>` element, nothing will appear on the page, but the audio file will automatically play upon loading.

```
1.   <audio src="jazz.ogg" autoplay></audio>
```

To display the `<audio>` element on a page, the `controls` Boolean attribute is necessary. When it's applied to the `<audio>` element, the `controls` Boolean attribute will display a browser's default audio controls, including play and pause, seek, and volume controls (see **Figure 9.9**).

```
1.   <audio src="jazz.ogg" controls></audio>
```

Figure 9.9 An audio clip with the default Google Chrome browser controls

When present on the `<audio>` element, the `loop` Boolean attribute will cause an audio file to repeat continually, from beginning to end.

Lastly, the `preload` attribute for the `<audio>` element helps identify what, if any, information about the audio file should be loaded before the clip is played. It accepts three values: `none`, `auto`, and `metadata`. The `none` value won't preload any information about an audio file, while the `auto` value will preload all information about an audio file. The `metadata` value sits in between the `none` and `auto` values, as it will preload any available metadata information about an audio file, such as the clip's length, but not all information.

When the `preload` attribute isn't present on the `<audio>` element, all information about an audio file is loaded, as if the value was set to `auto`. For this reason, using the `preload` attribute with a value of `metadata` or `none` is a good idea when an audio file is not essential to a page. It'll help to conserve bandwidth and allow pages to load faster.

Audio Fallbacks & Multiple Sources

At the moment, different browsers support different audio file formats, the three most popular of which are `ogg`, `mp3`, and `wav`. For the best browser support we'll need to use a handful of audio fallbacks, which will be included inside an `<audio>` element's opening and closing tags.

To begin, we'll remove the `src` attribute from the `<audio>` element. Instead, we'll use the `<source>` element, with a `src` attribute, nested inside the `<audio>` element to define a new source.

Using a `<source>` element and `src` attribute for each file format, we can list one audio file format after the other. We'll use the `type` attribute to quickly help the browser identify which audio types are available. When a browser recognizes an audio file format it will load that file and ignore all the others.

Because it was introduced in HTML5, some browsers may not support the `<audio>` element. In this case, we can provide a link to download the audio file after any `<source>` elements within the `<audio>` element (see **Figure 9.10**).

```
1.  <audio controls>
2.    <source src="jazz.ogg" type="audio/ogg">
3.    <source src="jazz.mp3" type="audio/mpeg">
4.    <source src="jazz.wav" type="audio/wav">
5.    Please <a href="jazz.mp3" download>download</a> the audio file.
6.  </audio>
```

Please <u>download</u> the audio file.

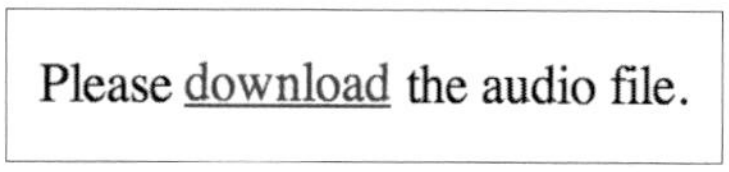

Figure 9.10 An anchor text audio fallback for when a browser doesn't support the `<audio>` element

To review the previous code, the <audio> element includes the `controls` Boolean attribute to ensure the audio player is displayed within browsers that support the element. The <audio> element does not include a `src` attribute and instead wraps three different <source> elements. Each <source> element includes a `src` attribute that references a different audio file format and a `type` attribute to identify the format of the audio file. As a last fallback, if a browser doesn't recognize any of the audio file formats, the anchor link to download the element will be displayed.

In addition to the <audio> element, HTML5 also introduced the <video> element, which shares quite a few similarities with the <audio> element.

Adding Video

Adding video in HTML5 is very similar to adding audio. We use the <video> element in place of the <audio> element. All of the same attributes (`src`, `autoplay`, `controls`, `loop`, and `preload`) and fallbacks apply here, too.

With the <audio> element, if the `controls` Boolean attribute isn't specified the audio clip isn't displayed. With videos, if the `controls` Boolean attribute is not specified the video will display. However, it is fairly difficult to view unless the `autoplay` Boolean attribute is also applied. In general, the best practice here is to include the `controls` Boolean attribute unless there is a good reason not to allow users to start, stop, or replay the video.

Figure 9.11 A video clip with the default Google Chrome browser controls

Since videos take up space on the page, it doesn't hurt to specify their dimensions, which is most commonly done with `width` and `height` properties in CSS. This helps ensure that the video isn't too large and stays within the implied layout of a page. Additionally, specifying a size, as with images, helps the browser render videos faster and allows it to allocate the proper space needed for the video to be displayed.

```
1.    <video src="earth.ogv" controls></video>
```

Customizing Audio & Video Controls

By default, the `<audio>` and `<video>` element controls are determined by each browser independently. Depending on the design of a website, more authority over the look and feel of the media player may be needed. If this is the case, a customized player can be built, but it will require a little JavaScript to work.

Poster Attribute

One additional attribute available for the `<video>` element is the `poster` attribute. The `poster` attribute allows us to specify an image, in the form of a URL, to be shown before a video is played. The example below uses a screen capture from the video as the poster for the Earth video.

```
1.    <video src="earth.ogv" controls poster="earth-video-screenshot.jpg"></video>
```

Figure 9.12 A video clip showing a poster image before it is played

Video Fallbacks

As with the `<audio>` element, video fallbacks are also necessary. The same markup format, with multiple `<source>` elements for each file type and a plain text fallback, also applies within the `<video>` element.

```
1.  <video controls>
2.    <source src="earth.ogv" type="video/ogg">
3.    <source src="earth.mp4" type="video/mp4">
4.    Please <a href="earth.mp4" download>download</a> the video.
5.  </video>
```

One additional fallback option that could be used in place of a plain text fallback is to use a YouTube or Vimeo embedded video. These video hosting websites allow us to upload our videos, provide a standard video player, and enable us to embed our videos onto a page using an inline frame.

HTML5 Audio & Video File Formats

Browser support for the `<audio>` and `<video>` elements varies, as do the file formats required with these elements. Each browser has its own preferred audio and video file formats.

There are a few tools that help to convert an audio or video file into different formats, and a quick search will provide an abundance of options.

Adding Inline Frames

Another way to add content to a page is to embed another HTML page within the current page. This is done using an inline frame, or `<iframe>` element. The `<iframe>` element accepts the URL of another HTML page within the `src` attribute value; this causes the content from the embedded HTML page to be displayed on the current page. The value of the `src` attribute may be a URL relative to the page the `<iframe>` element appears on or an absolute URL for an entirely external page.

Many pages use the `<iframe>` element to embed media onto a page from an external website such as Google Maps, YouTube, and others.

```
1.  <iframe src="https://www.google.com/maps/embed?..."></iframe>
```

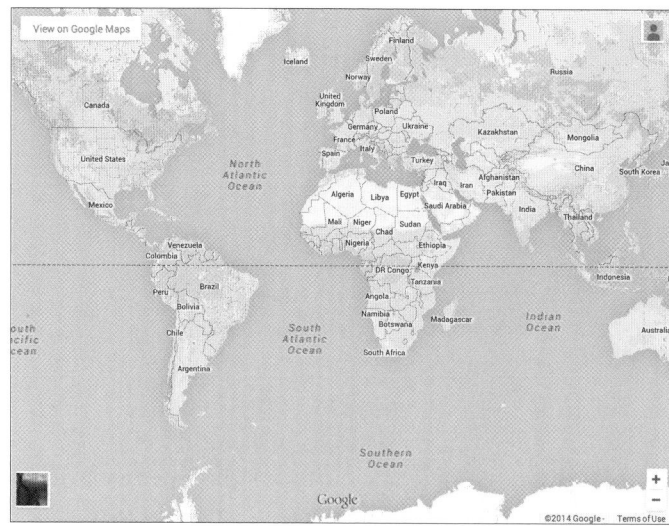

Figure 9.13 A page with an embedded HTML page that shows a map referenced from Google Maps

The `<iframe>` element has a few default styles, including an inset `border` and a `width` and `height`. These styles can be adjusted using the `frameborder`, `width`, and `height` HTML attributes or by using the `border`, `width`, and `height` CSS properties.

Seamless Inline Frames

Pages referenced within the `src` attribute of an `<iframe>` element play by their own rules, as they do not inherit any styles or behaviors from the page they are referenced on. Any styles applied to a page that includes an `<iframe>` element will not be inherited by the page referenced within the `<iframe>` element. Additionally, links within the page referenced within the `<iframe>` element will open inside that frame, leaving the page that contains the `<iframe>` element unchanged.

There will be times when we'll want to change these behaviors, and the `seamless` Boolean attribute will allow us to do just that. When present on the `<iframe>` element, the `seamless` Boolean attribute allows styles from the page that includes an `<iframe>` element to be inherited by the page referenced within the `<iframe>` element. Additionally, the `seamless` Boolean attribute allows links clicked on a page referenced within an `<iframe>` element to be opened within the same window as the original page that includes the `<iframe>` element.

```
1.    <iframe src="contact.html" seamless></iframe>
```

The `seamless` Boolean attribute is a new attribute introduced in HTML5. Although the browser support for this attribute is growing, it will not work within older browsers. It's advisable to test the `seamless` Boolean attribute before using it.

In Practice

Inline frames provide a great way to add dynamic content to a page. Let's give this a shot by updating our Venue page with some maps.

1. Before adding any maps or inline frames, let's first prepare our Venue page for a two-column grid. Below the leading section of the page we'll add a `<section>` element with the `class` attribute value of `row` to identify a new section of the page, and we'll include some general styles, such as a white `background` and some vertical `padding`.

    Directly inside this `<section>` element let's add a `<div>` element with the `class` attribute value of `grid`. The class of `grid` centers our content on the page and prepares for the one-third and two-thirds columns to follow.

    So far the main section of our `venue.html` file looks like this:

    ```
    1.   <section class="row">
    2.     <div class="grid">
    3.       ...
    4.     </div>
    5.   </section>
    ```

2. Within the `<div>` element with the `class` attribute value of `grid` we'll have two new sections, one for the conference venue and one for the conference hotel. Let's add two new `<section>` elements and give each of these `<section>` elements a unique class that corresponds to its content. We'll use these classes to add margins to the bottom of each section.

    Our HTML should now look like this:

    ```
    1.   <section class="row">
    2.     <div class="grid">
    3.
    4.       <section class="venue-theatre">
    5.         ...
    6.       </section>
    7.
    ```

continues

```
8.      <section class="venue-hotel">
9.         ...
10.     </section>
11.
12.    </div>
13. </section>
```

3. Now that we have a few classes to work with, let's create a new section within our main.css file for Venue page styles. We'll add a 66-pixel `margin` to the bottom of the `<section>` element with the `class` attribute value of `venue-theatre` to insert some space between it and the `<section>` element below it.

    Then, we'll add a 22-pixel `margin` to the bottom of the `<section>` element with the `class` attribute value of `venue-hotel` to provide some space between it and the `<footer>` element below it.

    The new venue section within the main.css file looks like the following:

```
1.  /*
2.      =========================================
3.      Venue
4.      =========================================
5.  */
6.
7.  .venue-theatre {
8.    margin-bottom: 66px;
9.  }
10. .venue-hotel {
11.   margin-bottom: 22px;
12. }
```

The `<section>` element with the `class` attribute value of `venue-hotel` has a smaller bottom `margin` than the `<section>` element with the `class` attribute value of `venue-theatre` because it sits next to the `padding` from the bottom of the `<section>` element with the `class` attribute of `row`. Adding that `margin` and `padding` together gives us the same value as the bottom `margin` on the `<section>` element with the `class` attribute value of `venue-theatre`.

4. Now it's time to create the two columns within each of the new `<section>` elements. We'll start by adding a `<div>` element with a `class` attribute value of `col-1-3` to establish a one-third column. After it we'll add an `<iframe>` element with a `class` attribute value of `col-2-3` to establish a two-thirds column.

    Keeping in mind that the column classes make both the `<div>` and `<iframe>` elements inline-block elements, we need to remove the empty space that will appear between them. To do so we'll open an HTML comment directly after the closing `<div>` tag, and we'll close the HTML comment immediately before the opening `<iframe>` tag.

    In all, our HTML for the columns looks like this:

```
1.  <section class="row">
2.    <div class="grid">
3.
4.      <section class="venue-theatre">
5.
6.        <div class="col-1-3"></div><!--
7.
8.        --><iframe class="col-2-3"></iframe>
9.
10.     </section>
11.
12.     <section class="venue-hotel">
13.
14.       <div class="col-1-3"></div><!--
15.
16.       --><iframe class="col-2-3"></iframe>
17.
18.     </section>
19.
20.   </div>
21. </section>
```

5. Within each of the `<div>` elements with a `class` attribute value of `col-1-3` let's add the venue's name within an `<h2>` element, followed by two `<p>` elements. In the first `<p>` element let's include the venue's address, and in the second `<p>` element let's include the venue's website (within an anchor link) and phone number.

Within each of the paragraphs, let's use the line-break element, `<br>`, to place breaks within the address and in between the website and phone number.

For the `<section>` element with the `class` attribute value of `venue-theatre`, the HTML looks like this:

```
1.   <section class="venue-theatre">
2.
3.     <div class="col-1-3">
4.       <h2>Chicago Theatre</h2>
5.       <p>175 N State St <br> Chicago, IL 60601</p>
6.       <p><a href="http://www.thechicagotheatre.com/">
           thechicagotheatre.com</a> <br> (312) 462-6300</p>
7.     </div><!--
8.
9.     --><iframe class="col-2-3"></iframe>
10.
11.  </section>
```

The same pattern shown here for the theatre should also be applied to the hotel (using, of course, the proper address, website, and phone number).

6. We can search for these addresses in Google Maps (google.com/maps/). Once we locate an address and create a customized map, we have the ability to embed that map into our page. Following the instructions on Google Maps for how to share and embed a map will provide us with the HTML for an `<iframe>` element.

   Let's copy the HTML—`<iframe>` element, `src` attribute, and all—onto our page where our existing `<iframe>` element resides. We'll do this for each location, using two different `<iframe>` elements.

   In copying over the `<iframe>` element from Google Maps we need to make sure we preserve the `class` attribute and value, `col-2-3`, from our existing `<iframe>` element. We also need to be careful not to harm the HTML comment that closes directly before our opening `<iframe>` tag.

   Looking directly at the `<section>` element with the `class` attribute value of `venue-theatre` again, the HTML looks like this:

```
1.   <section class="venue-theatre">
2.
3.     <div class="col-1-3">
4.       <h2>Chicago Theatre</h2>
```

```
5.      <p>175 N State St <br> Chicago, IL 60601</p>
6.      <p><a href="http://www.thechicagotheatre.com/">
        thechicagotheatre.com</a> <br> (312) 462-6300</p>
7.    </div><!--
8.
9.    --><iframe class="col-2-3" src="https://www.google.com/maps/
      embed?pb=!1m5!3m3!1m2!1s0x880e2ca55810a493%3A0x4700ddf60fcbfad6!
      2schicago+theatre!5e0!3m2!1sen!2sus!4v1388701393606"></iframe>
10.
11.  </section>
```

7. Lastly, we'll want to make sure that both `<iframe>` elements that reference Google Maps share the same height. To do this, we'll create a new class, `venue-map`, and apply it to each of the `<iframe>` elements alongside the existing `col-2-3` class attribute value.

The HTML for the `<section>` element with the `class` attribute value of `venue-theatre` now looks like this:

```
1.  <section class="venue-theatre">
2.
3.    <div class="col-1-3">
4.      <h2>Chicago Theatre</h2>
5.      <p>175 N State St <br> Chicago, IL 60601</p>
6.      <p><a href="http://www.thechicagotheatre.com/">
        thechicagotheatre.com</a> <br> (312) 462-6300</p>
7.    </div><!--
8.
9.    --><iframe class="venue-map col-2-3" src=
      "https://www.google.com/maps/embed?
      pb=!1m5!3m3!1m2!1s0x880e2ca55810a493%3A0x4700ddf60fcbfad6!
      2schicago+theatre!5e0!3m2!1sen!2sus!4v1388701393606"></iframe>
10.
11.  </section>
```

Once the `venue-map` class is applied to each `<iframe>` element, let's create the `venue-map` class rule set within our `main.css` file. It includes the `height` property with a value of 264 pixels.

The `venue-map` class rule set looks like this:

```
1.  .venue-map {
2.    height: 264px;
3.  }
```

We now have a Venue page (see **Figure 9.14**), complete with maps for the different locations of our conference.

Figure 9.14 Our Styles Conference Venue page, which now includes inline frames

The source code for the exercises within this lesson can be found at http://learn.shayhowe.com/html-css/adding-media.

Semantically Identifying Figures & Captions

With HTML5 also came the introduction of the `<figure>` and `<figcaption>` elements. These elements were created to semantically mark up self-contained content or media, commonly with a caption. Before HTML5 this was frequently done using an ordered list. While an ordered list worked, the markup was not semantically correct.

Figure

The `<figure>` block-level element is used to identify and wrap self-contained content, often in the form of media. It may surround images, audio clips, videos, blocks of code, diagrams, illustrations, or other self-contained media. More than one item of self-contained content, such as multiple images or videos, may be contained within the `<figure>` element at a time. If the `<figure>` element is moved from the main portion of a page to another location (for example, the bottom of the page), it should not disrupt the content or legibility of the page.

```
1.  <figure>
2.    <img src="dog.jpg" alt="A black, brown, and white dog wearing a
      kerchief">
3.  </figure>
```

Figure 9.15 A self-contained image placed within a `<figure>` element

Figure Caption

To add a caption or legend to the `<figure>` element, the `<figcaption>` element is used. The `<figcaption>` may appear at the top of, bottom of, or anywhere within the `<figure>` element; however, it may only appear once. When it's used, the `<figcaption>` element will serve as the caption for all content within the `<figure>` element.

Additionally, the `<figcaption>` element may replace an `<img>` element's `alt` attribute if the content of the `<figcaption>` element provides a useful description of the visual content of the image.

```
1.  <figure>
2.    <img src="dog.jpg">
3.    <figcaption>A beautiful black, brown, and white hound dog wearing
      a kerchief.</figcaption>
4.  </figure>
```

A beautiful black, brown, and white hound dog wearing a kerchief.

Figure 9.16 A self-contained image placed within a `<figure>` element, including a `<figcaption>` element

Not all forms of media need to be included within a `<figure>` element or include a `<figcaption>` element; only those that are self-contained and belong together as a group.

Summary

Alongside text, media is one of the largest parts of the web. Use of images, audio, and video has only grown over recent years, and it isn't likely to slow down. Now we know how to incorporate these forms of media into our designs and how we can use them to enrich the content on our websites.

Within this lesson we covered the following:

- The best ways to add images, audio clips, videos, and inline frames to a page

- Different ways to position images in different situations

- How to provide audio and video fallbacks for older browsers

- Common attributes available to audio clips and videos

- The `seamless` attribute, which allows us to make inline frames behave as if they are part of the page they are referenced from

- The semantic way to mark up self-contained content, including media

We're coming into the homestretch of learning HTML and CSS, with only a few more components left to introduce. Next on the list are forms.

Lesson 10

Building Forms

Forms are an essential part of the Internet, as they provide a way for websites to capture information from users and to process requests, and they offer controls for nearly every imaginable use of an application. Through controls or fields, forms can request a small amount of information—often a search query or a username and password—or a large amount of information— perhaps shipping and billing information or an entire job application.

We need to know how to build forms in order to acquire user input. In this lesson we'll discuss how to use HTML to mark up a form, which elements to use to capture different types of data, and how to style forms with CSS. We won't get too deep into how information from a form is processed and handled on the back end of a website. Form processing is a deeper topic, outside the realm of this book; for now we'll stick to the creation and styling of forms.

Initializing a Form

To add a form to a page, we'll use the `<form>` element. The `<form>` element identifies where on the page control elements will appear. Additionally, the `<form>` element will wrap all of the elements included within the form, much like a `<div>` element.

```
1.   <form action="/login" method="post">
2.     ...
3.   </form>
```

A handful of different attributes can be applied to the `<form>` element, the most common of which are `action` and `method`. The `action` attribute contains the URL to which information included within the form will be sent for processing by the server. The `method` attribute is the HTTP method browsers should use to submit the form data. Both of these `<form>` attributes pertain to submitting and processing data.

Text Fields & Textareas

When it comes to gathering text input from users, there are a few different elements available for obtaining data within forms. Specifically, text fields and textareas are used for collecting text- or string-based data. This data may include passages of text content, passwords, telephone numbers, and other information.

Text Fields

One of the primary elements used to obtain text from users is the `<input>` element. The `<input>` element uses the `type` attribute to define what type of information is to be captured within the control. The most popular `type` attribute value is `text`, which denotes a single line of text input.

Along with setting a `type` attribute, it is best practice to give an `<input>` element a `name` attribute as well. The `name` attribute value is used as the name of the control and is submitted along with the input data to the server (see **Figure 10.1**).

Figure 10.1 A self-contained text input created with the `<input>` element

```
1.   <input type="text" name="username">
```

The `<input>` element is self-contained, meaning it uses only one tag and it does not wrap any other content. The value of the element is provided by its attributes and their corresponding values.

Originally, the only two text-based `type` attribute values were `text` and `password` (for password inputs); however, HTML5 brought along a handful of new `type` attribute values. These values were added to provide clearer semantic meaning for inputs as well as to provide better controls for users. Should a browser not understand one of these HTML5 `type` attribute values, it will automatically fall back to the `text` attribute value. Below is a list of the new HTML5 input types.

- color
- date
- datetime
- email
- month
- number
- range
- search
- tel
- time
- url
- week

The following `<input>` elements show a few of these HTML5 `type` attribute values in use; **Figures 10.2** through **10.7** show how these unique values may look within iOS. Notice how the different values provide different controls, all of which make gathering input from users easier.

```
1.  <input type="date" name="birthday">
2.  <input type="time" name="game-time">
3.  <input type="email" name="email-address">
4.  <input type="url" name="website">
5.  <input type="number" name="cost">
6.  <input type="tel" name="phone-number">
```

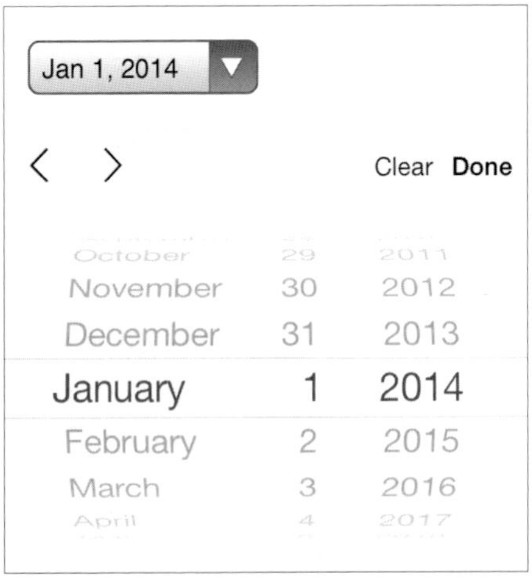

Figure 10.2 iOS7 controls for an `<input>` element with a `type` attribute value of `date`

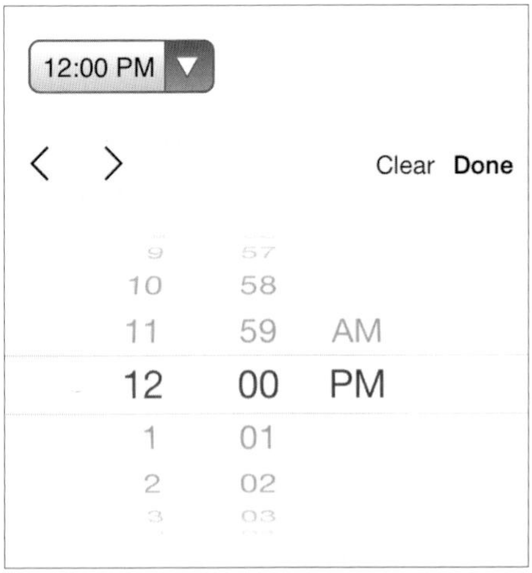

Figure 10.3 iOS7 controls for an `<input>` element with a `type` attribute value of `time`

Figure 10.4 iOS7 controls for an `<input>` element with a type attribute value of `email`

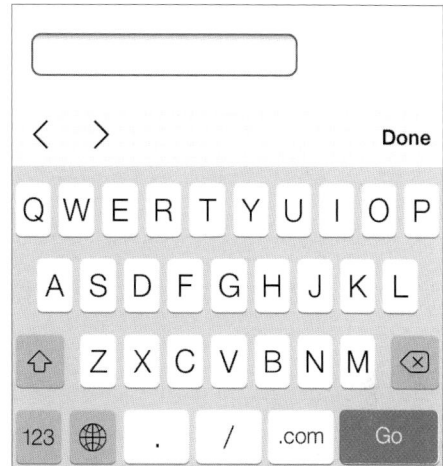

Figure 10.5 iOS7 controls for an `<input>` element with a type attribute value of `url`

Figure 10.6 iOS7 controls for an `<input>` element with a type attribute value of `number`

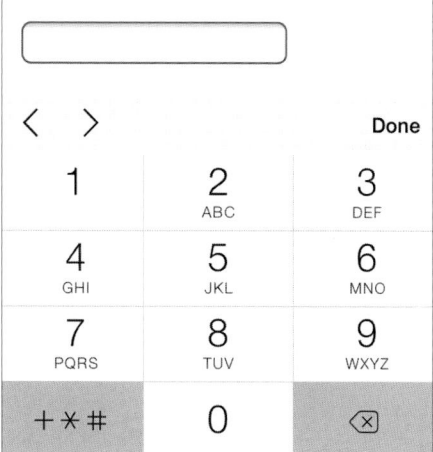

Figure 10.7 iOS7 controls for an `<input>` element with a type attribute value of `tel`

Textarea

Another element that's used to capture text-based data is the `<textarea>` element. The `<textarea>` element differs from the `<input>` element in that it can accept larger passages of text spanning multiple lines. The `<textarea>` element also has start and end tags that can wrap plain text. Because the `<textarea>` element only accepts one type of value, the `type` attribute doesn't apply here, but the `name` attribute is still used (see **Figure 10.8**).

Figure 10.8 An example of a `<textarea>` element

```
1.   <textarea name="comment">Add your comment here</textarea>
```

The `<textarea>` element has two sizing attributes: `cols` for width in terms of the average character width and `rows` for height in terms of the number of lines of visible text. The size of a textarea, however, is more commonly identified using the `width` and `height` properties within CSS.

Multiple Choice Inputs & Menus

Apart from text-based input controls, HTML also allows users to select data using multiple choice and drop-down lists. There are a few different options and elements for these form controls, each of which has distinctive benefits.

Radio Buttons

Radio buttons are an easy way to allow users to make a quick choice from a small list of options. Radio buttons permit users to select one option only, as opposed to multiple options.

To create a radio button, the `<input>` element is used with a `type` attribute value of `radio`. Each radio button element should have the same `name` attribute value so that all of the buttons within a group correspond to one another.

With text-based inputs, the value of an input is determined by what a user types in; with radio buttons a user is making a multiple choice selection. Thus, we have to define the input value. Using the `value` attribute, we can set a specific value for each `<input>` element.

Additionally, to preselect a radio button for users we can use the Boolean attribute `checked`.

```
1.   <input type="radio" name="day" value="Friday" checked> Friday
2.   <input type="radio" name="day" value="Saturday"> Saturday
3.   <input type="radio" name="day" value="Sunday"> Sunday
```

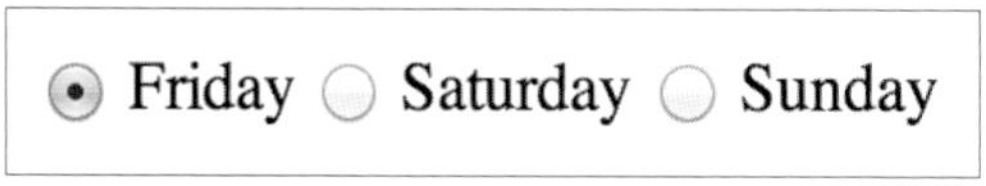

Figure 10.9 A group of radio buttons created by way of the `<input>` element with a `type` attribute value of `radio`

Check Boxes

Check boxes are very similar to radio buttons. They use the same attributes and patterns, with the exception of `checkbox` as their `type` attribute value. The difference between the two is that check boxes allow users to select multiple values and tie them all to one control name, while radio buttons limit users to one value.

```
1.   <input type="checkbox" name="day" value="Friday" checked> Friday
2.   <input type="checkbox" name="day" value="Saturday"> Saturday
3.   <input type="checkbox" name="day" value="Sunday"> Sunday
```

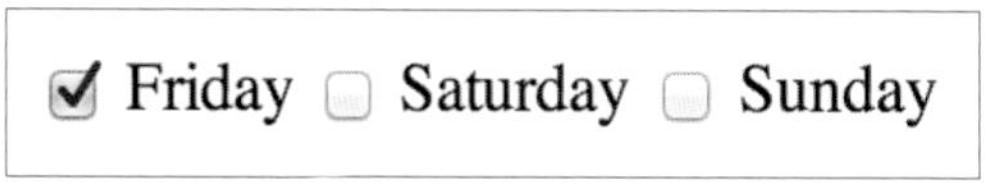

Figure 10.10 A group of check boxes created using the `<input>` element with a `type` attribute value of `checkbox`

Drop-Down Lists

Drop-down lists are a perfect way to provide users with a long list of options in a practical manner. A long column of radio buttons next to a list of different options is not only visually unappealing, it's daunting and difficult for users to comprehend, especially those on a mobile device. Drop-down lists, on the other hand, provide the perfect format for a long list of choices.

To create a drop-down list we'll use the `<select>` and `<option>` elements. The `<select>` element wraps all of the menu options, and each menu option is marked up using the `<option>` element.

The name attribute resides on the <select> element, and the value attribute resides on the <option> elements that are nested within the <select> element. The value attribute on each <option> element then corresponds to the name attribute on the <select> element.

Each <option> element wraps the text (which is visible to users) of an individual option within the list.

Much like the checked Boolean attribute for radio buttons and check boxes, drop-down menus can use the selected Boolean attribute to preselect an option for users.

```
1.   <select name="day">
2.     <option value="Friday" selected>Friday</option>
3.     <option value="Saturday">Saturday</option>
4.     <option value="Sunday">Sunday</option>
5.   </select>
```

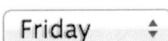

Figure 10.11 A drop-down menu created using the <input> and <option> elements

Multiple Selections

The Boolean attribute multiple, when added to the <select> element for a standard drop-down list, allows a user to choose more than one option from the list at a time. Additionally, using the selected Boolean attribute on more than one <option> element within the menu will preselect multiple options.

The size of the <select> element can be controlled using CSS and should be adjusted appropriately to allow for multiple selections. It may be worthwhile to inform users that to choose multiple options they will need to hold down the Shift key while clicking to make their selections.

```
1.   <select name="day" multiple>
2.     <option value="Friday" selected>Friday</option>
3.     <option value="Saturday">Saturday</option>
4.     <option value="Sunday">Sunday</option>
5.   </select>
```

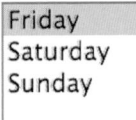

Figure 10.12 A drop-down list that allows users to select multiple options

Form Buttons

After a user inputs the requested information, buttons allow the user to put that information into action. Most commonly, a submit input or submit button is used to process the data.

Submit Input

Users click the submit button to process data after filling out a form. The submit button is created using the `<input>` element with a `type` attribute value of `submit`. The `value` attribute is used to specify the text that appears within the button (see **Figure 10.13**).

> Send

Figure 10.13 A submit button created by way of the `<input>` element with a `type` attribute value of `submit`

```
1.   <input type="submit" name="submit" value="Send">
```

Submit Button

As an `<input>` element, the submit button is self-contained and cannot wrap any other content. If more control over the structure and design of the input is desired—along with the ability to wrap other elements—the `<button>` element may be used.

The `<button>` element performs the same way as the `<input>` element with the `type` attribute value of `submit`; however, it includes opening and closing tags, which may wrap other elements. By default, the `<button>` element acts as if it has a `type` attribute value of `submit`, so the `type` attribute and value may be omitted from the `<button>` element if you wish.

Rather than using the `value` attribute to control the text within the submit button, the text that appears between the opening and closing tags of the `<button>` element will appear (see **Figure 10.14**).

> **Send Us a Message**

Figure 10.14 A submit button created using the `<button>` element

```
1.   <button name="submit">
2.     <strong>Send Us</strong> a Message
3.   </button>
```

Other Inputs

Besides the applications we've just discussed, the `<input>` element has a few other use cases. These include passing hidden data and attaching files during form processing.

Hidden Input

Hidden inputs provide a way to pass data to the server without displaying it to users. Hidden inputs are typically used for tracking codes, keys, or other information that is not pertinent to the user but is helpful when processing the form. This information is not displayed on the page; however, it can be found by viewing the source code of a page. It should therefore not be used for sensitive or secure information.

To create a hidden input, you use the `hidden` value for the `type` attribute. Additionally, include the appropriate `name` and `value` attribute values.

```
1.    <input type="hidden" name="tracking-code" value="abc-123">
```

File Input

To allow users to add a file to a form, much like attaching a file to an email, use the `file` value for the `type` attribute (see **Figure 10.15**).

```
1.    <input type="file" name="file">
```

Figure 10.15 An input to upload a file created by way of the `<input>` element with a `type` attribute value of `file`

Unfortunately, styling an `<input>` element that has a `type` attribute value of `file` is a tough task with CSS. Each browser has its own default input style, and none provide much control to override the default styling. JavaScript and other solutions can be employed to allow for file input, but they are slightly more difficult to construct.

Organizing Form Elements

Knowing how to capture data with inputs is half the battle. Organizing form elements and controls in a usable manner is the other half. When interacting with forms, users need to understand what is being asked of them and how to provide the requested information.

By using labels, fieldsets, and legends, we can better organize forms and guide users to properly complete them.

Label

Labels provide captions or headings for form controls, unambiguously tying them together and creating an accessible form for all users and assistive technologies. Created using the <label> element, labels should include text that describes the inputs or controls they pertain to.

Labels may include a for attribute. The value of the for attribute should be the same as the value of the id attribute on the form control the label corresponds to. Matching up the for and id attribute values ties the two elements together, allowing users to click on the <label> element to bring focus to the proper form control (see **Figure 10.16**).

```
1.  <label for="username">Username</label>
2.  <input type="text" name="username" id="username">
```

Figure 10.16 A label and form control that are bound together

If desired, the <label> element may wrap form controls, such as radio buttons or check boxes (see **Figure 10.17**). Doing so allows omission of the for and id attributes.

Figure 10.17 Form controls nested within a given label, allowing the omission of the for and id attributes

```
1.  <label>
2.    <input type="radio" name="day" value="Friday" checked> Friday
3.  </label>
4.  <label>
5.    <input type="radio" name="day" value="Saturday"> Saturday
6.  </label>
7.  <label>
8.    <input type="radio" name="day" value="Sunday"> Sunday
9.  </label>
```

Fieldset

Fieldsets group form controls and labels into organized sections. Much like a `<section>` or other structural element, the `<fieldset>` is a block-level element that wraps related elements, specifically within a `<form>` element, for better organization (see **Figure 10.18**). Fieldsets, by default, also include a border outline, which can be modified using CSS.

```
1.  <fieldset>
2.    <label>
3.      Username
4.      <input type="text" name="username">
5.    </label>
6.    <label>
7.      Password
8.      <input type="text" name="password">
9.    </label>
10. </fieldset>
```

Username _____   Password _____

Figure 10.18 Form controls and labels organized within a `<fieldset>` element

Legend

A legend provides a caption, or heading, for the `<fieldset>` element. The `<legend>` element wraps text describing the form controls that fall within the fieldset. The markup should include the `<legend>` element directly after the opening `<fieldset>` tag. On the page, the legend will appear within the top left part of the fieldset border (see **Figure 10.19**).

```
1.  <fieldset>
2.    <legend>Login</legend>
3.    <label>
4.      Username
5.      <input type="text" name="username">
6.    </label>
7.    <label>
8.      Password
9.      <input type="text" name="password">
```

```
10.    </label>
11.  </fieldset>
```

Login

Username [   ]   Password [   ]

Figure 10.19 Form controls and labels organized within a
`<fieldset>` element that includes a `<legend>` element

Form & Input Attributes

To accommodate all of the different form, input, and control elements, there are a number of attributes and corresponding values. These attributes and values serve a handful of different functions, such as disabling controls and adding form validation. Described next are some of the more frequently used and helpful attributes.

Disabled

The `disabled` Boolean attribute turns off an element or control so that it is not available for interaction or input. Elements that are disabled will not send any value to the server for form processing.

Applying the `disabled` Boolean attribute to a `<fieldset>` element will disable all of the form controls within the fieldset. If the `type` attribute has a `hidden` value, the `hidden` Boolean attribute is ignored.

Figure 10.20 A disabled input form control

```
1.  <label>
2.    Username
3.    <input type="text" name="username" disabled>
4.  </label>
```

Placeholder

The `placeholder` HTML5 attribute provides a hint or tip within the form control of an `<input>` or `<textarea>` element that disappears once the control is clicked in or gains focus (see **Figure 10.21**). This is used to give users further information on how the form input should be filled in, for example, the email address format to use.

Figure 10.21 An email input form control with a `placeholder` attribute

```
1.   <label>
2.     Email Address
3.     <input type="email" name="email-address"
       placeholder="name@domain.com">
4.   </label>
```

The main difference between the `placeholder` and `value` attributes is that the `value` attribute value text stays in place when a control has focus unless a user manually deletes it. This is great for pre-populating data, such as personal information, for a user but not for providing suggestions.

Required

The `required` HTML5 Boolean attribute enforces that an element or form control must contain a value upon being submitted to the server. Should an element or form control not have a value, an error message will be displayed requesting that the user complete the required field. Currently, error message styles are controlled by the browser and cannot be styled with CSS. Invalid elements and form controls, on the other hand, can be styled using the `:optional` and `:required` CSS pseudo-classes.

Validation also occurs specific to a control's type. For example, an `<input>` element with a `type` attribute value of `email` will require not only that a value exist within the control, but also that it is a valid email address (see **Figure 10.22**).

```
1.   <label>
2.     Email Address
3.     <input type="email" name="email-address" required>
4.   </label>
```

Figure 10.22
A required email input form control with an incorrect value

Additional Attributes

Other form and form control attributes include, but are not limited to, the following. Please feel free to research these attributes as necessary.

- accept
- autocomplete
- autofocus
- formaction
- formenctype

- formmethod
- formnovalidate
- formtarget
- max
- maxlength

- min
- pattern
- readonly
- selectionDirection
- step

Login Form Example

The following is an example of a complete login form that includes several different elements and attributes to illustrate what we've covered so far. These elements are then styled using CSS (see **Figure 10.23**).

Figure 10.23 An example of a login form

HTML

```
1.  <form>
2.    <fieldset class="account-info">
3.      <label>
4.        Username
5.        <input type="text" name="username">
6.      </label>
7.      <label>
8.        Password
9.        <input type="password" name="password">
10.     </label>
11.   </fieldset>
12.   <fieldset class="account-action">
13.     <input class="btn" type="submit" name="submit" value="Login">
14.     <label>
15.       <input type="checkbox" name="remember"> Stay signed in
16.     </label>
17.   </fieldset>
18. </form>
```

CSS

```
1.   *,
2.   *:before,
3.   *:after {
4.     -webkit-box-sizing: border-box;
5.        -moz-box-sizing: border-box;
6.             box-sizing: border-box;
7.   }
8.   form {
9.     border: 1px solid #c6c7cc;
10.    border-radius: 5px;
11.    font: 14px/1.4 "Helvetica Neue", Helvetica, Arial, sans-serif;
12.    overflow: hidden;
13.    width: 240px;
14.  }
15.  fieldset {
16.    border: 0;
17.    margin: 0;
18.    padding: 0;
19.  }
20.  input {
21.    border-radius: 5px;
22.    font: 14px/1.4 "Helvetica Neue", Helvetica, Arial, sans-serif;
23.    margin: 0;
24.  }
25.  .account-info {
26.    padding: 20px 20px 0 20px;
27.  }
28.  .account-info label {
29.    color: #395870;
30.    display: block;
31.    font-weight: bold;
32.    margin-bottom: 20px;
33.  }
34.  .account-info input {
35.    background: #fff;
36.    border: 1px solid #c6c7cc;
37.    -webkit-box-shadow: inset 0 1px 1px rgba(0, 0, 0, .1);
```

```
38.       -moz-box-shadow: inset 0 1px 1px rgba(0, 0, 0, .1);
39.            box-shadow: inset 0 1px 1px rgba(0, 0, 0, .1);
40.    color: #636466;
41.    padding: 6px;
42.    margin-top: 6px;
43.    width: 100%;
44.  }
45.  .account-action {
46.    background: #f0f0f2;
47.    border-top: 1px solid #c6c7cc;
48.    padding: 20px;
49.  }
50.  .account-action .btn {
51.    background: -webkit-linear-gradient(#49708f, #293f50);
52.    background:    -moz-linear-gradient(#49708f, #293f50);
53.    background:         linear-gradient(#49708f, #293f50);
54.    border: 0;
55.    color: #fff;
56.    cursor: pointer;
57.    font-weight: bold;
58.    float: left;
59.    padding: 8px 16px;
60.  }
61.  .account-action label {
62.    color: #7c7c80;
63.    font-size: 12px;
64.    float: left;
65.    margin: 10px 0 0 20px;
66.  }
```

In Practice

With an understanding of how to build forms in place, let's create a registration page for our Styles Conference website so that we can begin to gather interest and sell tickets for the event.

1. Jumping into our `register.html` file, we'll begin by following the same layout pattern we used on our Speakers and Venue pages. This includes adding a `<section>` element with a class attribute value of `row` just below the registration lead-in section

and nesting a `<div>` element with a class attribute value of `grid` directly inside the `<section>` element.

Our code just below the lead-in section for the Register page should look like this:

```
1.  <section class="row">
2.    <div class="grid">
3.      . . .
4.    </div>
5.  </section>
```

As a refresher, the `class` attribute value of `row` adds a white `background` and provides some vertical `padding`, while the class attribute value of `grid` centers our content in the middle of the page and provides some horizontal `padding`.

2. Inside the `<div>` element with a class attribute value of `grid` we're going to create two columns, one covering two-thirds of the page width and one covering one-third of the page width. The two-thirds column will be a `<section>` element on the left-hand side that tells users why they should register for our conference. The one-third column, then, will be a `<form>` element on the right-hand side providing a way for users to register for our conference.

    We'll add these two elements, and their corresponding `col-2-3` and `col-1-3` classes, directly inside the `<div>` element with a class attribute value of `grid`. Since both of these elements will be inline-block elements, we need to open a comment directly after the two-thirds column closing tag and then close that comment directly before the one-third column opening tag.

    In all, our code should look like this:

```
1.  <section class="row">
2.    <div class="grid">
3.
4.      <section class="col-2-3">
5.        . . .
6.      </section><!--
7.
8.      --><form class="col-1-3">
9.        . . .
10.     </form>
11.
12.   </div>
13. </section>
```

3. Now, inside our two-thirds column let's add some details about our event and why it's a good idea for aspiring designers and front-end developers to attend. We'll do so using a handful of different heading levels (along with their pre-established styles), a paragraph, and an unordered list.

In our `<section>` element with a class attribute value of `col-2-3`, the code should look like this:

```
1.   <section class="col-2-3">
2.
3.     <h2>Purchase a Conference Pass</h2>
4.     <h5>$99 per Pass</h5>
5.
6.     <p>Purchase your Styles Conference pass using the form to the
        right. Multiple passes may be purchased within the same order,
        so feel free to bring a friend or two along. Once your order is
        finished we&#8217;ll follow up and provide a receipt for your
        purchase. See you soon!</p>
7.
8.     <h4>Why Attend?</h4>
9.
10.    <ul>
11.      <li>Over twenty world-class speakers</li>
12.      <li>One full day of workshops and two full days of
          presentations</li>
13.      <li>Hosted at The Chicago Theatre, a historical landmark</li>
14.      <li>August in Chicago is simply amazing</li>
15.    </ul>
16.
17.  </section>
```

4. Currently our unordered list doesn't have any list item markers. All of the browser default styles have been turned off by the CSS reset we added all the way back in Lesson 1. Let's create some custom styles specifically for this unordered list.

To do so, let's add a `class` attribute value of `why-attend` to the unordered list.

```
1.   <ul class="why-attend">
2.     ...
3.   </ul>
```

With a class available to add styles to, let's create a new section for Register page styles at the bottom of our `main.css` file. Within this section let's use the class to select the unordered list and add a `list-style` of `square` and some bottom and left margins.

The new section at the bottom of our `main.css` file should look like this:

```
1.  /*
2.  ==========================================
3.  Register
4.  ==========================================
5.  */
6.
7.  .why-attend {
8.    list-style: square;
9.    margin: 0 0 22px 30px;
10. }
```

5. The details section of our registration page is complete, so now it's time to address our registration form. We'll start by adding the `action` and `method` attributes to the `<form>` element. Since we haven't set up our form processing, these attributes will simply serve as placeholders and will need to be revisited.

The code for our `<form>` element should look like this:

```
1.  <form class="col-1-3" action="#" method="post">
2.    ...
3.  </form>
```

6. Next, inside the `<form>` element we'll add a `<fieldset>` element. Inside the `<fieldset>` element we'll add a series of `<label>` elements that wrap a given form control.

We want to collect a user's name, email address, number of desired conference passes, and any potential comments. The name, email address, and number of conference passes are required fields, and we'll want to make sure we use the appropriate elements and attributes for each form control.

With a mix of different input types, select menus, textareas, and attributes, the code for our form should look like the following:

```
1.  <form class="col-1-3" action="#" method="post">
2.
3.    <fieldset>
```

```
4.
5.      <label>
6.        Name
7.        <input type="text" name="name" placeholder="Full name"
            required>
8.      </label>
9.
10.     <label>
11.       Email
12.       <input type="email" name="email" placeholder="Email address"
            required>
13.     </label>
14.
15.     <label>
16.       Number of Passes
17.       <select name="quantity" required>
18.         <option value="1" selected>1</option>
19.         <option value="2">2</option>
20.         <option value="3">3</option>
21.         <option value="4">4</option>
22.         <option value="5">5</option>
23.       </select>
24.     </label>
25.
26.     <label>
27.       Comments
28.       <textarea name="comments"></textarea>
29.     </label>
30.
31.   </fieldset>
32.
33.   <input type="submit" name="submit" value="Purchase">
34.
35. </form>
```

Here we can see each form control nested within a `<label>` element. The Name form control uses an `<input>` element with a `type` attribute value of `text`, while the Email form control uses an `<input>` element with a `type` attribute value of `email`.

Both the Name and Email form controls include the `required` Boolean attribute and a `placeholder` attribute.

The Number of Passes form control uses the `<select>` element and nested `<option>` elements. The `<select>` element itself includes the `required` Boolean attribute, and the first `<option>` element includes the `selected` Boolean attribute.

The Comments form control uses the `<textarea>` element without any special modifications. And lastly, outside of the `<fieldset>` element is the submit form control, which is formed by an `<input>` element with a `type` attribute value of `submit`.

7. With the form in place, it's time to add styles to it. We'll begin with a few default styles on the `<form>` element itself and on the `<input>`, `<select>`, and `<textarea>` elements.

    Within the register section of our `main.css` file we'll want to add the following styles:

    ```
    1.  form {
    2.    margin-bottom: 22px;
    3.  }
    4.  input,
    5.  select,
    6.  textarea {
    7.    font: 300 16px/22px "Lato", "Open Sans", "Helvetica Neue",
          Helvetica, Arial, sans-serif;
    8.  }
    ```

    We'll start by placing a 22-pixel margin on the bottom of our form to help vertically space it apart from other elements. Then we'll add some standard `font`-based styles—including `weight`, `size`, `line-height`, and `family`—for all of the `<input>`, `<select>`, and `<textarea>` elements.

    By default, every browser has its own interpretation of how the styles for form controls should appear. With this in mind, we have repeated the `font`-based styles from our `<body>` element to ensure that our styles remain consistent.

8. Let's add some styles to the elements within the `<fieldset>` element. Since we may add additional `<fieldset>` elements later on, let's add a class attribute value of `register-group` to our existing `<fieldset>` element, and from there we can apply unique styles to the elements nested within it.

    ```
    1.  <fieldset class="register-group">
    2.    ...
    3.  </fieldset>
    ```

Once the `register-group` class attribute value is in place, we'll add a few styles to the elements nested within the `<fieldset>` element. These styles will appear in our `main.css` file, below the existing form styles.

```css
1.  .register-group label {
2.    color: #648880;
3.    cursor: pointer;
4.    font-weight: 400;
5.  }
6.  .register-group input,
7.  .register-group select,
8.  .register-group textarea {
9.    border: 1px solid #c6c9cc;
10.   border-radius: 5px;
11.   color: #888;
12.   display: block;
13.   margin: 5px 0 27px 0;
14.   padding: 5px 8px;
15. }
16. .register-group input,
17. .register-group textarea {
18.   width: 100%;
19. }
20. .register-group select {
21.   height: 34px;
22.   width: 60px;
23. }
24. .register-group textarea {
25.   height: 78px;
26. }
```

You'll notice that most of these properties and values revolve around the box model, which we covered in Lesson 4. We're primarily setting up the size of different form controls, ensuring that they are laid out appropriately. Aside from adding some box model styles, we're adjusting the `color` and `font-weight` of a few elements.

9. So far, so good: our form is coming together quite nicely. The only remaining element yet to be styled is the submit button. As it's a button, we actually have some existing styles we can apply here. If we think back to our home page, our hero section contained a button that received some styles by way of the `btn` class attribute value.

Let's add this class attribute value, btn, along with a new class attribute value of btn-default to our submit button. Specifically we'll use the class name of btn-default since this button is appearing on a white background and will be the default style for buttons moving forward.

```
1.  <input class="btn btn-default" type="submit" name="submit"
    value="Purchase">
```

Now our submit button has some shared styles with the button on the home page. We'll use the btn-default class attribute value to then apply some new styles to our submit button specifically.

Going back to the buttons section of our main.css file, let's add the following:

```
1.  .btn-default {
2.    border: 0;
3.    background: #648880;
4.    padding: 11px 30px;
5.    font-size: 14px;
6.  }
7.  .btn-default:hover {
8.    background: #77a198;
9.  }
```

These new styles, which define the size and background of our submit button, are then combined with the existing btn class styles to create the final presentation of our submit button.

Our Register page is finished, and attendees can now begin to reserve their tickets (see **Figure 10.24**).

The source code for the exercises within this lesson can be found at http://learn.shayhowe.com/html-css/building-forms.

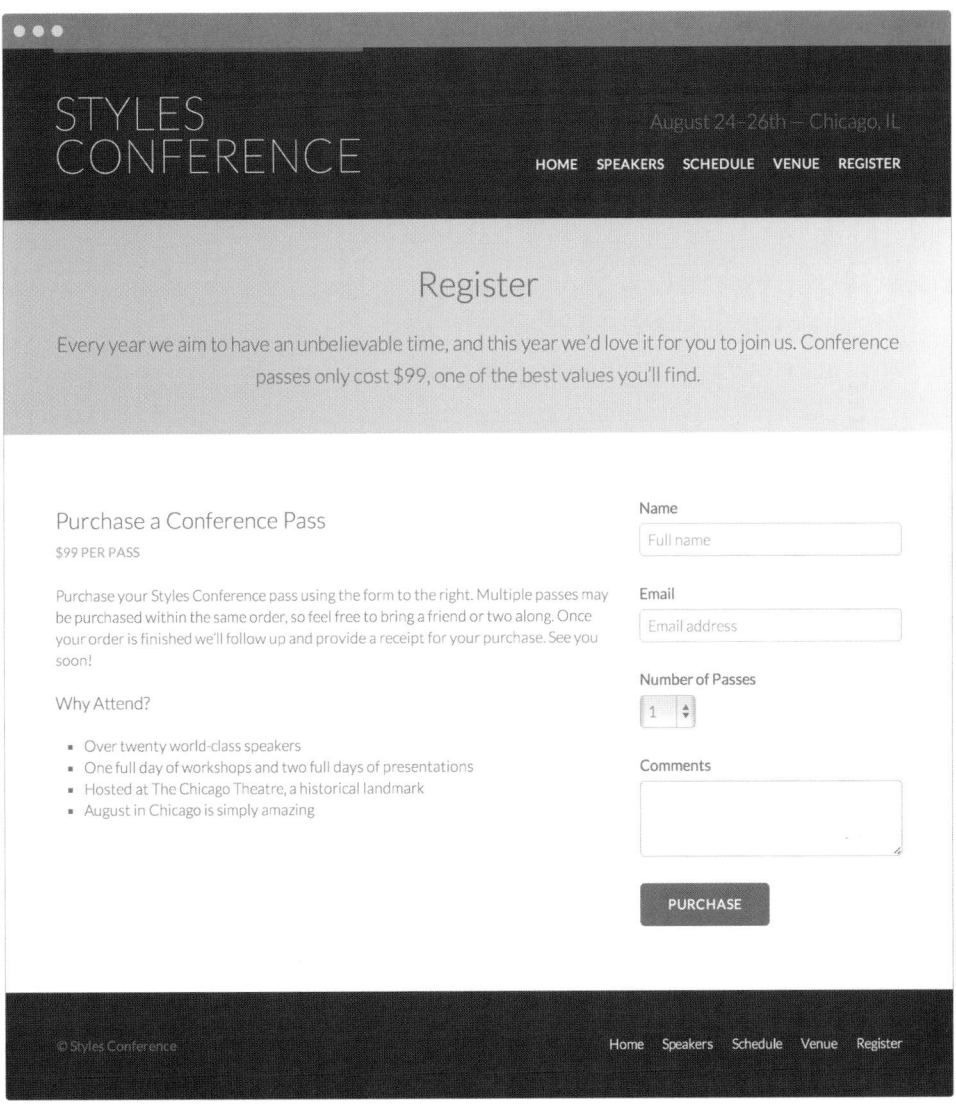

Figure 10.24 Our registration page, which includes a form

Summary

Forms play a large role in how users interact with, provide information to, and take action on websites. We've taken all the right steps to learn not only how to mark up forms but also how to style them.

To quickly recap, within this lesson we discussed the following:

- How to initialize a form
- Ways to obtain text-based information from users
- Different elements and methods for creating multiple choice options and menus
- Which elements and attributes are best used to submit a form's data for processing
- How best to organize forms and give form controls structure and meaning
- A handful of attributes that help collect more qualified data

Our understanding of HTML and CSS is progressing quite nicely, and we only have one more component to learn: tables. In the next chapter, we'll take a look at how to organize and present data with tables.

Lesson 11

Organizing Data with Tables

HTML tables were created to provide a straightforward way to mark up structured tabular data and to display that data in a form that is easy for users to read and digest.

When HTML was being developed, however, CSS was not widely supported in browsers, so tables were the primary means by which websites were built. They were used for positioning content as well as for building the overall layout of a page. This worked at the time, but it was not what table markup was intended for, and it led to many other associated problems.

Fortunately, we have come a long way since then. Today tables are used specifically for organizing data (like they should be), and CSS is free to get on with the jobs of positioning and layout.

Building data tables still has its challenges. How a table should be built in HTML depends largely on the data and how it is to be displayed. Then, once they're marked up in HTML, tables need to be styled with CSS to make the information more legible and understandable to users.

Creating a Table

Tables are made up of data that is contained within columns and rows, and HTML supplies several different elements for defining and structuring these items. At a minimum a table must consist of `<table>`, `<tr>` (table row), and `<td>` (table data) elements. For greater structure and additional semantic value, tables may include the `<th>` (table header) element and a few other elements as well. When all of these elements are working together, they produce a solid table.

Table

We use the `<table>` element to initialize a table on a page. Using the `<table>` element signifies that the information within this element will be tabular data displayed in the necessary columns and rows.

```
1.  <table>
2.    ...
3.  </table>
```

Table Row

Once a table has been defined in HTML, table rows may be added using the `<tr>` element. A table can have numerous table rows, or `<tr>` elements. Depending on the amount of information there is to display, the number of table rows may be substantial.

```
1.  <table>
2.    <tr>
3.      ...
4.    </tr>
5.    <tr>
6.      ...
7.    </tr>
8.  </table>
```

Table Data

Once a table is defined and rows within that table have been set up, data cells may be added to the table via the table data, or <td>, element. Listing multiple <td> elements one after the other will create columns within a table row (see **Figure 11.1**).

Don't Make Me Think by Steve Krug	In Stock	1 $30.02
A Project Guide to UX Design by Russ Unger & Carolyn Chandler	In Stock	2 $52.94 ($26.47 × 2)
Introducing HTML5 by Bruce Lawson & Remy Sharp	Out of Stock	1 $22.23
Bulletproof Web Design by Dan Cederholm	In Stock	1 $30.17

Figure 11.1 A table of books that includes multiple columns and rows

```
1.   <table>
2.     <tr>
3.       <td>Don&#8217;t Make Me Think by Steve Krug</td>
4.       <td>In Stock</td>
5.       <td>1</td>
6.       <td>$30.02</td>
7.     </tr>
8.     <tr>
9.       <td>A Project Guide to UX Design by Russ Unger &#38; Carolyn
         Chandler</td>
10.      <td>In Stock</td>
11.      <td>2</td>
12.      <td>$52.94 ($26.47 &#215; 2)</td>
13.    </tr>
14.    <tr>
15.      <td>Introducing HTML5 by Bruce Lawson &#38; Remy Sharp</td>
16.      <td>Out of Stock</td>
17.      <td>1</td>
18.      <td>$22.23</td>
19.    </tr>
20.    <tr>
21.      <td>Bulletproof Web Design by Dan Cederholm</td>
22.      <td>In Stock</td>
```

continues

```
23.        <td>1</td>
24.        <td>$30.17</td>
25.    </tr>
26. </table>
```

Table Header

To designate a heading for a column or row of cells, the table header element, <th>, should be used. The <th> element works just like the <td> element in that it creates a cell for data. The value to using the <th> element over the <td> element is that the table header element provides semantic value by signifying that the data within the cell is a heading, while the <td> element only represents a generic piece of data.

The difference between the two elements is similar to the difference between headings (<h1> through <h6> elements) and paragraphs (<p> elements). While a heading's content could be placed within a paragraph, it doesn't make sense to do so. Specifically using a heading adds more semantic value to the content. The same is true for table headers.

Table headers may be used within both columns and rows; the data within a table determines where the headers are appropriate. The scope attribute helps to identify exactly what content a table header relates to. The scope attribute indicates with the values col, row, colgroup, and rowgroup whether a table header applies to a row or column. The most commonly used values are col and row. The col value indicates that every cell within the column relates directly to that table header, and the row value indicates that every cell within the row relates directly to that table header.

Using the <th> element, along with the scope attribute, tremendously helps screen readers and assistive technologies make sense of a table. Therefore, they are also beneficial to those browsing a web page using those technologies.

Additionally, depending on the browser, table headers may receive some default styling, usually bold and centered (see **Figure 11.2**).

```
1.  <table>
2.    <tr>
3.      <th scope="col">Item</th>
4.      <th scope="col">Availability</th>
5.      <th scope="col">Qty</th>
6.      <th scope="col">Price</th>
7.    </tr>
8.    <tr>
```

```
9.    <td>Don&#8217;t Make Me Think by Steve Krug</td>
10.   <td>In Stock</td>
11.   <td>1</td>
12.   <td>$30.02</td>
13.  </tr>
14.  <tr>
15.   <td>A Project Guide to UX Design by Russ Unger &#38;
      Carolyn Chandler</td>
16.   <td>In Stock</td>
17.   <td>2</td>
18.   <td>$52.94 ($26.47 &#215; 2)</td>
19.  </tr>
20.  <tr>
21.   <td>Introducing HTML5 by Bruce Lawson &#38; Remy Sharp</td>
22.   <td>Out of Stock</td>
23.   <td>1</td>
24.   <td>$22.23</td>
25.  </tr>
26.  <tr>
27.   <td>Bulletproof Web Design by Dan Cederholm</td>
28.   <td>In Stock</td>
29.   <td>1</td>
30.   <td>$30.17</td>
31.  </tr>
32. </table>
```

Item	Availability	Qty	Price
Don't Make Me Think by Steve Krug	In Stock	1	$30.02
A Project Guide to UX Design by Russ Unger & Carolyn Chandler	In Stock	2	$52.94 ($26.47 × 2)
Introducing HTML5 by Bruce Lawson & Remy Sharp	Out of Stock	1	$22.23
Bulletproof Web Design by Dan Cederholm	In Stock	1	$30.17

Figure 11.2 A table of books that includes table headers

Getting data into a table is only the beginning. While we've scratched the surface of how to semantically add data to a table, there is more we can do to define the structure of our tables.

The Headers Attribute

The `headers` attribute is very similar to the `scope` attribute. By default, the `scope` attribute may only be used on the `<th>` element. In the case that a cell, either a `<td>` or `<th>` element, needs to be associated with a different header, the `headers` attribute comes into play. The value of the `headers` attribute on a `<td>` or `<th>` element needs to match the `id` attribute value of the `<th>` element that cell pertains to.

Table Structure

Knowing how to build a table and arrange data is extremely powerful; however, there are a few additional elements to help us organize the data and structure of a table. These elements include `<caption>`, `<thead>`, `<tbody>`, and `<tfoot>`.

Table Caption

The `<caption>` element provides a caption or title for a table. A caption will help users identify what the table pertains to and what data they can expect to find within it. The `<caption>` element must come immediately after the opening `<table>` tag, and it is positioned at the top of a table by default (see **Figure 11.3**).

```
1.  <table>
2.    <caption>Design and Front-End Development Books</caption>
3.    ...
4.  </table>
```

Design and Front-End Development Books			
Item	**Availability**	**Qty**	**Price**
Don't Make Me Think by Steve Krug	In Stock	1	$30.02
A Project Guide to UX Design by Russ Unger & Carolyn Chandler	In Stock	2	$52.94 ($26.47 × 2)
Introducing HTML5 by Bruce Lawson & Remy Sharp	Out of Stock	1	$22.23
Bulletproof Web Design by Dan Cederholm	In Stock	1	$30.17

Figure 11.3 A table of books with a caption that shows what the table relates to

Table Head, Body, & Foot

The content within tables can be broken up into multiple groups, including a head, a body, and a foot. The `<thead>` (table head), `<tbody>` (table body), and `<tfoot>` (table foot) elements help to structurally organize tables.

The table head element, `<thead>`, wraps the heading row or rows of a table to denote the head. The table head should be placed at the top of a table, after any `<caption>` element and before any `<tbody>` element.

After the table head may come either the `<tbody>` or `<tfoot>` elements. Originally the `<tfoot>` element had to come immediately after the `<thead>` element, but HTML5 has provided leeway here. These elements may now occur in any order so long as they are never parent elements of one another. The `<tbody>` element should contain the primary data within a table, while the `<tfoot>` element contains data that outlines the contents of a table (see **Figure 11.4**).

```
1.   <table>
2.     <caption>Design and Front-End Development Books</caption>
3.     <thead>
4.       <tr>
5.         <th scope="col">Item</th>
6.         <th scope="col">Availability</th>
7.         <th scope="col">Qty</th>
8.         <th scope="col">Price</th>
9.       </tr>
10.    </thead>
11.    <tbody>
12.      <tr>
13.        <td>Don&#8217;t Make Me Think by Steve Krug</td>
14.        <td>In Stock</td>
15.        <td>1</td>
16.        <td>$30.02</td>
17.      </tr>
18.      ...
19.    </tbody>
20.    <tfoot>
21.      <tr>
22.        <td>Subtotal</td>
```

continues

```
23.        <td></td>
24.        <td></td>
25.        <td>$135.36</td>
26.      </tr>
27.      <tr>
28.        <td>Tax</td>
29.        <td></td>
30.        <td></td>
31.        <td>$13.54</td>
32.      </tr>
33.      <tr>
34.        <td>Total</td>
35.        <td></td>
36.        <td></td>
37.        <td>$148.90</td>
38.      </tr>
39.    </tfoot>
40.  </table>
```

Design and Front-End Development Books			
Item	**Availability**	**Qty**	**Price**
Don't Make Me Think by Steve Krug	In Stock	1	$30.02
A Project Guide to UX Design by Russ Unger & Carolyn Chandler	In Stock	2	$52.94 ($26.47 × 2)
Introducing HTML5 by Bruce Lawson & Remy Sharp	Out of Stock	1	$22.23
Bulletproof Web Design by Dan Cederholm	In Stock	1	$30.17
Subtotal			$135.36
Tax			$13.54
Total			$148.90

Figure 11.4 A table of books complete with caption, table head, table body, and table foot elements

Combining Multiple Cells

Often, two or more cells need to be combined into one without breaking the overall row and column layout. Perhaps two cells next to each other contain the same data, there's an empty cell, or the cells should be combined for styling purposes. In these cases we can use the colspan and rowspan attributes. These two attributes work on either the <td> or <th> elements.

The colspan attribute is used to span a single cell across multiple columns within a table, while the rowspan attribute is used to span a single cell across multiple rows. Each attribute accepts an integer value that indicates the number of cells to span across, with 1 being the default value.

Using the table of books from before, we can now remove the empty table cells within the table footer as well as clean up the table header (see **Figure 11.5**).

```
1.   <table>
2.     <caption>Design and Front-End Development Books</caption>
3.     <thead>
4.       <tr>
5.         <th scope="col" colspan="2">Item</th>
6.         <th scope="col">Qty</th>
7.         <th scope="col">Price</th>
8.       </tr>
9.     </thead>
10.    <tbody>
11.      <tr>
12.        <td>Don&#8217;t Make Me Think by Steve Krug</td>
13.        <td>In Stock</td>
14.        <td>1</td>
15.        <td>$30.02</td>
16.      </tr>
17.      ...
18.    </tbody>
19.    <tfoot>
20.      <tr>
21.        <td colspan="3">Subtotal</td>
22.        <td>$135.36</td>
23.      </tr>
```

continues

```
24.     <tr>
25.       <td colspan="3">Tax</td>
26.       <td>$13.54</td>
27.     </tr>
28.     <tr>
29.       <td colspan="3">Total</td>
30.       <td>$148.90</td>
31.     </tr>
32.   </tfoot>
33. </table>
```

Design and Front-End Development Books			
Item		**Qty**	**Price**
Don't Make Me Think by Steve Krug	In Stock	1	$30.02
A Project Guide to UX Design by Russ Unger & Carolyn Chandler	In Stock	2	$52.94 ($26.47 × 2)
Introducing HTML5 by Bruce Lawson & Remy Sharp	Out of Stock	1	$22.23
Bulletproof Web Design by Dan Cederholm	In Stock	1	$30.17
Subtotal			$135.36
Tax			$13.54
Total			$148.90

Figure 11.5 A table of books that contains a couple of cells that span multiple columns or rows

Table Borders

Effective use of borders can help make tables more comprehensible. Borders around a table or individual cells can make a large impact when a user is trying to interpret data and quickly scan for information. When styling table borders with CSS there are two properties that will quickly come in handy: `border-collapse` and `border-spacing`.

Border Collapse Property

Tables consist of a parent `<table>` element as well as nested `<th>` or `<td>` elements. When we apply borders around these elements those borders will begin to stack up, with the border of one element sitting next to that of another element. For example, if we put a 2-pixel border around an entire table and then an additional 2-pixel border around each table cell, there would be a 4-pixel border around every cell in the table.

The `border-collapse` property determines a table's border model. There are three values for the `border-collapse` property: `collapse`, `separate`, and `inherit`. By default, the `border-collapse` property value is `separate`, meaning that all of the different borders will stack up next to one another, as described above. The `collapse` property, on the other hand, condenses the borders into one, choosing the table cell as the primary border (see **Figure 11.6**).

```
1.  table {
2.    border-collapse: collapse;
3.  }
4.  th,
5.  td {
6.    border: 1px solid #c6c7cc;
7.    padding: 10px 15px;
8.  }
```

Item		Qty	Price
Don't Make Me Think by Steve Krug	In Stock	1	$30.02
A Project Guide to UX Design by Russ Unger & Carolyn Chandler	In Stock	2	$52.94 ($26.47 × 2)
Introducing HTML5 by Bruce Lawson & Remy Sharp	Out of Stock	1	$22.23
Bulletproof Web Design by Dan Cederholm	In Stock	1	$30.17
Subtotal			$135.36
Tax			$13.54
Total			$148.90

Figure 11.6 A table with collapsed borders

Border Spacing Property

As the `border-collapse` property with the `separate` value allows borders to be stacked up against one another, the `border-spacing` property can determine how much space, if any, appears between the borders.

For example, a table with a 1-pixel border around the entire table and a 1-pixel border around each cell will have a 2-pixel border all around every cell because the borders stack up next to one another. Adding in a `border-spacing` value of 4 pixels separates the borders by 4 pixels (see **Figure 11.7**).

```
1.  table {
2.    border-collapse: separate;
3.    border-spacing: 4px;
4.  }
5.  table,
6.  th,
7.  td {
8.    border: 1px solid #c6c7cc;
9.  }
10. th,
11. td {
12.   padding: 10px 15px;
13. }
```

Item		Qty	Price
Don't Make Me Think by Steve Krug	In Stock	1	$30.02
A Project Guide to UX Design by Russ Unger & Carolyn Chandler	In Stock	2	$52.94 ($26.47 × 2)
Introducing HTML5 by Bruce Lawson & Remy Sharp	Out of Stock	1	$22.23
Bulletproof Web Design by Dan Cederholm	In Stock	1	$30.17
Subtotal			$135.36
Tax			$13.54
Total			$148.90

Figure 11.7 A table with separated borders

The `border-spacing` property works only when the `border-collapse` property value is `separate`, its default value. If the `border-collapse` property hasn't been previously used, we can use the `border-spacing` property without worry.

Additionally, the `border-spacing` property may accept two length values: the first value for horizontal spacing and the second value for vertical spacing. The declaration `border-spacing: 5px 10px;`, for example, will place 5 pixels of horizontal spacing between borders and 10 pixels of vertical spacing between borders.

Adding Borders to Rows

Adding borders to a table can be tricky at times, particularly when putting borders between rows. Within a table, borders cannot be applied to `<tr>` elements or table structural elements, so when we want to put a border between rows some thought is required.

We'll begin by making sure the table's `border-collapse` property value is set to `collapse`, and then we'll add a bottom `border` to each table cell, regardless of whether it's a `<th>` or `<td>` element. If we wish, we can remove the bottom `border` from the cells within the last row of the table by using the `last-child` pseudo-class selector to select the last `<tr>` element within the table and target the `<td>` elements within that row. Additionally, if a table is using the structural elements, we'll want to make sure to prequalify the last row of the table as being within the `<tfoot>` element (see **Figure 11.8**).

```
1.   table {
2.     border-collapse: collapse;
3.   }
4.   th,
5.   td {
6.     border-bottom: 1px solid #c6c7cc;
7.     padding: 10px 15px;
8.   }
9.   tfoot tr:last-child td {
10.     border-bottom: 0;
11.   }
```

Item		Qty	Price
Don't Make Me Think by Steve Krug	In Stock	1	$30.02
A Project Guide to UX Design by Russ Unger & Carolyn Chandler	In Stock	2	$52.94 ($26.47 × 2)
Introducing HTML5 by Bruce Lawson & Remy Sharp	Out of Stock	1	$22.23
Bulletproof Web Design by Dan Cederholm	In Stock	1	$30.17
Subtotal			$135.36
Tax			$13.54
Total			$148.90

Figure 11.8 A table with borders between each row

Table Striping

In the effort to make tables more legible, one common design practice is to "stripe" table rows with alternating background colors. This makes the rows clearer and provides a visual cue for scanning information. One way to do this is to place a class on every other <tr> element and set a background color to that class. Another, easier way is to use the :nth-child pseudo-class selector with an even or odd argument to select every other <tr> element.

Here, our table of books uses the :nth-child pseudo-class selector with an even argument to select all even table rows within the table and apply a gray background. Consequently, every other row within the table body is gray (see **Figure 11.9**).

```
1.  table {
2.    border-collapse: separate;
3.    border-spacing: 0;
4.  }
5.  th,
6.  td {
7.    padding: 10px 15px;
8.  }
9.  thead {
10.    background: #395870;
11.    color: #fff;
```

```
12. }
13. tbody tr:nth-child(even) {
14.   background: #f0f0f2;
15. }
16. td {
17.   border-bottom: 1px solid #c6c7cc;
18.   border-right: 1px solid #c6c7cc;
19. }
20. td:first-child {
21.   border-left: 1px solid #c6c7cc;
22. }
```

Item	Qty		Price
Don't Make Me Think by Steve Krug	In Stock	1	$30.02
A Project Guide to UX Design by Russ Unger & Carolyn Chandler	In Stock	2	$52.94 ($26.47 × 2)
Introducing HTML5 by Bruce Lawson & Remy Sharp	Out of Stock	1	$22.23
Bulletproof Web Design by Dan Cederholm	In Stock	1	$30.17
Subtotal			$135.36
Tax			$13.54
Total			$148.90

Figure 11.9 A table with striped rows

Within this code there are a few intricacies worth mentioning. To begin, the `<table>` element has an explicit `border-collapse` property set to `separate` and a `border-spacing` property set to 0. The reason for this is that the `<td>` elements include borders, while the `<th>` elements do not. Without the `border-collapse` property set to `separate` the borders of the `<td>` elements would make the body and foot of the table wider than the head.

Since the `border-collapse` property is set to `separate` we need to be careful as to how borders are applied to `<td>` elements. Here borders are set to the right and bottom of all `<td>` elements. Then, the very first `<td>` element within a `<tr>` element will receive a left `border`. As all of the `<td>` elements stack together so do their borders, providing the appearance of a solid border around each element.

Lastly, all `<th>` elements receive a blue `background`, and every even `<tr>` element receives a gray `background` by way of the `:nth-child` pseudo-class selector.

Aligning Text

In addition to table borders and striping, the alignment of text within cells, both horizontal and vertical, plays an integral role in table formatting. Names, descriptions, and so forth are commonly flush left, while numbers and other figures are flush right. Other information, depending on its context, may be centered. We can move text horizontally using the `text-align` property in CSS, as we covered in Lesson 6, "Working with Typography."

To align text vertically, however, the `vertical-align` property is used. The `vertical-align` property works only with inline and table-cell elements—it won't work for block, inline-block, or any other element levels.

The `vertical-align` property accepts a handful of different values; the most popular values are `top`, `middle`, and `bottom`. These values vertically position text in relation to the table cell, for table-cell elements, or to the closest parent element, for inline-level elements.

By revising the HTML and CSS to include the `text-align` and `vertical-align` properties, we can clean up the layout of our table of books. Note that the data within the table becomes much clearer and more digestible (see **Figure 11.10**).

Item		Qty	Price
Don't Make Me Think by Steve Krug	In Stock	1	$30.02
A Project Guide to UX Design by Russ Unger & Carolyn Chandler	In Stock	2	$52.94 $26.47 × 2
Introducing HTML5 by Bruce Lawson & Remy Sharp	Out of Stock	1	$22.23
Bulletproof Web Design by Dan Cederholm	In Stock	1	$30.17
		Subtotal	$135.36
		Tax	$13.54
		Total	$148.90

Figure 11.10
A table with multiple text alignments

HTML

```
1.  <table>
2.    <thead>
3.      <tr>
4.        <th scope="col" colspan="2">Item</th>
5.        <th scope="col">Qty</th>
6.        <th scope="col">Price</th>
7.      </tr>
8.    </thead>
9.    <tbody>
10.     <tr>
11.       <td>
12.         <strong class="book-title">Don&#8217;t Make Me Think
              </strong> by Steve Krug
13.       </td>
14.       <td class="item-stock">In Stock</td>
15.       <td class="item-qty">1</td>
16.       <td class="item-price">$30.02</td>
17.     </tr>
18.     <tr>
19.       <td>
20.         <strong class="book-title">A Project Guide to UX Design
              </strong> by Russ Unger &#38; Carolyn Chandler
21.       </td>
22.       <td class="item-stock">In Stock</td>
23.       <td class="item-qty">2</td>
24.       <td class="item-price">$52.94 <span class="item-multiple">
            $26.47 &#215; 2</span></td>
25.     </tr>
26.     <tr>
27.       <td>
28.         <strong class="book-title">Introducing HTML5</strong> by
              Bruce Lawson &#38; Remy Sharp
29.       </td>
30.       <td class="item-stock">Out of Stock</td>
31.       <td class="item-qty">1</td>
32.       <td class="item-price">$22.23</td>
```

continues

```
33.    </tr>
34.    <tr>
35.      <td>
36.        <strong class="book-title">Bulletproof Web Design</strong>
             by Dan Cederholm
37.      </td>
38.      <td class="item-stock">In Stock</td>
39.      <td class="item-qty">1</td>
40.      <td class="item-price">$30.17</td>
41.    </tr>
42.  </tbody>
43.  <tfoot>
44.    <tr>
45.      <td colspan="3">Subtotal</td>
46.      <td>$135.36</td>
47.    </tr>
48.    <tr>
49.      <td colspan="3">Tax</td>
50.      <td>$13.54</td>
51.    </tr>
52.    <tr>
53.      <td colspan="3">Total</td>
54.      <td>$148.90</td>
55.    </tr>
56.  </tfoot>
57. </table>
```

CSS

```
1.  table {
2.    border-collapse: separate;
3.    border-spacing: 0;
4.    color: #4a4a4d;
5.    font: 14px/1.4 "Helvetica Neue", Helvetica, Arial, sans-serif;
6.  }
7.  th,
8.  td {
9.    padding: 10px 15px;
10.   vertical-align: middle;
```

```
11. }
12. thead {
13.   background: #395870;
14.   color: #fff;
15. }
16. th:first-child {
17.   text-align: left;
18. }
19. tbody tr:nth-child(even) {
20.   background: #f0f0f2;
21. }
22. td {
23.   border-bottom: 1px solid #c6c7cc;
24.   border-right: 1px solid #c6c7cc;
25. }
26. td:first-child {
27.   border-left: 1px solid #c6c7cc;
28. }
29. .book-title {
30.   color: #395870;
31.   display: block;
32. }
33. .item-stock,
34. .item-qty {
35.   text-align: center;
36. }
37. .item-price {
38.   text-align: right;
39. }
40. .item-multiple {
41.   display: block;
42. }
43. tfoot {
44.   text-align: right;
45. }
46. tfoot tr:last-child {
47.   background: #f0f0f2;
48. }
```

Completely Styled Table

So far our table of books is looking pretty good. Let's take it one step further by rounding some corners and styling some of the text just a little more. (see **Figure 11.11**).

ITEM		QTY	PRICE
Don't Make Me Think by Steve Krug	In Stock	1	$30.02
A Project Guide to UX Design by Russ Unger & Carolyn Chandler	In Stock	2	$52.94 $26.47 × 2
Introducing HTML5 by Bruce Lawson & Remy Sharp	Out of Stock	1	$22.23
Bulletproof Web Design by Dan Cederholm	In Stock	1	$30.17
		Subtotal	$135.36
		Tax	$13.54
		Total	**$148.90**

Figure 11.11
A full-featured table of books, now completely styled

HTML

```
1.   <table>
2.     <thead>
3.       <tr>
4.         <th scope="col" colspan="2">Item</th>
5.         <th scope="col">Qty</th>
6.         <th scope="col">Price</th>
7.       </tr>
8.     </thead>
9.     <tbody>
10.      <tr>
11.        <td>
12.          <strong class="book-title">Don&#8217;t Make Me Think
             </strong>
13.          <span class="text-offset">by Steve Krug</span>
14.        </td>
```

```
15.      <td class="item-stock">In Stock</td>
16.      <td class="item-qty">1</td>
17.      <td class="item-price">$30.02</td>
18.    </tr>
19.    <tr>
20.      <td>
21.        <strong class="book-title">A Project Guide to UX Design
           </strong>
22.        <span class="text-offset">by Russ Unger &#38; Carolyn
           Chandler</span>
23.      </td>
24.      <td class="item-stock">In Stock</td>
25.      <td class="item-qty">2</td>
26.      <td class="item-price">$52.94 <span class="text-offset
         item-multiple">$26.47 &#215; 2</span></td>
27.    </tr>
28.    <tr>
29.      <td>
30.        <strong class="book-title">Introducing HTML5</strong>
31.        <span class="text-offset">by Bruce Lawson &#38; Remy
           Sharp</span>
32.      </td>
33.      <td class="item-stock">Out of Stock</td>
34.      <td class="item-qty">1</td>
35.      <td class="item-price">$22.23</td>
36.    </tr>
37.    <tr>
38.      <td>
39.        <strong class="book-title">Bulletproof Web Design</strong>
40.        <span class="text-offset">by Dan Cederholm</span>
41.      </td>
42.      <td class="item-stock">In Stock</td>
43.      <td class="item-qty">1</td>
44.      <td class="item-price">$30.17</td>
45.    </tr>
46.  </tbody>
47.  <tfoot>
```

continues

```
48.    <tr class="text-offset">
49.      <td colspan="3">Subtotal</td>
50.      <td>$135.36</td>
51.    </tr>
52.    <tr class="text-offset">
53.      <td colspan="3">Tax</td>
54.      <td>$13.54</td>
55.    </tr>
56.    <tr>
57.      <td colspan="3">Total</td>
58.      <td>$148.90</td>
59.    </tr>
60.  </tfoot>
61. </table>
```

CSS

```
1.   table {
2.     border-collapse: separate;
3.     border-spacing: 0;
4.     color: #4a4a4d;
5.     font: 14px/1.4 "Helvetica Neue", Helvetica, Arial, sans-serif;
6.   }
7.   th,
8.   td {
9.     padding: 10px 15px;
10.    vertical-align: middle;
11.  }
12.  thead {
13.    background: #395870;
14.    background: -webkit-linear-gradient(#49708f, #293f50);
15.    background:    -moz-linear-gradient(#49708f, #293f50);
16.    background:         linear-gradient(#49708f, #293f50);
17.    color: #fff;
18.    font-size: 11px;
19.    text-transform: uppercase;
20.  }
21.  th:first-child {
22.    border-top-left-radius: 5px;
```

```
23.    text-align: left;
24.  }
25.  th:last-child {
26.    border-top-right-radius: 5px;
27.  }
28.  tbody tr:nth-child(even) {
29.    background: #f0f0f2;
30.  }
31.  td {
32.    border-bottom: 1px solid #c6c7cc;
33.    border-right: 1px solid #c6c7cc;
34.  }
35.  td:first-child {
36.    border-left: 1px solid #c6c7cc;
37.  }
38.  .book-title {
39.    color: #395870;
40.    display: block;
41.  }
42.  .text-offset {
43.    color: #7c7c80;
44.    font-size: 12px;
45.  }
46.  .item-stock,
47.  .item-qty {
48.    text-align: center;
49.  }
50.  .item-price {
51.    text-align: right;
52.  }
53.  .item-multiple {
54.    display: block;
55.  }
56.  tfoot {
57.    text-align: right;
58.  }
59.  tfoot tr:last-child {
```

continues

```
60.    background: #f0f0f2;
61.    color: #395870;
62.    font-weight: bold;
63. }
64. tfoot tr:last-child td:first-child {
65.    border-bottom-left-radius: 5px;
66. }
67. tfoot tr:last-child td:last-child {
68.    border-bottom-right-radius: 5px;
69. }
```

In Practice

Now that we know how to create and style tables, let's wrap up the last remaining page of our Styles Conference website, the schedule.

1. We'll begin our Schedule page by opening up the `schedule.html` file and adding a `<section>` element with a class attribute value of `row`, much like we've done with all of the other subpages. Within this new `<section>` element let's also add a `<div>` element with a class attribute value of `container`.

    ```
    1.  <section class="row">
    2.    <div class="container">
    3.      ...
    4.    </div>
    5.  </section>
    ```

    With these elements and classes we've created a new section of the page with a white `background` and vertical `padding`, and we've centered our content on the page. What's different here from all of the other subpages is the `container` class attribute value in place of the `grid` class attribute value on the `<div>` element. Since we're not using any of the `col`-based classes we'll forgo the `grid` class attribute value in favor of the `container` class attribute value.

2. Within the new section we'll add three tables, one for each day of the conference. The tables will display the events of each day using three columns and multiple rows and will include a table head and table body.

    To get started let's outline the structure of the first table, including the `<table>`, `<thead>`, and `<tbody>` elements.

```
1.   <section class="row">
2.      <div class="container">
3.
4.        <table>
5.          <thead>
6.            ...
7.          </thead>
8.          <tbody>
9.            ...
10.          </tbody>
11.        </table>
12.
13.      </div>
14.   </section>
```

3. Currently, even though our first table doesn't contain any data, it does have some styles applied to it. Specifically, the reset we added back in Lesson 1 to tone down all of the default browser styles has added the `border-collapse` property with a value of `collapse` and the `border-spacing` property with a value of `0` to the table. We want these styles, so we'll leave them alone; however, let's create a new section in our `main.css` file to add some additional styles.

In our new section of styles specifically for the Schedule page (which will appear just below the styles for the Speakers page), let's set our `<table>` elements to have a `width` of `100%` and a bottom `margin` of `44` pixels.

Then, using the `:last-child` pseudo-class selector to identify the last `<table>` element within the section, let's set its bottom `margin` to `0` pixels. Doing so prevents this table from conflicting with the bottom `padding` belonging to the `<section>` element with a class attribute value of `row`.

So far, the new section within our `main.css` file looks like this:

```
1.   /*
2.   ========================================
3.   Schedule
4.   ========================================
5.   */
6.
7.   table {
```

continues

```
8.    margin-bottom: 44px;
9.    width: 100%;
10. }
11. table:last-child {
12.   margin-bottom: 0;
13. }
```

4. Now let's add some data to our table. We'll begin with the first day of our conference, the workshop day on August 24.

    Within the `<thead>` element of the table let's add a `<tr>` element. The first cell within the row will be a `<th>` element noting the focus of the day: "Workshops" for this specific day. Since the `<th>` element is the heading for the row we'll also add the `scope` attribute with a value of `row` to it.

    After the `<th>` element comes a `<td>` element with the date, "August 24th" in this case. Now, more often than not we'll have three columns, the first being a table heading that identifies a time of day and the second two columns being regular table cells that identify speakers for that given time. Since this row doesn't feature two separate speakers we'll want to add the `colspan` attribute with a value of 2 to the `<td>` element, forcing it to span two columns.

    Our code for the table now looks like this:

```
1.  <table>
2.    <thead>
3.      <tr>
4.        <th scope="row">
5.          Workshops
6.        </th>
7.        <td colspan="2">
8.          August 24th
9.        </td>
10.     </tr>
11.   </thead>
12.   <tbody>
13.     ...
14.   </tbody>
15. </table>
```

5. Inside the <tbody> element let's fill out the day's activities. We'll begin by adding a <tr> element with a <th> and a <td> element directly inside the row.

On the <th> element, and all subsequent <th> elements, we'll add the scope attribute with a value of row to semantically identify this element as the header for the row. Then within the <th> element let's add a <time> element that shows the time of the first activity of the day, "8:30 AM" in this case. We'll also include a datetime attribute on the <time> element with a value noting the time in hours, minutes, and seconds, 08:30:00.

In the <td> element that follows the <th> element we'll include the activity name (since there aren't any speakers at this time), which is "Registration" in this case. Since there is only one activity at this time we'll also include the colspan attribute with a value of 2 on the <td> element.

In all, the code for our first table looks like this:

```
1.  <table>
2.    <thead>
3.      <tr>
4.        <th scope="row">
5.          Workshops
6.        </th>
7.        <td colspan="2">
8.          August 24th
9.        </td>
10.     </tr>
11.   </thead>
12.   <tbody>
13.     <tr>
14.       <th scope="row">
15.         <time datetime="08:30:00">8:30 AM</time>
16.       </th>
17.       <td colspan="2">
18.         Registration
19.       </td>
20.     </tr>
21.   </tbody>
22. </table>
```

6. For the second row within the `<tbody>` element let's add a `<tr>` element just below our previous row. Then let's add a `<th>` element with the `scope` attribute with a value of `row`, and again add a `<time>` element with the appropriate time and `datetime` attribute value within that `<th>` element.

After the `<th>` element let's add two `<td>` elements for the two speakers presenting at that time. Directly inside each `<td>` element we'll add an `<a>` element, which will link back to where that speaker is positioned on the Speakers page. Remember, we added `id` attributes with each speaker's name to the parent elements for each speaker. Using that `id` attribute value preceded by the `speakers.html` filename and a pound/hash sign, #, we can link directly to that speaker's talk description and biography on the Speakers page.

Within the `<a>` element we'll include an `<h4>` element with the speaker's name followed by the talk title.

The code for the first two workshops looks like this:

```
1.   <table>
2.     <thead>
3.       <tr>
4.         <th scope="row">
5.           Workshops
6.         </th>
7.         <td colspan="2">
8.           August 24th
9.         </td>
10.      </tr>
11.    </thead>
12.    <tbody>
13.      <tr>
14.        <th scope="row">
15.          <time datetime="08:30:00">8:30 AM</time>
16.        </th>
17.        <td colspan="2">
18.          Registration
19.        </td>
20.      </tr>
21.      <tr>
```

```
22.        <th scope="row">
23.          <time datetime="09:00:00">9:00 AM</time>
24.        </th>
25.        <td>
26.          <a href="speakers.html#adam-connor">
27.            <h4>Adam Connor</h4>
28.            Lights! Camera! Interaction! Design Inspiration from
                 Filmmakers
29.          </a>
30.        </td>
31.        <td>
32.          <a href="speakers.html#jennifer-jones">
33.            <h4>Jennifer Jones</h4>
34.            What Designers Can Learn from Parenting
35.          </a>
36.        </td>
37.      </tr>
38.    </tbody>
39.  </table>
```

7. From here, we can repeat this pattern for each activity and speaker to finish our first table and then add the next two tables for the second two days of the conference.

    While doing this, keep in mind that the table head will always include a table heading noting the events of the day and a table cell spanning two columns showing the date.

    Then, within the body of each table, every row will have a table heading that shows the time of day. After the table heading will be an activity, a speaker, or multiple speakers. Activities without speakers will reside within a single <td> element that spans two columns. If only one speaker is presenting at a certain time, that speaker will reside within a single <td> element that spans two columns as well, <a> and <h4> elements and all.

    If there are two speakers for a given time then each speaker will reside within his or her own <td> element, just as before.

The full code for all three tables can be found at http://learn.shayhowe.com/
html-css/organizing-data-with-tables. For reference, the table for the first day,
which includes lunch and two more speakers, looks like this:

```
1.   <table>
2.     <thead>
3.       <tr>
4.         <th scope="row">
5.           Workshops
6.         </th>
7.         <td colspan="2">
8.           August 24th
9.         </td>
10.      </tr>
11.    </thead>
12.    <tbody>
13.      <tr>
14.        <th scope="row">
15.          <time datetime="08:30:00">8:30 AM</time>
16.        </th>
17.        <td colspan="2">
18.          Registration
19.        </td>
20.      </tr>
21.      <tr>
22.        <th scope="row">
23.          <time datetime="09:00:00">9:00 AM</time>
24.        </th>
25.        <td>
26.          <a href="speakers.html#adam-connor">
27.            <h4>Adam Connor</h4>
28.            Lights! Camera! Interaction! Design Inspiration from
                 Filmmakers
29.          </a>
30.        </td>
31.        <td>
32.          <a href="speakers.html#jennifer-jones">
```

```
33.          <h4>Jennifer Jones</h4>
34.          What Designers Can Learn from Parenting
35.        </a>
36.      </td>
37.    </tr>
38.    <tr>
39.      <th scope="row">
40.        <time datetime="12:30:00">12:30 PM</time>
41.      </th>
42.      <td colspan="2">
43.        Lunch
44.      </td>
45.    </tr>
46.    <tr>
47.      <th scope="row">
48.        <time datetime="14:00">2:00 PM</time>
49.      </th>
50.      <td>
51.        <a href="speakers.html#tessa-harmon">
52.          <h4>Tessa Harmon</h4>
53.          Crafty Coding: Generating Knitting Patterns
54.        </a>
55.      </td>
56.      <td>
57.        <a href="speakers.html#russ-unger">
58.          <h4>Russ Unger</h4>
59.          From Muppets to Mastery: Core UX Principles from Mr. Jim
             Henson
60.        </a>
61.      </td>
62.    </tr>
63.  </tbody>
64. </table>
```

8. Now that our tables are taking shape, it's time to add a little style to them. Let's begin by adding some general styles to the <th> and <td> elements. For both the <th> and <td> elements let's add a bottom padding of 22 pixels and a vertical alignment of top. For <th> elements specifically let's add a right padding of 45 pixels, a text alignment of right, and a width of 20%. Then, for <td> elements let's add a width of 40%.

Below our existing table and schedule styles, our code should look like this:

```
1.  th,
2.  td {
3.    padding-bottom: 22px;
4.    vertical-align: top;
5.  }
6.  th {
7.    padding-right: 45px;
8.    text-align: right;
9.    width: 20%;
10. }
11. td {
12.   width: 40%;
13. }
```

9. Next, let's style the table head and the elements within the table head. We'll set a line-height of 44 pixels on the <thead> element only, and a color of #648880 and a font-size of 24 pixels on all <th> elements nested within a <thead> element. Our new styles include the following:

```
1.  thead {
2.    line-height: 44px;
3.  }
4.  thead th {
5.    color: #648880;
6.    font-size: 24px;
7.  }
```

10. The table head is looking good, so let's also add some styles for the table body. We'll begin with `<th>` elements nested within the `<tbody>` element: changing their `color`, adding some `font-` and `text`-based styles, and adding some top `padding`.

```
1.  tbody th {
2.    color: #a9b2b9;
3.    font-size: 14px;
4.    font-weight: 400;
5.    padding-top: 22px;
6.    text-transform: uppercase;
7.  }
```

11. We'll also add some styles to `<td>` elements nested within the `<tbody>` element, beginning with a top `border` and `padding`. We'll style the `<td>` elements that span only one column by adding 15 pixels of right `padding` to those that form the left column and 15 pixels of left `padding` to those that form the right column. Doing so puts a total of 30 pixels of `padding` between the two columns while keeping each cell the same size. We don't need to apply any left or right `padding` to the `<td>` elements that span two columns.

We'll add all of these horizontal paddings using the `:first-of-type`, `:last-of-type`, and `:only-of-type` pseudo-class selectors. These pseudo-class selectors work very similarly to the `:last-child` pseudo-class selector we've used before.

The `:first-of-type` pseudo-class selector will select the first element of its type within a parent element. In our case, the `td:first-of-type` selector will select the first `<td>` element within a `<tr>` element. Then, the `:last-of-type` pseudo-class selector will select the last element of its type within a parent element.

Again, in our case, the `td:last-of-type` selector will select the last `<td>` element within a `<tr>` element. Lastly, the `:only-of-type` pseudo-class selector will select an element if it's the only element of its type within a parent element. Here, the `td:only-of-type` selector will only select a `<td>` element if it's the only `<td>` element within a `<tr>` element, such as when a `<td>` element spans two columns.

Our styles are a little complex, but they're flexible in addressing the needs of our table. These new styles include the following:

```
1.  tbody td {
2.    border-top: 1px solid #dfe2e5;
3.    padding-top: 21px;
4.  }
```

continues

```
5.    tbody td:first-of-type {
6.      padding-right: 15px;
7.    }
8.    tbody td:last-of-type {
9.      padding-left: 15px;
10.   }
11.   tbody td:only-of-type {
12.     padding-left: 0;
13.     padding-right: 0;
14.   }
```

12. Our schedule—and the tables that display it—is coming together. Let's adjust a few
     of the styles on existing elements to clean up the design. We'll start by making all of
     the links within the table a medium gray. If we target only the <a> elements within a
     table, our headings with the speaker's name within the links will remain green, while
     the talk titles will be gray, creating a nice contrast between the two.

     While we're adjusting the styles of the entries for the talks, let's also remove the bot-
     tom margin on the <h4> elements within the table, allowing the speaker's name to
     sit closer to her or his title. We can implement these styles with the following code:

```
1.    table a {
2.      color: #888;
3.    }
4.    table h4 {
5.      margin-bottom: 0;
6.    }
```

13. Lastly, let's create some visual contrast among the different types of activities hap-
     pening throughout the day. All of the talks look good with our latest changes. For
     all of the other activities, such as registration, lunch, and breaks (which are within
     the table body) as well as for the date (which is within the table header) let's use a
     subtle gray.

     We'll do so by creating a new class, schedule-offset, and assigning a color of
     #a9b2b9 to it.

```
1.    .schedule-offset {
2.      color: #a9b2b9;
3.    }
```

Once the class is in place, let's add it to all of the <td> elements that span two columns and include either the day's date or a designated activity—registration, lunch, or a break. Looking back to our table for the first day, the workshops day, the HTML will look like this:

```
1.  <table>
2.   <thead>
3.     <tr>
4.       <th scope="row">
5.         Workshops
6.       </th>
7.       <td class="schedule-offset" colspan="2">
8.         August 24th
9.       </td>
10.    </tr>
11.   </thead>
12.   <tbody>
13.     <tr>
14.       <th scope="row">
15.         <time datetime="08:30:00">8:30 AM</time>
16.       </th>
17.       <td class="schedule-offset" colspan="2">
18.         Registration
19.       </td>
20.     </tr>
21.     ...
22.     <tr>
23.       <th scope="row">
24.         <time datetime="12:30:00">12:30 PM</time>
25.       </th>
26.       <td class="schedule-offset" colspan="2">
27.         Lunch
28.       </td>
29.     </tr>
30.     ...
31.   </tbody>
32. </table>
```

Tables, which may appear simple on the surface, can be quite complex, and that is the case with our Styles Conference schedule. The good news is that our schedule is now complete, and it's looking great (see **Figure 11.12**).

The source code for the exercises within this lesson can be found at http://learn.shayhowe.com/html-css/organizing-data-with-tables.

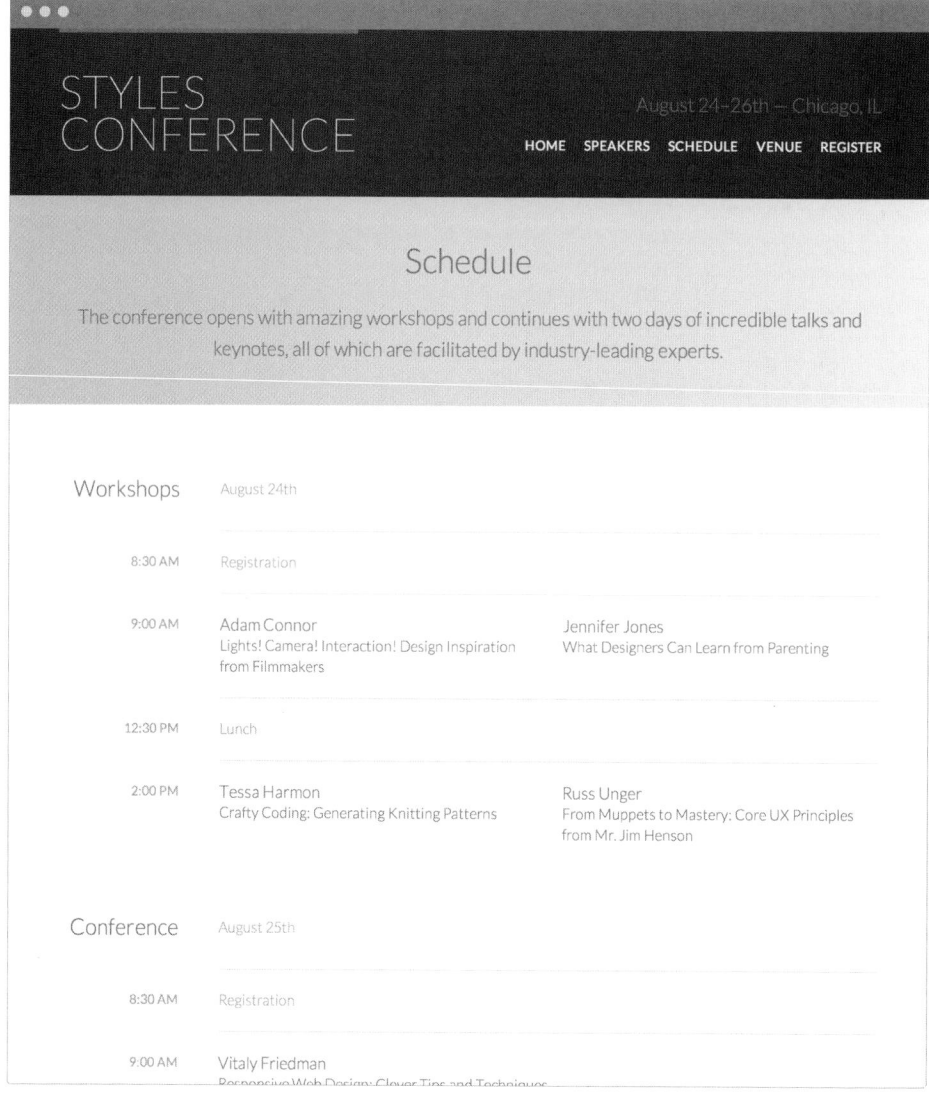

Figure 11.12 The Schedule page, which includes multiple tables, for Styles Conference

Summary

All right, we now know how to semantically lay out tabular data within HTML while also making it intuitive with CSS. Discussing tables was our last major hurdle in learning HTML and CSS, and we have now officially finished our Styles Conference website.

To review, within this lesson we covered the following:

- The best ways to semantically create tables
- How to make individual table cells span multiple columns or rows
- The structural elements that make up tables
- Different ways to style borders on a table, and how different border properties affect a table's appearance
- How to vertically align text within a table

We've done a great job at putting all of our new skills to use, and we're miles beyond where we were a few lessons ago. Let's end on a high note, tie up some loose ends, and look at ways to write our best possible code.

Lesson 12

Writing Your Best Code

There's a lot to learn—different elements, attributes, properties, values, and more—in order to write HTML and CSS. Every lesson until this point has had the primary objective of explaining these various components of HTML and CSS, in hopes of helping you to understand the core fundamentals of both languages. This lesson takes a step back and looks at a more abstract picture of HTML and CSS.

More specifically, this lesson focuses on the best coding practices for both HTML and CSS. These coding practices serve as an over-arching framework for writing HTML and CSS. They apply to every lesson and should always be kept in mind when programming.

When you're reviewing these best practices think about how they may be used in other areas or programming languages, too. For example, the use of comments to organize code (as we cover in this lesson) is beneficial in all programming languages. Keep an open mindset and consider how you can fully utilize each practice.

HTML Coding Practices

A lot of coding best practices emphasize keeping code lean and well organized. The general practices within HTML are no different. The goal is to write well-structured and standards-compliant markup. The guidelines described here provide a brief introduction to HTML coding practices; this is by no means an exhaustive list.

Write Standards-Compliant Markup

HTML, by nature, is a forgiving language that allows poor code to execute and render to varying levels of accuracy. Successful rendering, however, does not mean that our code is semantically correct or guarantee that it will validate as standards compliant. In addition, poor code is unpredictable, and you can't be certain what you're going to get when it renders. We have to pay close attention when writing HTML and be sure to nest and close all elements correctly, to use IDs and classes appropriately, and to always validate our code.

The code that follows has multiple errors, including using the `intro` ID attribute value multiple times when it should be a unique value, closing the `<p>` and `<strong>` elements in the wrong order within the first paragraph, and not closing the `<p>` element at all in the second paragraph.

BAD CODE

```
1.  <p id="intro">New items on the menu today include <strong>caramel
    apple cider and breakfast crepes</p>.</strong>
2.  <p id="intro">The caramel apple cider is delicious.
```

GOOD CODE

```
1.  <p class="intro">New items on the menu today include
    <strong>caramel apple cider and breakfast crepes</strong>.</p>
2.  <p class="intro">The caramel apple cider is delicious.</p>
```

Make Use of Semantic Elements

The library of elements in HTML is fairly large, with well over 100 elements available for use. Deciding which elements to use to describe different content may be difficult, but these elements are the backbone of semantics. We need to research and double-check our code to ensure we are using the proper semantic elements. Users will thank us in the long run for building a more accessible website, and your HTML will arguably be easier to style. If you are ever unsure of your code, find a friend to help out and perform routine code reviews.

Here the HTML doesn't use the proper heading and paragraph elements; instead, it uses meaningless elements to style and group content.

BAD CODE

```
1.    <span class="heading"><strong>Welcome Back</span></strong>
2.    <br><br>
3.    It has been a while. What have you been up to lately?
4.    <br><br>
```

GOOD CODE

```
1.    <h1>Welcome Back</h1>
2.    <p>It has been a while. What have you been up to lately?</p>
```

Use the Proper Document Structure

As previously mentioned, HTML is a forgiving language and, therefore, pages will render without the use of the <!DOCTYPE html> doctype or <html>, <head>, and <body> elements. Without a doctype and these structural elements, pages will not render properly in every browser.

We must always be sure to the use proper document structure, including the <!DOCTYPE html> doctype, and the <html>, <head>, and <body> elements. Doing so keeps our pages standards compliant and fully semantic, and helps guarantee they will be rendered as we wish.

BAD CODE

```
1.    <html>
2.      <h1>Hello World</h1>
3.      <p>This is a web page.</p>
4.    </html>
```

GOOD CODE

```
1.   <!DOCTYPE html>
2.   <html>
3.     <head>
4.       <title>Hello World</title>
5.     </head>
6.     <body>
7.       <h1>Hello World</h1>
8.       <p>This is a web page.</p>
9.     </body>
10. </html>
```

Keep the Syntax Organized

As pages grow, managing HTML can become quite a task. Thankfully there are a few quick rules that can help us keep our syntax clean and organized. These include the following:

- Use lowercase letters within element names, attributes, and values
- Indent nested elements
- Strictly use double quotes, not single or completely omitted quotes
- Remove the forward slash at the end of self-closing elements
- Omit the values on Boolean attributes

Observing these rules will help keep our code neat and legible. Looking at the two sets of HTML here, the good code is easier to digest and understand.

BAD CODE

```
1.   <Aside>
2.   <h3>Chicago</h3>
3.   <H5 HIDDEN='HIDDEN'>City in Illinois</H5>
4.   <img src=chicago.jpg alt="Chicago, the third most populous city
       in the United States" />
5.   <ul>
6.   <li>234 square miles</li>
7.   <li>2.715 million residents</li>
8.   </ul>
9.   </ASIDE>
```

GOOD CODE

```
1.  <aside>
2.    <h3>Chicago</h3>
3.    <h5 hidden>City in Illinois</h5>
4.    <img src="chicago.jpg" alt="Chicago, the third most populous city
      in the United States">
5.    <ul>
6.      <li>234 square miles</li>
7.      <li>2.715 million residents</li>
8.    </ul>
9.  </aside>
```

Use Practical ID & Class Values

Creating ID and class values can be one of the more difficult parts of writing HTML. These values need to be practical, relating to the content itself, not the style of the content. Using a value of red to describe red text isn't ideal, as it describes the presentation of the content. Should the style of the text ever need to be changed to blue, not only does the CSS have to be changed, but so does the HTML in every instance where the class red exists.

The HTML here assumes that the alert message will be red. However, should the style of the alert change to orange the class name of red will no longer make sense and will likely cause confusion.

BAD CODE

```
1.  <p class="red">Error! Please try again.</p>
```

GOOD CODE

```
1.  <p class="alert">Error! Please try again.</p>
```

Use the Alternative Text Attribute on Images

Images should always include the `alt` attribute. Screen readers and other accessibility software rely on the `alt` attribute to provide context for images.

The `alt` attribute value should be very descriptive of what the image contains. If the image doesn't contain anything of relevance, the `alt` attribute should still be included; however, the value should be left blank so that screen readers will ignore it rather than read the name of the image file.

Additionally, if an image doesn't have a meaningful value—perhaps it is part of the user interface, for example—it should be included as a CSS background image if at all possible, not as an `<img>` element.

BAD CODE

```
1.   <img src="puppy.jpg">
```

GOOD CODE

```
1.   <img src="puppy.jpg" alt="A beautiful, two-year-old hound mix puppy">
```

Separate Content from Style

Never, ever, use inline styles within HTML. Doing so creates pages that take longer to load, are difficult to maintain, and cause headaches for designers and developers. Instead, use external style sheets, using classes to target elements and apply styles as necessary.

Here, any desired changes to styles within the bad code must be made in the HTML. Consequently, these styles cannot be reused, and the consistency of the styles will likely suffer.

BAD CODE

```
1.   <p style="color: #393; font-size: 24px;">Thank you!</p>
```

GOOD CODE

```
1.   <p class="alert-success">Thank you!</p>
```

Avoid a Case of "Divitis"

When writing HTML, it is easy to get carried away adding a `<div>` element here and a `<div>` element there to build out any necessary styles. While this works, it can add quite a bit of bloat to a page, and before too long we're not sure what each `<div>` element does.

We need to do our best to keep our code lean and to reduce markup, tying multiple styles to a single element where possible. Additionally, we should use the HTML5 structural elements where suitable.

BAD CODE

```
1.  <div class="container">
2.    <div class="article">
3.      <div class="headline">Headlines Across the World</div>
4.    </div>
5.  </div>
```

GOOD CODE

```
1.  <div class="container">
2.    <article>
3.      <h1>Headlines Across the World</h1>
4.    </article>
5.  </div>
```

Continually Refactor Code

Over time websites and code bases continue to evolve and grow, leaving behind quite a bit of cruft. Remember to remove old code and styles as necessary when editing a page. Let's also take the time to evaluate and refactor our code after we write it, looking for ways to condense it and make it more manageable.

CSS Coding Practices

Similar to those for HTML, the coding practices for CSS focus on keeping code lean and well organized. CSS also has some additional principles regarding how to work with some of the intricacies of the language.

Organize Code with Comments

CSS files can become quite extensive, spanning hundreds of lines. These large files can make finding and editing our styles nearly impossible. Let's keep our styles organized in logical groups. Then, before each group, let's provide a comment noting what the following styles pertain to.

Should we wish, we can also use comments to build a table of contents at the top of our file. Doing so reminds us—and others—exactly what is contained within the file and where the styles are located.

BAD CODE

```
1.   header { ... }
2.   article { ... }
3.   .btn { ... }
```

GOOD CODE

```
1.   /* Primary header */
2.   header { ... }
3.
4.   /* Featured article */
5.   article { ... }
6.
7.   /* Buttons */
8.   .btn { ... }
```

Write CSS Using Multiple Lines & Spaces

When writing CSS, it is important to place each selector and declaration on a new line. Then, within each selector we'll want to indent our declarations.

After a selector and before the first declaration comes the opening curly bracket, {, which should have a space before it. Within a declaration, we need to put a space after the colon, :, that follows a property and end each declaration with a semicolon, ;.

Doing so makes the code easy to read as well as edit. When all of the code is piled into a single line without spaces, it's hard to scan and to make changes.

BAD CODE

```
1.    a,.btn{background:#aaa;color:#f60;font-size:18px;padding:6px;}
```

GOOD CODE

```
1.    a,
2.    .btn {
3.      background: #aaa;
4.      color: #f60;
5.      font-size: 18px;
6.      padding: 6px;
7.    }
```

Comments & Spacing

These two recommendations, organizing code with comments and using multiple lines and spaces, are not only applicable to CSS, but also to HTML or any other language. Overall we need to keep our code organized and well documented. If a specific part of our code is more complex, let's explain how it works and what it applies to within comments. Doing so helps others working on the same code base, as well as ourselves when we revisit our own code down the road.

Use Proper Class Names

Class names (or values) should be modular and should pertain to content within an element, not appearance, as much as possible. These values should be written in such a way that they resemble the syntax of the CSS language. Accordingly, class names should be all lowercase and should use hyphen delimiters.

BAD CODE

```
1.   .Red_Box { ... }
```

GOOD CODE

```
1.   .alert-message { ... }
```

Build Proficient Selectors

CSS selectors can get out of control if they are not carefully maintained. They can easily become too long and too location specific.

The longer a selector is and the more prequalifiers it includes, the higher specificity it will contain. And the higher the specificity the more likely a selector is to break the CSS cascade and cause undesirable issues.

Also in line with keeping the specificity of our selectors as low as possible, let's not use IDs within our selectors. IDs are overly specific, quickly raise the specificity of a selector, and quite often break the cascade within our CSS files. The cons far outweigh the pros with IDs, and we are wise to avoid them.

Let's use shorter and primarily direct selectors. Nest them only two to three levels deep, and remove as many location-based qualifying selectors as possible.

BAD CODE

```
1.   #aside #featured ul.news li a { ... }
2.   #aside #featured ul.news li a em.special { ... }
```

GOOD CODE

```
1.   .news a { ... }
2.   .news .special { ... }
```

Use Specific Classes When Necessary

There are times when a CSS selector is so long and specific that it no longer makes sense. It creates a performance lag and is strenuous to manage. In this case, using a class alone is advised. While applying a class to the targeted element may create more code within HTML, it will allow the code to render faster and will remove any managing obstacles.

For example, if an `<em>` element is nested within an `<h1>` element inside of an `<aside>` element, and all of that is nested within a `<section>` element, the selector might look something like `aside h1 em`. Should the `<em>` element ever be moved out of the `<h1>` element the styles will no longer apply. A better, more flexible selector would use a class, such as `text-offset`, to target the `<em>` element.

BAD CODE

```
1.   section aside h1 em { ... }
```

GOOD CODE

```
1.   .text-offset { ... }
```

Use Shorthand Properties & Values

One feature of CSS is the ability to use shorthand properties and values. Most properties and values have acceptable shorthand alternatives. As an example, rather than using four different `margin`-based property and value declarations to set the margins around all four sides of an element, use one single `margin` property and value declaration that sets the values for all four sides at once. Using the shorthand alternative allows us to quickly set and identify styles.

When we're only setting one value, though, shorthand alternatives should not be used. If a box only needs a bottom `margin`, use the `margin-bottom` property alone. Doing so ensures that other `margin` values will not be overwritten, and we can easily identify which side the `margin` is being applied to without much cognitive effort.

BAD CODE

```
1.   img {
2.     margin-top: 5px;
3.     margin-right: 10px;
```

```
4.     margin-bottom: 5px;
5.     margin-left: 10px;
6.   }
7.   button {
8.     padding: 0 0 0 20px;
9.   }
```

GOOD CODE

```
1.   img {
2.     margin: 5px 10px;
3.   }
4.   button {
5.     padding-left: 20px;
6.   }
```

Use Shorthand Hexadecimal Color Values

When available, use the three-character shorthand hexadecimal color value, and always use lowercase characters within any hexadecimal color value. The idea, again, is to remain consistent, prevent confusion, and embrace the syntax of the language the code is being written in.

BAD CODE

```
1.   .module {
2.     background: #DDDDDD;
3.     color: #FF6600;
4.   }
```

GOOD CODE

```
1.   .module {
2.     background: #ddd;
3.     color: #f60;
4.   }
```

Drop Units from Zero Values

One way to easily cut down on the amount of CSS we write is to remove the unit from any zero value. No matter which length unit is being used—pixels, percentages, em, and so forth—zero is always zero. Adding the unit is unnecessary and provides no additional value.

BAD CODE

```
1.  div {
2.    margin: 20px 0px;
3.    letter-spacing: 0%;
4.    padding: 0px 5px;
5.  }
```

GOOD CODE

```
1.  div {
2.    margin: 20px 0;
3.    letter-spacing: 0;
4.    padding: 0 5px;
5.  }
```

Group & Align Vendor Prefixes

With CSS3, vendor prefixes gained some popularity, adding quite a bit of code to CSS files. The added work of using vendor prefixes is often worth the generated styles; however, they have to be kept organized. In keeping with the goal of writing code that is easy to read and modify, it's best to group and indent individual vendor prefixes so that the property names stack vertically, as do their values.

Depending on where the vendor prefix is placed, on the property or the value, the alignment may vary. For example, the following good code keeps the background property aligned to the left, while the prefixed linear-gradient() functions are indented to keep their values vertically stacked. Then, the prefixed box-sizing property is indented as necessary to keep the box-sizing properties and values vertically stacked.

As always, the objective is to make the styles easier to read and to edit.

BAD CODE

```
1.  div {
2.    background: -webkit-linear-gradient(#a1d3b0, #f6f1d3);
3.    background: -moz-linear-gradient(#a1d3b0, #f6f1d3);
4.    background: linear-gradient(#a1d3b0, #f6f1d3);
5.    -webkit-box-sizing: border-box;
6.    -moz-box-sizing: border-box;
7.    box-sizing: border-box;
8.  }
```

GOOD CODE

```
1.  div {
2.    background: -webkit-linear-gradient(#a1d3b0, #f6f1d3);
3.    background:    -moz-linear-gradient(#a1d3b0, #f6f1d3);
4.    background:         linear-gradient(#a1d3b0, #f6f1d3);
5.    -webkit-box-sizing: border-box;
6.      -moz-box-sizing: border-box;
7.           box-sizing: border-box;
8.  }
```

Vendor Prefixes

When using vendor prefixes we need to make sure to place an unprefixed version of our property and value last, after any prefixed versions. Doing so ensures that browsers that support the unprefixed version will render that style according to its placement within the cascade, reading styles from the top of the file to the bottom.

The good news is that browsers are largely moving away from using vendor prefixes. Over time this will become less of a concern; however, for now we're well advised to double-check which styles require a vendor prefix and to keep those prefixes organized.

Modularize Styles for Reuse

CSS is built to allow styles to be reused, specifically with the use of classes. For this reason, styles assigned to a class should be modular and available to share across elements as necessary.

If a section of news is presented within a box that includes a border, background color, and other styles, the class of news might seem like a good option. However, those same styles may also need to be applied to a section of upcoming events. The class of news doesn't fit in this case. A class of feat-box would make more sense and may be widely used across the entire website.

BAD CODE

```
1.   .news {
2.     background: #eee;
3.     border: 1px solid #ccc;
4.     border-radius: 6px;
5.   }
6.   .events {
7.     background: #eee;
8.     border: 1px solid #ccc;
9.     border-radius: 6px;
10.  }
```

GOOD CODE

```
1.   .feat-box {
2.     background: #eee;
3.     border: 1px solid #ccc;
4.     border-radius: 6px;
5.   }
```

Summary

Hopefully the principles of writing beautiful HTML and CSS are starting to become clear here. While each language does have its own intricacies, the majority of these practices can be shared across the two languages—and many other computer languages.

Individually we need to do our best to uphold these practices, and when working on a team we need to do our best to help educate the team on these practices, too. Likewise, our teams may have valuable suggestions and practices that we should work together to follow.

To highlight some of the overarching themes of this lesson, our HTML and CSS should always

- Be well organized, so that it is easy to read, edit, and maintain
- Be modular and flexible, allowing us to reuse code and patterns as necessary
- Look as if one person wrote it, even if several people contributed

These practices are only the beginning, and as the languages evolve and we write more and more HTML and CSS, we'll develop new ones. It's all part of the beauty of knowing HTML and CSS.

You're now equipped with some very powerful knowledge about how to build websites with HTML and CSS, and I'm excited to see what you do with it. Keep me posted on how it goes, and happy building!

Index

- (hyphen), 38
; (semicolon), 8, 274
: (colon), 8
. (period), 10
{ } (curly brackets), 8, 9, 274
& (ampersand), 31
# (hash sign), 10, 46
< > (angle brackets), 2
% unit notation, 51

A

<a> element, 29
absolute lengths, 50
absolute paths, 30
absolute positioning, 96–98
absolute value, 96–98
action attribute, 205
Adobe Kuler, 47
alert message example, 136–137
alignment
    float values and, 114
    images, 185–186
    list items, 170
    text, 114, 121, 122
    vendor prefixes, 278–279
    vertical, 91
alpha channels, 48
alt attribute, 179, 271
alt (alternative) text, 179
alternative (alt) text, 179
ampersand (&), 31
anchor elements, 29
anchor links, 3, 29
anchor tags, 3
angle brackets < >, 2
<article> element, 25
<aside> element, 26, 76, 78
aspect ratio, 180
attributes
    for, 213
    action, 205
    alt, 179, 271

audio, 189–190
autoplay, 189, 191
charset, 5
checkbox, 209
cite, 129, 130–131
class, 3, 10
cols, 208
colspan, 237–238
container class, 244
controls, 189, 191
datetime, 255
described, 3–4
disabled, 215
headers, 234
height, 180–181
hidden, 215
hidden, 215
href, 3, 11, 12, 30
id, 3, 10, 213, 234, 256
ID, 172
intro ID value, 267
loop, 189, 191
method, 205
multiple, 210
name, 205, 208, 210
placeholder, 216
poster, 192
preload, 189–190, 191
rel, 11
required, 216
reversed, 158–160
rows, 208
rowspan, 237–238
scope, 232, 234, 255
seamless, 194–195
selected, 210
src, 3, 179, 189, 190
start, 159
target, 31
type, 190, 205–208
value, 160, 208
width, 180–181
audio, 189–191

buttons
    background color, 43
    font size, 43
    forms, 208–209, 211
    radio, 208–209
    styles, 138–139

C

capitalize value, 116
<caption> element, 234
captions
    figures, 202
    table, 234
cascade, 37–38
cascading properties, 37–38
Cascading Style Sheets. *See* CSS
cells, combining, 237–238
cf class, 83
characters
    encodings, 2
    hexadecimal colors, 46, 277
    special, 28
charset attribute, 5
check boxes, 209
checkbox attribute, 209
Chrome browser, 65, 67–68
citations, 128, 129, 130–131
cite attribute, 129, 130–131
<cite> element, 128, 130–131
class attribute, 3, 10
class selectors, 10, 38
class values, 270
classes
    multiple, 42–43
    names, 275
    pseudo-classes, 106
    tips for, 275, 276
    values, 275
clear property, 80
clearfix, 83
clearfix class, 83
clearing floats, 80
closing tags, 3
code validation, 6
coding best practices, 266–281
    CSS, 273–280
    general guidelines, 281

HTML, 267–272
    reusable layouts, 90–94
col value, 232
colon (:), 8
color
    background, 37–38, 133, 137, 242–243
    borders, 62
    gradients, 146–147
    hexadecimal values, 46–47, 277
    HSL/HSLa, 49–50
    keyword, 44–45
    links, 137–138
    margins and, 62
    opacity, 48
    padding and, 62
    RGB/RGBa, 48
    sRGB, 44
    in tables, 242–243
    text, 100, 138
    transparent, 48
color channels, 46–50
color property, 100
color stops, 146–147
color values, 42–50
color wheel, 47
cols attribute, 208
colspan attribute, 237–238
comments
    in CSS, 19, 273, 274
    in HTML code, 19
contain keyword value, 154
container class, 69
container class attribute, 252
content, 74–98. *See also* media
    absolute positioning, 96–98
    centering, 69
    embeddable, 3
    grouping, 25
    positioning with floats, 75–86
    positioning with inline-block, 87–89
    related, 26
    relative positioning, 95–96
    reusable layouts, 90
    self-contained, 25
    semantic decisions and, 25, 267–268
    separating from style, 271
    source for, 3
    in tables, 234–235
    wrapping, 79

content boxes, 65
content-box value, 65, 155-156
controls attribute, 189, 191
cover keyword value, 154
creative works, citing, 128
cross-browser compatibility, 12-13
cross-browser testing, 13
CSS (Cascading Style Sheets)
    best practices, 273-280
    calculating specificity, 38-39
    cascading properties, 37-38
    class names/values, 275
    code validators, 6
    color values, 42-50
    comments in, 19, 273, 274
    considerations, 2
    described, 2, 36
    dropping units from zero values, 278
    good vs. bad code examples, 273-280
    length values, 50-52
    modularized styles, 280
    multiple lines and, 274
    property values, 44-52
    referencing, 11-12
    reusable layouts, 90
    shorthand alternatives. *See* shorthand values
    spacing and, 274
    terminology, 7-9
    units of measurement, 50-52
    vendor prefixes, 278-279
.css extension, 11
CSS pseudo-classes, 106
CSS resets, 12-15, 28
CSS selectors
    IDs and, 275
    tips for, 275
CSS3 gradient generators, 146
CSS3 gradients, 146
curly brackets { }, 8, 9, 274

D

data, table, 231-232, 254
datetime attribute, 255
<dd> element, 160-161
description lists, 160-161
developer tools, 67-68

dialogue citation, 129
dialogue quotation, 129
disabled attribute, 215
display property, 54-55, 167, 182
display value, 77, 169
<div> element, 18-19, 25, 272
divisions, 18-19, 25
<dl> element, 160-161
<!DOCTYPE html> declaration, 4, 5
Dreamweaver, 4
drop-down lists, 209-210
<dt> element, 160-161

E

elements
    absolute positioning, 96-98
    block-level, 18, 29, 54, 55
    borders, 62-64
    classifying, 3
    described, 2
    displaying, 54-55
    floating, 76
    height of, 57-58, 59
    hiding, 55
    identifying, 3
    indenting, 5
    inline, 18, 54, 55
    margins, 59-62
    nested, 5
    padding, 60-62
    relative positioning, 95-96
    self-closing, 5
    text-based, 20-23
    width of, 57-58
em unit notation, 51
em units, 51
<em> element, 22-23, 276
email addresses
    linking to, 30-31
    validation, 216
Eric Meyer's reset, 12, 13
error message styles, 216
external citation, 130-131
external quotation, 130
external style sheets, 11, 12

F

fallback options
    audio, 190-191
    backgrounds, 133
    fonts, 101
    video, 191, 193
fields, text, 205-207
fieldsets, 214
`<figcaption>` element, 202
`<figure>` element, 201-202
figures, 201-202
file input, 212
files
    adding to forms, 212
    audio, 189-191
    comments, 19
    CSS, 273, 275, 278
    external, 4, 24
    gradient image, 142
    links to, 24
    organizing, 19
Firefox browser, 65
`:first-of-type` pseudo-class selector, 261
`float` property, 75, 77, 79, 114, 167, 182
floating
    clearing floats, 80
    considerations, 95
    containing floats, 80-83
    content, 75-86
    images, 182-183
    lists, 167-168
font families, 101
`font` property, 104
font variants, 102
`@font-face` at-rule, 124
`font-family` property, 101, 124
fonts
    bold, 102-103
    considerations, 99, 125
    described, 100
    embedded, 99, 124-127
    example code, 105-106
    fallback options, 101
    Google Fonts, 125
    italics, 102
    licensing issues, 125
    practice exercise, 106-113

    properties, 101-113
    shorthand values, 104
    size, 51, 101
    styles, 102
    vs. typefaces, 100
    web-safe, 123-124
    weights, 102-103
`font-size` property, 101
`font-style` property, 102
`font-variant` property, 102
`font-weight` property, 102-103, 126, 127
`<footer>` element, 26, 28
footers, 26, 235
`for` attribute, 213
`<form>` element, 205
forms, 204-228
    adding files to, 212
    adding to pages, 205
    buttons, 208-209, 211
    check boxes, 209
    disabling elements/controls, 215
    drop-down lists, 209-210
    example code, 217-219
    fieldsets, 214
    hidden inputs, 212
    initializing, 205
    input attributes/values, 215-217
    labels, 213
    legends, 214-215
    login, 217-219
    multiple selections, 210
    organizing elements in, 212-215
    overview, 204
    placeholder controls, 216
    practice example, 219-226
    required values, 216
    text fields, 205-207
    textareas, 208
    validation, 216

G

`gif` format, 180
Google Chrome browser, 65, 67-68
Google Fonts, 125
gradient backgrounds, 142-151
    changing direction of, 143-144
    color stops, 146-147

considerations, 142
CSS3, 146
example code, 147–148
linear, 142–144
practice example, 148–151
radial, 145–146
vendor prefixes, 142
gradients
background. *See* gradient backgrounds
`grid` class attribute, 91, 92, 171, 195, 220, 252.
`group` class, 81

H

`<h>` element, 5, 20, 24
hash sign (#), 10, 46
`<head>` element, 4, 5, 11, 24
`<header>` element, 24, 27
headers
table, 232–234, 235
text, 24, 27
`headers` attribute, 234
headings, 5, 20
`height` attribute, 180–181
`height` property, 56, 58, 59, 180
hexadecimal colors, 46–47, 277
hexadecimal values, 100, 133, 147
`hidden` attribute, 215
hidden inputs, 212
hiding elements, 55
`:hover` pseudo-class, 106
`href` attribute, 3, 11, 12, 30
`hsl()` function, 49
HSLa value, 133
HSL/HSLa colors, 49–50
HTML (HyperText Markup Language), 2–4
HTML code
best practices, 267–272
class values, 270
comments in, 19
considerations, 2
described, 2
divisions, 18–19
document structure, 268–269
example of basic code, 4–5
good vs. bad code examples, 267–272

headings, 20
hyperlinks. *See* hyperlinks
ID values, 270
inline styles and, 271
paragraphs, 21
refactoring code, 272
referencing CSS in, 11–12
removing code, 272
reusable layouts, 90
semantics in, 18, 267–268
spans, 18–19
standards-compliant markup, 267
structural elements, 23–29
syntax organization, 269–270
terminology, 2–4
text-based elements, 20–23
validators, 6
version, 4
HTML document structure, 4–7
`.html` extension, 4
`<html>` element, 4, 5
hyperlink reference. *See* `href`
hyperlinks
adding, 32–35
anchor, 3, 29
background images, 134
to citations, 128, 129
colors, 137–138
creating, 29–35
described, 29
to email addresses, 30–31
navigation, 24
opening links in new window, 31
to other pages of website, 30
to parts of same page, 32
to quotations, 129
specifying, 3
HyperText Markup Language. *See* HTML
hyphen (-), 38

I

`<i>` element, 22–23
icons, 180
`id` attribute, 3, 10, 213, 234, 256
ID attributes, 172
ID selectors, 10, 38, 39

ID values, 270
`<iframe>` element, 193-195
image elements, 183
image formats, 180
images, 179-188
  adding to pages, 179
  alignment, 185-186
  `alt` attribute, 271
  aspect ratio, 180
  background. *See* background images
  borders, 182
  distorted, 180
  embedded, 179
  floating, 182-183
  flush left/right, 182-183
  margins, 182-183
  padding, 182
  positioning, 181-183
  practice exercise, 183-188
  sizing, 180-181
  spacing, 182-183
`<img>` element, 179, 181, 183
indenting text, 115
`index.html` file, 15
inline elements, 18
inline frames, 193-195
inline styles, 11, 271
`inline` value, 54, 166-167
inline-block elements
  positioning content with, 87-89
  removing spaces between, 88-89
  sizing, 59
  space between, 55
`inline-block` value, 55, 166-167
inline-level elements, 59
`<input>` element, 205
`inside` property value, 165, 166
internal style sheets, 11
Internet Explorer, 65
`intro` ID attribute value, 267
italicized text, 22-23, 102

J

`jpg` format, 180

K

key selector, 40
keyword color values, 44-45, 47

L

`<label>` element, 213
labels, 213
`:last-child` pseudo-class selector, 170, 241, 253
`:last-of-type` pseudo-class selector, 261
leading, 103-104
legends, 214-215
length values, 50-52
letter spacing, 117
`letter-spacing` property, 117
`<li>` element, 158
linear gradients, 142-143
`linear-gradient ()` function, 143, 149
`line-height` property, 103-104
`<link>` element, 11-12, 125-126
links
  adding, 32-35
  anchor, 3, 29
  background images, 134
  to citations, 128, 129
  colors, 137-138
  creating, 29-35
  described, 29
  to email addresses, 30-31
  navigation, 24
  opening links in new window, 31
  to other pages of website, 30
  to parts of same page, 32
  to quotations, 129
  specifying, 3
list item markers
  floating and, 167
  setting content of, 163-165
  using images as, 164-165
list items
  alignment, 170
  styling, 163-166
lists, 157-177
  changing values in, 160
  considerations, 157
  description, 160-161

drop-down, 209–210
floating, 167–168
horizontally displaying, 166–169
navigational, 168–169
nesting, 162–163
numbered, 158–160
ordered, 158–160
overview, 157
practice example, 169–176
reverse order, 158–160
sample code, 168–169
unordered, 158
list-style property value, 166
list-style-position property, 165–166
list-style-type property, 163–165
login forms, 217–219
loop attribute, 189, 191
lowercase value, 116

M

"magic corners," 144
mailto:, 31
main.css file, 12
margin property, 59–62, 182–183
margins
    images, 182–183
    overview, 59–62
measurement, units of, 50–52
media, 178–203. *See also* content
    audio, 189–191
    considerations, 178
    embedded, 193
    images. *See* images
    inline frames, 193–195
    video, 191–193
media player, 192
<meta> element, 5
method attribute, 205
mp3 format, 190
multiple attribute, 210

N

name attribute, 205, 208, 210
<nav> element, 24
navigation menus, 33–34, 168–169

navigational links, 24
navigational lists, 168–169
nested elements, 5
nesting lists, 162–163
none value, 55
Normalize.css, 12–13
Notepad++, 4
:nth-child pseudo-class selector, 242–243
number sign (#), 10, 46
numbered lists, 158–160

O

offset class, 96
ogg format, 190
<ol> element, 158–160
:only-of-type pseudo-class selector, 261
opacity, 48
opening tags, 3
<option> elements, 208
ordered lists, 158–160
outside property value, 165

P

<p> element, 5, 21
padding, 60–62, 66, 182
padding property
    box model, 60–62, 66
    tables, 260–262
padding-box value, 66, 155–156
pages. *See* web pages
paragraphs, 21
paths
    absolute, 30
    hyperlink, 134
    relative, 30
pattern, background, 180
percentages, 51
performance, 276
period (.), 10
photographs, 180
pixels, 50
placeholder attribute, 216
placeholder controls, 216
png format, 180
position property, 95–98

poster attribute, 192
pound sign (#), 10, 46
preload attribute, 189-190, 191
properties
    background, 133, 134, 142, 164, 183
    background-clip, 155-156
    background-color, 133
    background-image, 134, 142, 183
    background-origin, 155-156
    background-position, 135
    background-repeat, 134
    background-size, 153-155
    border, 62-64
    border-collapse, 238-239, 241, 243
    border-spacing, 240-241
    box-shadow, 116
    box-sizing, 64-67
    cascading, 37-38
    cascading properties, 37-38
    clear, 80
    color, 100
    described, 8
    display, 54-55, 167, 182
    float, 75, 77, 79, 114, 167, 182
    font, 104
    font-based, 101-113
    font-family, 101, 124
    fonts, 101-113
    font-size, 101
    font-style, 102
    font-variant, 102
    font-weight, 102-103, 126, 127
    height, 56, 58, 59, 180
    letter-spacing, 117
    line-height, 103-104
    list-style, 166
    list-style-position, 165-166
    list-style-type, 163-165
    margin, 59-62, 182-183
    padding, 60-62, 66, 260-262
    position, 95-98
    text, 113-123
    text-align, 114, 244-247
    text-based, 101-123
    text-decoration, 114
    text-indent, 115
    text-shadow, 115-116
    text-transform, 116
    vertical-align, 244
    width, 57-58, 180
    word-spacing, 117
prose citation, 129
prose quotation, 129
pseudo-class selectors, 261
px unit notation, 50

Q

<q> element, 128, 129
quotations, 128, 129, 130

R

radial gradients, 145-146
radial-gradient() function, 145
radio buttons, 208-209
rel attribute, 11
relative lengths, 51
relative paths, 30
relative positioning, 95-96
relative value, 95-96
required attribute, 216
reusable layouts, 90-94
reversed attribute, 158-160
rgb() function, 48
rgba() function, 48
RGB/RGBa colors, 48
root directory, 12
row value, 232
rows
    adding borders to, 241-242
    gradient background, 148
    styles, 139-140
    table, 230
rows attribute, 208
rowspan attribute, 237-238

S

Safari browser, 65
scope attribute, 232, 234, 255
seamless attribute, 194-195
<section> elements, 25, 27, 76, 140, 149
<select> element, 210